Errand to the World

WILLIAM R. HUTCHISON

Errand to the World

AMERICAN PROTESTANT THOUGHT
AND FOREIGN MISSIONS

The University of Chicago Press
Chicago and London

WILLIAM R. HUTCHISON is Charles Warren Professor of the History of Religion in America at Harvard University. He is the author of *The Transcendentalist Ministers: Church Reform in the New England Renaissance* and *The Modernist Impulse in American Protestantism,* editor of *American Protestant Thought in the Liberal Era,* and coeditor of *Missionary Ideologies in the Imperialist Era.*

The University of Chicago Press, Chicago 60637
The University of Chicago Press, Ltd., London
© 1987 by William R. Hutchison
All rights reserved. Published 1987
Printed in the United States of America
96 95 94 93 92 91 90 89 88 87   54321

Library of Congress Cataloging-in-Publication Data

Hutchison, William R.
  Errand to the world.

  Bibliography: p.
  Includes index.
  1. Missions, American—History. 2. Messianism,
Political—United States. I. Title. II. Title:
American Protestant thought and foreign missions.
BV2410.H87 1987 266'.023'73   86-24960
ISBN 0-226-36309-0

Contents

List of Illustrations   ix

Acknowledgments   xi

Introduction: God's Mission and America's   1

1. "Civilizing": From Necessity to Virtue   15
   SOURCES IN ROMAN CATHOLIC MISSIONS   16
   PROTESTANTS AND THE INDIANS   23
   AGAINST THE GRAIN: THE QUAKERS AND ROGER WILLIAMS   33
   MISSIONS AND MILLENNIUM   38

2. New Nation, New Errand   43
   HOME BASE AND FOREIGN FOOTHOLDS   45
   MISSION APOLOGETICS   46
   THE LANGUAGE OF SPIRITUAL EXPANSIONISM   51
   LEGACIES   60

3. Christ, Not Culture   62
   "LITTLE ELSE THAN DISAPPOINTMENT": LESSONS FROM THE
   AMERICAN-INDIAN MISSIONS   63
   HAWAII AND THE PERILS OF SUCCESS   69
   RUFUS ANDERSON AND THE NEW MISSION POLICY   77

4. A Moral Equivalent for Imperialism   91
   THERMIDOR: RESISTANCE TO THE ANDERSON POLICIES   95
   PROTESTANT LIBERALISM AND MISSIONS   102
   RELIGIOUS CONSERVATISM AND CULTURAL FAITH   112
   MAINTAINING CONSENSUS:
       THE WATCHWORD AND ITS SPOKESMEN   118

5. Activism under Fire   125
   "ACTIVISM": THE VIEW FROM EUROPE   126
   FUNDAMENTALIST OBJECTIONS   138

6. Tradition under Fire 146
   VISION AND REVISION 150
   WILLIAM E. HOCKING: RE-THINKING MISSIONS 158
   CRITICIZING THE CRITICS:
      THE BATTLE OVER THE LAYMEN'S REPORT 164

7. Familiar Debates in an Unfamiliar World 176
   THE ECUMENICAL-EVANGELICAL STANDOFF 177
   A CHURCH FOR OTHERS: THE HOEKENDIJK PRESCRIPTION 183
   CONTESTING RIGHTS TO THE HERITAGE 186
   REALIGNMENTS AND SECOND THOUGHTS 192

Afterword: Mission for a "People Among Peoples" 203

Bibliography 211

Index 221

Illustrations

"Come and Help Us," 1630   10
"Come and Help Us," 1920   11
John Eliot   34
David Brainerd   35
Adoniram Judson   50
Edward Dorr Griffin   57
The Indian school at Cornwall, Connecticut   66
Hiram Bingham   73
Asa and Lucy Thurston   74
Rufus Anderson   83
Robert E. Speer and John R. Mott   94
Newly appointed Congregational missionaries, 1915   101
Arthur T. Pierson   114
A Student Volunteer Movement convention, 1920   130
World map showing placement of Student Volunteers, 1920   131
Gustav Warneck   134
Heinrich Frick   137
Augustus Strong   142
John D. Rockefeller, Jr.   149
Daniel Johnson Fleming   153
William Ernest Hocking   160
J. Gresham Machen   166
Robert E. Speer   167
Pearl Buck   167
Johannes Hoekendijk   187
Donald McGavran   189

Acknowledgments

My interest in the missionary movement undoubtedly is rooted in family history—my parents having spent several years as educational missionaries in Iran, my wife's parents having served for many years with the YMCA in Cairo. As an American historian, however, I had paid little attention to the subject until John Fairbank, in the early 1970s, enlisted me in one of his projects in the history of American–East Asian relations. Shortly after that, Martin Marty encouraged me to undertake, for the University of Chicago Press, the study that has eventuated in this book. I have enjoyed the venture, and am grateful to both of these friends.

Over the past decade I have tried out my ideas, and received invaluable aid and stimulation, in more settings than I could possibly acknowledge here. But I am particularly aware of having received good advice, along with clues to complex and divergent attitudes about foreign missions, in meetings of the Harvard Colloquium in American religious history, the Boston Area Historians seminar, the American Historians' dinner group at Harvard, the Church History and International colloquia of the Boston Theological Institute, the Massachusetts Historical Society, and the Harvard Divinity School faculty seminar.

Overseas, I was able to discuss this subject with colleagues in two conferences (1977 and 1981) of the International Commission for Comparative Ecclesiastical History; at seminars in Hyderabad, Madras, and Colombo in 1981; and with lecture audiences in 1983 at the Theological College of the Pacific in Fiji, the University of Papua, New Guinea, and the Lutheran seminary at Lae (PNG). In the spring of 1980 I tried some of my conclusions on Bengt Sundkler, Carl Hallencreutz, and their doctoral students in Uppsala, and on Emilio Castro and his co-workers at the World Council of Churches in Geneva. I was helped greatly by all these encounters.

Others who deserve special thanks, for critiquing the entire manuscript or for aiding me at crucial points in its development, are John Carman, the late Torben Christensen, Charles Forman, Roger Martin, John Piper, Leroy Rouner, Lamin Sanneh, Grant Wacker, and David Watt. I am grateful, in addition, to the editors of the *Indian Journal of American Studies* and of the *Proceedings* of the Massachusetts Historical

Society for allowing me to republish material that appeared earlier in those publications. I also thank those who have supplied, located, or identified photographs for the book, and those who have given us permission to use them.

My research assistant during earlier phases of this work was Robert A. Schneider. Erick Schenkel took over in time to incur the heavy burdens of checking and rationalizing my annotations, and of finding or soliciting photographs and permissions. Kay Shanahan has performed brilliantly and faithfully at all stages of manuscript preparation.

I am composing these acknowledgments in my Widener Library study on a Saturday that is also my thirty-fourth wedding anniversary. The reaction of my children and students to that intelligence would be entirely predictable: "It figures." My own response is once again to express deep gratitude to my remarkable wife, Virginia Quay Hutchison—for existing; for putting up with all this; for encouraging, admonishing, and supporting. Also, of course, for winning only 60 percent of our tennis matches, and pretending that winning that many involves a certain amount of effort.

Introduction: God's Mission and America's

Don't apologize. All Americans are missionaries.

Arnold Rose

The foreign mission enterprise in its heyday (about 1880 to 1930) was a massive affair, involving tens of thousands of Americans abroad and millions at home. Even in the early nineteenth century, as a movement of huge aspiration but more modest dimensions, it exceeded most other reform or benevolent organizations in size and resources.[1] It sent abroad, through most of its history, not only the largest contingents of Americans—dwarfing all other categories except that of short-term travelers—but also the most highly educated. Missionaries on the whole belonged to the tiny cohort of the college-trained; and male missionaries generally had been educated beyond college. If deficient from a modern point of view in sensitivity to foreign cultures, they were measurably superior in that regard to most contemporaries at home or abroad.

The missionaries' considerable influence among other peoples and in America, while hard to quantify, has usually been acknowledged both by those who feel kindly disposed toward them and by others who wish fervently that these religious couriers had stayed home. People of varying persuasions may wince at John K. Fairbank's listing of ten Chinese Communist programs originated by the missionaries, but few could take factual exception to it. Nor would they be likely to dispute the conclusion, now common in the scholarly literature, that the missionaries were the chief interpreters of remote cultures for the people at home, and as such played a central role in the shaping of American public attitudes. The large number of missionary offspring that ob-

[1]Annual reports reveal, for example, that in the 1820s, when the income of the American Board of Commissioners for Foreign Missions ranged around $40,000 a year, that of the American Temperance Society was one-third that size. Those of the Prison Discipline Society and American Peace Society were each one-tenth as large as the ABCFM's. By 1900 the annual income of the most affluent mission society (the northern Methodist) had passed a million dollars, while those of the Anti-Saloon League and the American Federation of Labor were $18,000 and $71,000 respectively. Arnold Rose gave the response quoted in the epigraph when a fellow academic, at a conference in India, admitted to having been a missionary. Leroy S. Rouner, conversation with the author.

servers noted among the foreign-culture experts of the Second World War era (roughly 50 percent came from such a background) suggested that the enterprise had had many forms of continuing impact, and perhaps vouched for a certain quality in the original personnel.[2]

One could, however, make more modest claims for the movement and still find it remarkable that missionaries and their sponsors have on the whole remained shadowy figures in narrations of religious and general history. The reason for such neglect is plain enough: these overseas Americans and their best-known objectives have seemed more than a little embarrassing, and especially so to those who might have struck some balance between appreciation and criticism; that is, to those engaged in the study of religion.[3]

The problem has been that the missionaries' stated purposes, while expressive of service and sacrifice, bespoke a supercilious and often demeaning attitude toward religions that the recipient peoples considered integral to their own cultures. The missionaries who embodied such complexities have seemed too admirable to be treated as villains, yet too obtrusive and self-righteous to be embraced as heroes. The most common reaction, therefore, has been simple avoidance.

Distortion, in the form both of hagiography and of negative stereotyping, was available to fill some of the vacuum. Whether the missionaries, when recognized in these ways, suffered more at the hands of detractors or of admirers would be hard to say; both types of biographer created abstract and unreal figures. Stereotyping led to more avoidance and disdain, and the more we disdained the less we learned; thus the cycle of neglect and bad history became well established.

From the outset, of course, there were noteworthy exceptions—historians who viewed missionaries as typical Americans working abroad and who dealt with the movement as they would any other. Then, in the Vietnam era, amid an increasing sense on all sides that we must learn what our overseas compatriots of the past had done and thought, the cycle was broken. Like the study of Puritanism in the 1930s, or of Protestant revivalism in the 1950s and of Indian missions in the 1960s, the study of foreign mission history began in the 1970s to take its place as a worthwhile subject for ordinary scholarly inquiry and classroom discussion. In this latest instance of revision, as in the Puritan and other

[2]Fairbank, *Missionary Enterprise,* p. 2; Phillips, *Protestant America,* p. vii. Thomson, *Sentimental Imperialists,* p. 59; Hogg, "Role," p. 372. For an overview of missionary influence on foreign relations, see Grabill, "Invisible Missionary."

[3]The reference here, and later, is to what might be called "mainline" scholarship, as carried out in secular or liberal-religious institutions. Under more conservative auspices, emphases have changed but the subject has never suffered neglect.

cases, it was "secular" scholars, more than those associated with seminaries or religion departments, who called for a new look at a neglected subject.[4]

Though developments even then were scarcely epochal, one could adopt a modest biblical phrasing to say that in the 1970s many ran to and fro, and knowledge of foreign missions was increased. But it increased unevenly, rapidly with respect to some vital foreign areas (such as China), scarcely at all in relation to others (Iran, Korea). And despite a highly developed scholarship on related matters of American ideology—dealing, for example, with Americans' sense of themselves as a chosen people and a redeemer nation—the ideological assumptions behind foreign missions were as yet touched only incidentally and sporadically. Several years earlier, Pierce Beaver of the University of Chicago had agreed to discuss missionary ideas and motivation in a volume of "reinterpretations" in American religious history; but he had remarked wryly that the task was really not feasible since "first interpretation" had not occurred. Even an adequate narrative of American participation, he argued, had not yet appeared.[5] By the 1980s, despite noticeably increased interest and effort, Beaver's observation still held.

In some respects the goal of adequate generalization and chronicling came to seem farther away than ever. Historians of missions for some time had known that in reconstructing the story they would have to look beyond official pronouncements and publicity, and beyond the sanitized reports in mission-board archives, into the actual day-to-day experience of workers in the field. But by the 1980s they also realized that women, both at home and abroad, had constituted a clear if relatively silent majority in the movement; and that women's experience must be heeded far more than it had been. They saw that they must consider the ventures and ideas of American Catholics, blacks, pentecostals, and other distinctive groups outside the Protestant mainline even though foreign mission activity in most such cases had been minimal, and theorizing nonexistent, before the Second World War. Finally, scholars grasped that beyond all this they would need to view the enterprise through the eyes and sensibilities of those whom the missionaries had set out to convert. If adequate accounts could be achieved

[4]The initiatives that are usually credited to Perry Miller in Puritan scholarship, to William McLoughlin and Bernard Weisberger in the study of revivalism, and to Alden Vaughan in the area of Indian missions, all came from outside of "Church history," as did those of John Fairbank and his students on the subject of foreign missions. In the 1980s, John Hersey's *The Call* constituted a further demythologizing of the missionary experience. For Fairbank's complaint that the missionary had been "the invisible man of American history," see his "Assignment for the '70's," p. 877.

[5]Beaver, "Missionary Motivation," p. 113.

of what mainline Protestants had done, and of what their mostly male theorists had said and written, that would be only a beginning.

Yet beginnings must be attempted. If one does presume at this point to offer a general analysis, he or she must be content either to write a preliminary institutional survey, or else to trace a limited theme or relationship. As a student of American thought with little background in "missiology" or even in institutional Church history I found it more natural and engrossing to adopt the second of these approaches, and to do so with an emphasis on the ideas that informed the movement. I have chosen, therefore, to explore the changing relations between missionary ideology (here meaning simply "body of ideas") and several pertinent and well-known themes in American thought. I have responded to the need for choice and limitation by looking intently at the missionary (or mission theorist) as American.

To adopt such a line of inquiry could mean that one is actually reducing American missionary operatives *to* their American identity, and contending that they were little more than spokespersons for national and societal values. I do not mean to fall into that common simplification. Confusing as it may be, missionaries and mission theorists claimed a number of identities, and with something like equal conviction. They always, by explicit career choice and almost by definition, insisted that their Christian identity transcended any other. They were aware, moreover, to a greater degree than most of us would have suspected, that Western forms, language, and cultural trappings could complicate or nullify what they considered was their essential witness. But none of this prevented them from acknowledging and glorying in their identities as Westerners and as Americans.

Which is to say that in the missionary context as in its other manifestations the "Christ and culture" dilemma was almost never put to rest by a simple choice. For most missionaries, as for most Christians, such a choice would have seemed unnecessary; but in any case it was just not possible. Customarily, for example, they assumed both a deeply affirming and a sharply critical stance toward their own culture. They were not alienated from it, but neither were they about to identify it, straight out, with Christ or Christianity: preachers and Christian workers did not, just because they became overseas missionaries, cease to feel strongly about debaucheries and structural evils in American society. Since the missionaries, once they had fashioned a satisfactory working relation between their own religious and cultural identities, had to make this formula effective within a quite different milieu, the difficulties in balancing its various elements were especially complex. The missionary's problem was, one might say, the Christ-and-culture problem squared.

Solutions—in particular, the formulas for relating Christian outreach to its Western cultural embodiment and vocabulary—were correspondingly varied, indeed multitudinous; and they of course changed over time as well as in response to the challenges presented by particular overseas situations. One can best chart a path through these mission ideologies, can begin to organize the varied prescriptions without doing violence to them, by calling attention at the outset to the ways in which mission theories affirmed Western and American culture; and then to the ways in which they either disavowed elements of both, or attempted for practical reasons to divorce the Christian message and outreach from the cultural trappings.[6]

The movement in its culturally affirmative mode drew, first of all, upon many of the biblical ideas and metaphors that historians have discerned in American literary expression and the rhetoric of secular expansionism. Convictions about the Adamic or Christlike innocence of the Americans, a national destiny made manifest in biblical prophecy, and America's redemptive role within the divine plan were as evident, especially in the founding years of the missionary movement, as was the biblical injunction to "go into all the world and preach the gospel." The latter, the so-called Great Commission, authorized foreign missions; biblical typologies, read as expressing God's clear intent for the New World societies, explained why the Americans bore special obligations toward foreign missions.

Among the several explanations of America's unique responsibility that were offered by biblical models, the most directly appropriate was the one that had been phrased in the latter part of the seventeenth century as a Puritan "errand into the wilderness." While the imagery of a city on a hill suggested the influence of an exemplary society, that of an errand into the wilderness suggested a heightened activism—the actual transporting of a message and witness to unknown, possibly fearsome and uncivilized places.

Among Puritans and other early Americans who drew on this set of ideas, "wilderness" meant the environment into which the Church flees for protection and nurture, but also the Church's resting-place on the way to triumphs for Christ in a wider world. Insofar as the errand had looked to the saving or improving of others, it had involved a fitful concern about the Indians, and a somewhat steadier sense of obligation

[6]Unless otherwise indicated, I am in all instances using the term "culture" in the anthropologist's sense; that is, to designate the entire secondary or humanly made environment. In phrases that juxtapose "religion" and "culture," the latter is shorthand for what, strictly speaking, should read "the rest of culture" or "secular culture."

toward England and Protestant Europe: colonial spokesmen, during the Cromwellian era and recurrently thereafter, looked to Europe as they elaborated John Winthrop's famous warning that "the eyes of all people are upon us." The more sanguine expected the societies on the North American strand to provide examples, but also active instigation and personnel, for a British and European renovation that must occur before the Church could fulfill her destiny throughout the world.[7]

Such aspirations, limited though they were, ended in defeat. Or so Puritan leaders lamented during their seasons of discouragement. The historian Perry Miller suggested in an influential essay of the 1950s that the Stuart restoration of 1660 persuaded many that, though God was surely noting the successes of his American couriers, Englishmen were not. Miller concluded poignantly that the colonists, with all Europe ignoring and slighting them, found themselves "left alone with America."[8]

Yet the ideal, far from being permanently defeated or suppressed, was revived repeatedly, often in grander forms. The epoch of the American and French revolutions constituted another great cycle of hope and despair; an ecstatic conviction, as the French Revolution began, that wicked old Europe was at last listening and taking note; then a new round of disappointment, lasting from the Thermidorean reaction through the Napoleonic era; and after 1815 a resigned determination on the part of Americans to tend their own garden and come to terms with the American environment. Again the world had not heard, or not heard well; and our frustration, we have thought, helped engender the various forms of cultural nationalism and hemispheric thinking that marked the period from 1820 to the Civil War. Somewhat later, the American retreat from internationalism after the First World War and the Versailles Conference provided merely the most acute latter-day instance of a dialectical process evident throughout American history.

As that term "dialectical" suggests, even the periods that have seemed clearly isolationist or clearly internationalist have shown contrary tendencies that complicate the historian's simpler generalizations. A parochial nationalism after 1815 could be transmuted almost overnight, by a Latin American or Central European revolution, into something recalling older commitments to an American errand. "Young America" in the mid-nineteenth century not only could feel kinship for Young

---

[7]See Williams, *Wilderness and Paradise,* pp. 84–87, 109.

[8]Miller, *Errand Into the Wilderness,* p. 15; Theodore Dwight Bozeman, "The Puritan 'Errand into the Wilderness' Reconsidered," *New England Quarterly* 59 (June 1986): 231–51. Bozeman warns, as have others, against the common tendency to exaggerate the centrality and pervasiveness of the "errand" idea, especially for the first decade of settlement.

Germany or Young Hungary (as Americans lined the parade routes for the Hungarian insurgent Kossuth); it could also take pride in having provided an example and a set of instructions. The dream of renovating old Europe and the world never fully receded.

The American foreign mission enterprise of the early nineteenth century is best understood not as a majority expression—whether it was that, even at its apogee a hundred years later, can be questioned— but as one of these countercyclical gestures of openness to the world in a period better known for cultural nationalism and relative isolationism. As the movement grew, dispatching some two thousand missionaries over a sixty-year period, it could be said to represent a substantial bloc of Americans who after the disappointments of the Napoleonic era had resolved to do what the preachers of the "Jeremiads" had always instructed them to do at such junctures: to pick themselves up and try again; to repent their own sinfulness as well as indict that of the wicked uncaring world; to reaffirm their covenant with God. In this new version of the errand they would seek to establish "that true Church which is to be as a garden in the wilderness of the world beyond the seas."[9]

Even more than earlier embodiments of the errand ideal, the foreign mission effort placed a premium on activism and motion, doing and going. To set an example, to send forth beams from the American hilltop, was seen as essential but not sufficient. Americans as Christ's special messengers were a people sent as well as chosen. Later, when the movement had grown to huge proportions and great public notice, those who could not go were admonished that the foreign missionaries were couriers on their behalf; that this was the mission of an entire, favored people. In moments of special enthusiasm or compulsiveness, for example during the campus recruitments for the Student Volunteer Movement at the end of the century, Christians were made to feel they must justify, to God if to no one else, a decision not to run the errand themselves. Those with compelling reasons for staying home were in effect expected to pay for a substitute by tithing or otherwise supporting the effort in a sacrificial way.

The missionaries, on their part, were obliged to report back to the home churches. This was not merely to inspire or shame those who stayed behind, or to assure them the job was being done; it was also because the missionaries were considered important to the renovation of their own churches and society. In that respect this nineteenth-century errand retained much of the Puritans' sense of going into the wilderness to nurture and preserve Christ's church. One of the most common

[9]Williams, *Wilderness and Paradise*, p. 87.

arguments for missions (also one of the most problematic as a contribution to the way Americans conceive their relations to others) was that missions must be pursued for the health and fulfillment of the churches at home. Christianity itself would expire, mission publicists warned, if it denied its true nature and ceased to expand over all the world.

Once more, as in the Puritan formulation of the American errand, spokesmen referred constantly to the manner in which God's providence had opened the way for the couriers. In that earlier instance God had provided Protestant winds that defeated Romish armadas or that propelled settlers off-course to New England; he had sent plagues to reduce the numbers of "savages" and make it evident that the white men were to occupy their lands; above all, God had wondrously kept the New World hidden from human knowledge until the Protestant movement had gained leverage against Antichrist and could assure settlement under the auspices of true religion. In the analogous thinking of nineteenth-century mission spokesmen, God had given his signs in the new winds of Western technology and power, in the timely debilitation of rival religions, and in the opening of treaty ports through which religion could flow along with commerce. The potential converts, in both epochs, were said to be pleading with Christ's servants to bring them the Gospel. Whenever the work seemed to be faltering, in the later instance as in the earlier one, the tendency was to conclude, not that God's intent or the natives' wishes had been misinterpreted, but rather that Christians had been failing in their clear obligations.

To propose that the analogies between the Puritan migration and the missionary enterprise are exact, or the continuities complete, would be mistaken and is by no means necessary. What does seem reasonable is to interpret this major nineteenth-century movement, in its American expressions, as rooted both in a Christian, a-nationalistic zeal for expansion and active evangelization, and equally in a fervent belief, less obviously Christian but just as religious, that Americans were under special obligation to save and renovate the world.

In theory, the first of these motivations could have operated without aid from the second. American promoters of foreign missions, conscious of an active and continuing collaboration with British and other European colleagues, could plausibly have contended that Christian world obligations were essentially unrelated to national ideology. In fact, however, they seldom advanced such an argument; they were much less concerned to disentangle Christian missions and the American mission than later apologists have been on their behalf. The religious rationale did have to be primary; and as far as possible the Gospel was to be offered in universal rather than parochial terms. But, given those caveats, spokesmen were comfortable with formulations that pictured a universal, nonparochial faith being carried to the world by certain clearly chosen emissaries: by the Protestant West, by the Anglo-Americans, and above all by God's New Israel.

Cultural affirmation in these very fundamental forms deserves to be called a dominant motif in this nineteenth-century version of the American errand. Indeed the affirmations, responding to the youthful enthusiasm of the Americans in nearly all their endeavors, tended to be extreme or at least ebullient. While sharing the Puritans' confidence in the renovating possibilities of Reformed Christianity, the nineteenth-century envoys far exceeded the Puritans in their certitude that they represented a society in which the possibilities were being realized. Yet the elements of tension between Christ and culture, between the religion the missionaries sought to represent and the civilization or society of which they were a part, qualified this affirmation, greatly complicated the missionaries' task and their seemingly straightforward agenda, and accounted for much of the controversy within and surrounding the movement. Three forms of this tension stand out.

One form, already mentioned, was an intense disapproval of certain features of the sending culture. The missionary coming out of a revivalist tradition was most likely to deplore the sins, back home, that were associated with individual morality, while the "Social Gospel" missionary common in the later stages of the movement deplored collective sins. Because neither was prone to hang out this dirty linen when preaching to benighted heathen, one might be tempted to suppose that such reservations were unimportant. But they were enormously important, and in very practical ways. The missionaries and mission boards frequently clashed with the commercial, the military, and even the diplomatic representatives of their own and other Western countries—with the rumrunners, landgrabbers, slavetraders, and other less flagrantly evil compatriots. The missionary interests, if restrained about discussing these hostilities before foreign audiences, made them part of the rhetoric when exhorting the folks at home. In the latter setting they complained loudly about the ways in which imperfections in the Western societies, of whatever description, were undercutting their best efforts.

Another form of the Christ-and-culture tension, rarely encountered yet providing prophetic counterpoint when it did occur, extended these selective reservations into much broader indictments of the home culture. From the sixteenth-century Spanish priest Bartolomé de Las Casas, railing against a society that had institutionalized Indian slavery; through

"Come and Help Us," 1630. An early seal of the Massachusetts Bay Colony. From Nehemiah Adams, *The Life of John Eliot* (Boston: Sabbath School Society, 1847), frontispiece.

Roger Williams, proclaiming the superior virtue of the native Americans; to the premillennialists and social radicals of the late nineteenth and early twentieth centuries; one could always hear a few voices within the churches and the missionary enterprise raising sharp questions about the purported overall superiority of Western or American civilization.

Far more common than either of these forms of outright hostility was a third form of tension between Christ and culture that related less to missionary ideals than to missionary practice. Mission theorists debated incessantly about the extent to which Western and American culture, however one might evaluate them, were what the missionary was commissioned to transmit; whether the cultural baggage the mis-

WORLD SUNDAY
SCHOOL NUMBER

COME OVER
INTO ASIA
AND HELP US

"Come and Help Us," 1920. Cover illustration for *Missionary Review of the World* 43 (May 1920). Courtesy of the Publications Office, World Council of Churches.

sionary carried did not in fact get in the way of his or her proper business.

The Christ-culture dialectic in this milder but exceedingly troublesome form provides the main theme and "problematic" for most of the chapters that follow. Until the late nineteenth century, the issue was commonly posed in an entirely Eurocentric way as one of evangelization vs. civilization; after that, many spoke of education, medical missions, social reform and social service without using an umbrella-term—"civilization" or "civilizing"—that they knew to be invidious. Although either-or choices between evangelization and its competitors were avoided, disagreements in this area were intense and often acrimonious.

A persistent minority, throughout the history of the missionary movement, questioned the right to impose one's own cultural forms, however God-given and glorious; and doubted the complementary "right" to suppress or seek to displace another culture, however crude or benighted. When an abstract right of cultural displacement was conceded (as it usually was, especially in the early decades), the question nonetheless arose whether it was politic to act on that right; whether the urging of particular cultural forms aided or impeded the reception of the religious message. Finally, if one did espouse aggressive civilizing aims, serious questions remained about the sequence: must one educate and civilize before evangelization can be effective? Or should one concentrate upon evangelization, confident that civilization will follow? Or should the two processes be simultaneous?

Here again, as in the matter of cultural self-criticism, we could question whether tortured, seemingly abstract issues of "evangelization or civilization" carried much meaning for working missionaries, or even for mission executives with their tidy public pronouncements. Certainly the executives and theorists, the people mainly under scrutiny in this book, spent more time and ink on these controverted issues than on the straightforward advocacy and cheerleading for which they were best known. From the beginning, mission boards, executives, and all but the most superficial advocates dealt constantly with the "cultural" questions: whether or not to teach in English; whether to send out "farmers and mechanicks" or only preachers; how to relate to governments and other secular entities.

As for missionaries in the field (it is well to remember, incidentally, that many theorists had themselves been missionaries in the field), they not only cared about such issues; they confronted them as matters of daily experience, as truly agonizing questions affecting their own sense of duty and purpose. The dispiriting gap between the generally tiny harvests of converts and the plethora of successful civilizing ventures (a gap that was not emphasized in reports to the home churches, yet was well understood by both missionaries and executives) made the issue of "civilizing or evangelizing" a personal and often painful one for devoted workers who had been recruited to evangelize the world. Even for the many missionaries, perhaps a majority, who went about their teaching or healing with little sense of personal strain, the questions that others were debating as grand theory impinged in a thousand disconcerting ways. Whether the captive audiences of proud Moslems or Buddhists in a hospital ward were to be preached to and prayed over, or just healed, was the sort of symbolic and practical issue that could determine the nature, and sometimes the fate, of any missionary endeavor.

Both for individual missionaries and for the movement at large, moreover, the built-in difficulties were intensified by outside criticism that, intentionally or not, presented them with a classic "no-win situation." If, recognizing the dangers and counterproductive effects of imposing their cultural forms, they resolved to preach "Christ only," they would be criticized for ignoring the need for material and social amelioration. If they came to see, intuitively or otherwise, that the attempt to undermine someone's religion is the ultimate cultural aggression; and if, as happened repeatedly, they therefore turned from proselytizing to social amelioration coupled with personal witness; they were then criticized as relatively unsanctified promoters of Western technology and ideology. If, finally, they tried to ignore criticism and go about their business for Christ, they were rewarded with a reputation for insular thinking.

All three missionary responses were common, and all are highly important to an understanding of the changing contours of the movement. The third stance—Bunyan's brave "I'll care not what men say"— was probably the most usual reaction. As such it goes far to explain what was most heroic in the mission enterprise, as well as what was most mundanely productive. But it also helps account for a fortress mentality more intense and pervasive than that of most other religious movements.

None of this means that the dilemmas of missions and of missionary rationales were manufactured by captious critics. The quandaries were real enough, and indeed intrinsic not just to this enterprise but, it would seem, to any venture in which one culture attempts to apply its ideals and technologies to the supposed benefit of another.

By the same token, the dilemmas are still with us. This is not to say that the historian's criticism is out of order; the missionaries and their sponsors were guilty of miscalculations and lapses of logic that are such not merely in privileged hindsight but by the light of their own knowledge and their own Bible. Yet the fact that a later, purportedly more enlightened age makes similar errors in a more dangerous world means that any wholesale condescension toward the religious and cultural ambassadors of an earlier century would clearly be inappropriate. Mr. William Buckley, in his heartwarming tribute to the people of Boston, allowed that he would rather be governed by a random two thousand Bostonians than by the Harvard faculty. At some points in the more recent history of American outreach to the world, many of us could well have wished that foreign policy and cultural relations might be handled by the first two thousand persons in the missionary directory of 1900. Retrospective criticism is in order but, to use John Higham's useful distinction, retrospective judging probably is not.[10]

If the missionaries' most frustrating problems, as well as their successes, lived on in the five hundred agencies, private and governmental, that offered overseas education and technical assistance in the 1980s, it was also true that more Americans than ever before were, at that later time, engaged in overseas evangelism. By then, the "mainline" missions treated in this book had dwindled; their ten-to-one numerical preponderance of the 1930s had been more than reversed. Yet the total number of American career missionaries abroad (many, to be sure, operating in Europe or elsewhere in the Christian world) had increased threefold—from the 11,000 of 1935 to 35,000 in 1980.[11] While many of the newer mission organizations—generally classified as evangelical or conservative evangelical—differed from the traditional movement in cultural or even religious assumptions, others adhered to nineteenth-century modes and rhetoric. In this respect, too, the story of the foreign missionary movement in its classic era has import as something more than past history.

[10]John Higham, "Beyond Consensus: The Historian as Moral Critic," *American Historical Review* 67 (April 1962): 609–25. For the Buckley *mot*, see his *Rumbles Left and Right* (New York: G. P. Putnam's Sons, 1963), p. 134.

[11]Coote, "Uneven Growth," p. 120.

CHAPTER 1

"Civilizing": From Necessity to Virtue

I find it absolutely necessary to carry on civility with Religion.

John Eliot, 1649

The Sacred Congregation for the Propagation of the Faith, founded by Pope Gregory XV in 1622 and commonly known as the Propaganda, instructed missionaries of the mid-seventeenth century not to regard it as their task to change the "manners, customs, and uses" of the people they served except where such usages were "evidently contrary to religion and sound morals." People everywhere, the Roman authorities advised, treasure their own country and customs; and nothing alienates them so readily as an attack on those customs, which may well go back to a venerable antiquity. Still more offensive is the connected effort to install European usages. God's emissaries should therefore do their utmost to adapt themselves to the native customs. "What could be more absurd," the Propaganda asked, "than to transport France, Spain, Italy or some other European country to China? Do not introduce all of that to them, but only the faith."[1]

Missionaries have been offered this sort of advice, though usually in less outright terms, with some regularity from the time of St. Paul to the present. And the pattern of responses seems consistent from one age to the next. At one extreme (though representing a majority in some eras) are those who have been so heedless, or so caught up in the self-confidence of a particular culture, that they have shunned the advice altogether. At the other are organizations like the early Jesuit order or individuals like Roger Williams who have carried respect for indigenous cultures so far as to get themselves into serious trouble.

Between the extremes have been the John Eliots of the missionary enterprise, the people whose struggles with this question come closest to telling the story of the movement. These were the missionaries and leaders who tried gallantly to separate the realms of God and of Caesar in their own cultures; who tried to distinguish in the receiving societies between customs "contrary to religion and sound morals" and customs that should be left alone; and who suffered varying degrees of distress

[1]Quoted in Neill, *Missions,* p. 179.

because all of these operations proved impossible or extraordinarily difficult.

Both Roman Catholic experience (the only kind available before the mid-eighteenth century) and the early, sporadic Protestant ventures in Asia and North America provided abundant illustrations of each response. These were known and built upon in the nineteenth century even though American Protestants rarely referred approvingly to the Catholic models, and exercised some selectivity in citing the Protestant ones.

SOURCES IN ROMAN CATHOLIC MISSIONS

The great surge of Catholic mission activity occurred in the period bounded by the rise and decline of the Jesuits, from the founding of the order in 1540 until its temporary suppression by the Roman authorities in 1773. For somewhat less than half of this time, missionary work was controlled by the religious orders themselves, in collaboration with the Spanish and Portuguese monarchs, who had divided between them the areas that were being discovered and explored. After the mid-seventeenth century, the administration of overseas missions was centralized in Rome, with results pertinent to the civilization issue. The new arrangement, which lessened rivalry among the orders, also virtually closed down such culturally adaptive ventures as the training of natives to the priesthood and the amalgamating of Christian and indigenous religious forms.

Missionary success varied with the fortunes of conquest and the degree of welcome or resistance offered by rulers; and the very definition of success varied according to one's estimate of what was required for genuine conversion. In some areas such as the Philippines, Vietnam, and much of Latin America, the church won at least nominal adherents in the thousands and created permanent establishments of Catholic faith. In others such as Japan and sub-Sahara Africa, successes were temporary, and Catholics would need to begin again in the nineteenth century. In still others, as in the surprising case of French Canada, heroic and dedicated efforts over many decades brought almost no results in the conversion of native peoples.

Against this variegated background, both persisting aims and recurring dilemmas stand out with special clarity. The most distinctive and also fundamental trait of the missionaries themselves was their sincerity in the evangelistic endeavor. There were many exceptions, and much can be said about the priests' complicity in the less godly aims of others. Yet it is fair to conclude, as Herbert E. Bolton did in a pivotal essay of 1917 on the Spanish establishments, that the missionaries' "principal work was to spread the Faith, first, last, and always." To doubt this, Bolton wrote, "is to confess complete and disqualifying ignorance of the great mass of existing missionary correspondence . . . so fraught with unmistakable proofs of the religious zeal and devotion of the vast majority of the missionaries." It is hard to question the genuineness of Jean de Brébeuf's plea to the Jesuit brethren who would follow him in working among the Hurons and who might, like Brébeuf, face martyrdom: "You must have sincere affection for the savages,— looking upon them as ransomed by the blood of the son of God, and as our brethren with whom we are to pass the rest of our lives."[2]

Behind the zeal and good will stood a conviction—missing in most other world religions, generally strong in Christianity—that the faith must be actively extended. Evangelization was seen as an absolute requirement, not just a desideratum or a matter of vocation; this was made impressively plain by the missionaries' persistence in the face of martyrdom, and in pursuit of what seemed largely a losing cause. Zenobé Membré, some nine years before his own violent death, recorded the meager results that he and other Franciscans had achieved in the Illinois country. "With regard to conversions," he wrote, "I can not rely on any. . . . There is in these savages such an alienation from the faith . . . that great time would be needed . . . for any fruit. . . . We baptized some dying children, and two or three dying persons who manifested proper dispositions." When his colleague Father Gabriel was murdered by a band of Kickapoos, and his scalp displayed in their villages as that of an Iroquois, Membré remarked that "surely he deserved a better fate, if, indeed, we can desire a happier one before God, than to die in the exercise of the apostolic functions, by the hands of nations to whom we are sent by God."[3]

The purposes of those who sponsored or accompanied the missionaries were less likely to be unequivocally religious. Philip II of Spain, chartering the expedition to settle Florida in the 1560s, emphasized "the teaching and conversion of the natives of those provinces, and the bringing them into our Holy Catholic Faith." He ordered Pedro Menéndez de Avilés, the leader of the expedition, to pursue "the good and the salvation of those souls." But for the monarch, and for most of those engaged in overseas expansion, spiritual and physical conquest were not only compatible; they were quite inseparable. It was natural for Philip to commend, in one breath, Menéndez's zeal "for the service

[2]Herbert E. Bolton, *The Mission as a Frontier Institution in the Spanish-American Colonies* [1917] (El Paso: Academic Reprints, 1960), p. 6; Ellis, *Documents,* 1: 49.
[3]Ibid., pp. 72–74.

of God Our Lord, and for the increase to the Royal Crown of these kingdoms."[4]

The missionaries, while they can be quoted to the same effect, were often at odds with the entrepreneurs or the secular authorities, and not only in mundane matters of territoriality or relative status. Even where one finds the kings and the captains at their God-fearing best, or finds priests to have been less than saintly, differences of basic objective were sufficient to complicate the tasks of both. The missionary, acutely conscious of these differences, was generally vocal about the need to close the gap by saving and civilizing his compatriots. The spiritual expansionists, to be sure, were obliged to acknowledge their integral and inescapable relation to the secular ones. They knew they relied for protection and well-being on the military arm, though not usually the commercial arm, of the sending society. But this very dependence could increase resentments against secular associates, and the sense of moral superiority to them.

The historian Stephen Neill declares flatly that the single greatest obstacle to the evangelizing goals of the Spanish missionaries was "the cruelty with which [the natives] were treated by the Spanish colonists."[5] That kind of observation, which would apply in some degree to most missions, may be especially plain in retrospect, but it was also vehemently asserted at the time. The need for some independence from the political authorities and from the kinds of conquest and exploitation they were prone to sponsor, spurred the centralizing of mission activities effected through the Propaganda. In general, the missionary's resistance to full collaboration with his own society meant that the determination to civilize was, from the start, more problematic than the commitment to spread the faith.

In some respects, certainly, the missionaries' acceptance of a civilizing function was unqualified. They believed that almost any form of civilization was superior to barbarism, and that Christendom was clearly preferable to alternative forms of civilization. Most of them, undoubtedly, looked forward to the eventual displacement of many elements in the native culture. However forcefully they might effect tactful or tolerant concessions, it had to be expected that the assumptions of superiority would show through, would in fact color every action.

The missionary, in addition, felt obliged to impose his civilization wherever, as the Propaganda put it, the customs of the people were "evidently contrary to religion and sound morals." Here the absoluteness

[4]Ibid., p. 13.
[5]*Missions,* p. 170.

of the Christianizing imperative served, repeatedly, to tip the scales in favor of civilizing intrusions. The list of "customs contrary to religion" might be very short; missionaries in the field have frequently, throughout history, scandalized home authorities with the brevity of such lists. But they were often long enough to reach into every corner of a people's mode of living.

Bishop Calderón of Cuba, who operated with one of the longer lists, assured the Spanish Queen Mother in the 1670s that he had secured decent clothing for "four thousand and eighty-one women, whom I found in the villages naked from the waist up and from the knees down." Father Louis Hennepin, reporting less successful ventures in the St. Lawrence and Mississippi valleys at about the same time, blamed his difficulties not only on the Indians' alleged lack of any idea of a deity, but also on their feeling that it was silly to confine oneself to one wife.[6]

Hennepin deplored another, deeper cultural trait: the Indians' infuriating tolerance. While the murdering of missionaries obviously thwarted evangelism, a perplexed Hennepin seemed almost equally appalled by the lack of any religious motives for such acts. One "hindrance" to the work of conversion, he wrote,

> lies in a Custom of theirs, not to contradict any Man; they think every one ought to be left to his own Opinion. . . .
> *America* is no place to go out of a desire to suffer Martyrdom, taking the Word in a Theological Sense: The Savages never put any Christian to death on the score of his Religion. . . . They don't kill people, but in particular Quarrels, or when they are brutish, or drunk. . . . They are incapable of taking away any Person's life out of hatred of his Religion.[7]

To see the Christian missionary having to deal, as evangelist, with matters as rudimentary as clothing or as fundamental as a people's inbred tolerance, is to realize how difficult it was to keep the offer of the Gospel from appearing, and being, a cultural proposition. Yet the fact that the priests attempted such a feat, and in many respects did distance themselves from their own culture, deserves recognition.

The best-known, indeed classic, missionary outburst against the secular authorities came in the impassioned protests of the Spanish priest Las Casas against the rapacity of his countrymen, and in particular against the paternalistic and oppressive labor system called *encomienda*. In debates of 1650–51 with the scholar Sepulveda, who insisted that military suppression must precede Christianization, Las Casas argued

[6]Ellis, *Documents,* 1: 21, 80.
[7]Ibid., pp. 80–81.

that these are people who define the Good, and the good life, quite differently from Europeans, and "who care little for your Philosophy or your Theology. . . . If you go naked, and carry the load of a horse upon your back, as they do, then you would be wise according to their doctrine, and would be recognized as a great man, otherwise not." In the case of Robert de Nobili, cultural accommodation led to what later generations would call "going native." Nobili learned Tamil, Telugu, and Sanskrit, converting himself so far as possible into a *sannyāsi guru,* or Hindu holy man. To avoid all associations that Indians might see as contaminating, he in fact cut himself off from contact with the church.[12]

Nobili, though he was removed from his mission at Madurai and died in poverty in 1656, seems not to have been scorned. If anything, his successes among the Indians were exaggerated and romanticized. His kind of accommodationism was, however, repudiated at the end of the century. In some fields of conquest and mission, notably those under direct Portuguese control, such principles had not made headway in the first place. In places where they had, new generations of missionaries, shocked by what they regarded as compromises with native religions, called for retrenchment. They helped pressure the Roman authorities into a series of decisions that by the mid-eighteenth century had reinstated most of the practices that Indians, Chinese, and others had found offensive. As Neill writes, "the first great attempt at 'accommodation' had failed. Rome had ruled that Roman practice, exactly as it was at Rome, was to be in every detail the law for the missions." That stance, or one very close to it, was to govern Catholic missionary practice for the next two hundred years.[13]

In cultural settings that Europeans considered more primitive than those of Japan or India, the pressure to renounce "accommodation" was likely to come from a different direction; not in the form of directives from the home authorities, but as a reluctant decision on the part of missionaries that the native peoples must be educated in European modes, and otherwise prepared, before they could be approached with the Gospel. Father Hennepin described his own change of mind in terms that expressed assumptions about native character sharply at variance with those of the romantics quoted earlier. Writing in 1697, he explained that his predecessors had "always given it for their opinion, and I now own 'tis mine, that the way to succeed in converting the Barbarians, is to endeavor to make them men before we go about to make them Christians." Taking measures to combat a nomadic lifestyle, one must "fix the Barbarians to a certain dwelling place,

[12]Ellis, *Documents,* 1: 49–50; Neill, *Missions,* p. 184.
[13]Neill, *Missions,* p. 194.

and introduce our Customs and Laws amongst them. . . . Colleges might be founded to breed up the young Savages in the Christian Faith, which might in time contribute very much to the Conversion of their Country-men."

Hennepin's reduced estimate of native culture and character did not, however, imply any high degree of satisfaction with the Europeans who were his putative allies in civilizing endeavors. He complained that the establishment of the desired communities, in which whites and Indians would dwell together, had consistently been impeded by "the covetousness of those [European merchants] who are for getting a great deal in a short time," and who did not see settled communities as advancing their own greedy interests.[14]

But those priests who, like Hennepin, saw the natives as "miserable dark Creatures . . . blind wretches" who were "naturally very vitious," could also be goaded, in effect, into more cordial relations with the forces of conquest and exploitation. The speech of Father Claude Allouez in 1671, informing the Indians of Sault Sainte Marie of their good fortune in being subjected to Louis XIV, conveys little of the compassion and cultural tolerance enunciated by colleagues like Brébeuf. "Cast your eyes upon the Cross raised so high above your heads," Allouez instructed the Indians.

> There it was that JESUS CHRIST . . . was pleased to be fastened and to die. . . . He is the master of our lives, of Heaven, of Earth, and of Hell. Of him I have always spoken to you, and his name and word I have borne into all these countries. But look likewise at that other post, to which are affixed the armorial bearings of the great Captain of France whom we call King. . . . He has slain so many with his sword that he does not count their scalps, but [counts] the rivers of blood which he sets flowing.

After much more about the blood of Christ and the blood of France's enemies, the ceremony was closed with a bonfire around which, according to another of the priests, "the Te Deum was sung to thank God, on behalf of those poor peoples, that they were now the subjects of so great and powerful a Monarch."[15]

PROTESTANTS AND THE INDIANS

Protestant mission interests, once these had been aroused after a long period of indifference during and after the Reformation, embodied much

[14]Ellis, *Documents,* 1: 75–76.
[15]Ibid., pp. 75–79, 61–63.

the same range of aspirations as those of the Catholics, and a similar range of formulas for achieving them. But among the English and other Europeans who sought to convert native Americans in areas of the future United States, the need "to carry on civility with religion" was more generally acknowledged than it had been in other times and places.

In most respects the elements in mission ideology were simply continuous with those of the past. Puritan missionaries, for example, gave first place to evangelization; believed, at the same time, in their power and responsibility to civilize; and commonly began with the intention of subordinating or even forgoing the second of these functions in order to concentrate on the first. Clearly, though, for these Protestants the majority experience was the one recorded by Eliot: they found that civilizing was a prerequisite for converting, and that it required much more emphasis than they would have liked. In both a substantive and a temporal sense, the civilizing strategy adopted by Hennepin and others marked the starting point for New World Protestant missionaries. It was "where they came in."

Until the latter part of the eighteenth century, Protestant missions in North America consisted of little beyond the admonitions in company charters and, after the initiation of John Eliot's work in Massachusetts, a few celebrated attempts to respond to them. The marching orders of the Dutch and English colonizers, much like those of their Catholic predecessors, displayed prominent humanitarian and conversionary intentions. Sir Humphrey Gilbert, heading in 1583 for the northernmost American regions, was ordered to seek the salvation of the "poor infidels, it seeming probable that God hath reserved these Gentiles to be introduced into Christian civility by the English nation." In the Massachusetts charter, a desire "to win and invite the natives of the country to the knowledge of the only true God and Savior" was proclaimed not merely as an official motive of colonization but as the principal motive. Perry Miller found that in the case of Virginia as well—despite long historiographic traditions to the contrary—this was the "most obvious theme" in the charters and early literature.[16]

Among the various "small beginnings" of worldwide Protestant missions, the smallest seem to have had the greatest effect, or at least were to be most honored as progenitors of the massive nineteenth-century movements. Large-scale successes seemed more dubious, even at the time. The Dutch could claim to have converted tens of thousands in Indonesia, Ceylon, and Formosa. Yet by the late eighteenth century, while many had been baptized, only a tenth of those baptized had

---

[16]Neill, *Missions*, pp. 220–25; Miller, *Errand*, p. 101.

become communicants. The religious (as distinguished from political) scale of the operation is suggested by the fact that in 1776 all of Indonesia was served by twenty-two Christian ministers, of whom five spoke the native languages.[17] It was the less grandiose and less official ventures, stemming from Pietism on the Continent and from the Puritan and early evangelical movements in Great Britain, that fueled enthusiasm and emulation. These provided, in retrospect at least, influential models for the generally independent and individualistic missions that later Protestants would be inclined, and best equipped, to undertake. The mixed and meager successes of German missionaries in India, and of an odd lot of Puritan, Presbyterian, and German Moravian missionaries to the North American Indians, would provide most of the historical inspiration for the nineteenth-century movement.

Among English and other Protestants on the North American continent, the familiar motives favoring an emphasis on civilization were augmented in two respects. First, like the French in Canada but with a greater sense of cultural difference, the Protestants were addressing their efforts to people whose civilization they perceived as primitive or nonexistent. Second, the Protestant missionaries were forced to operate without the kind of institutional support afforded in most Catholic instances by monarchs, powerful religious orders, or a collaboration between the two.

The first of these determinants, the gap between cultures, seemed especially formidable to Protestant Europeans who did not readily mix or cohabit with other peoples; whose exuberant missionary aims had not been tempered by experience in such highly literate and (in Western terms) sophisticated cultures as those of China or Japan; and whose religious style, unlike that of the Catholics, placed a premium on the written word and a convert's ability to understand it.

When the inevitable difficulties arose, and the forms of persuasion effective in converting other Europeans failed to move native Americans, the alternatives available to the Spanish or French in the form of collective conversions were ordinarily not options for Englishmen and Germans. There were exceptions, as in the religious-political ingathering of the Mohawk nation in the mid-eighteenth century; but by and large the Protestants, nearly all dissenters in their own countries, were in no position to secure entire tribes "for Crown and Church." Nor could they count on the kind of support, either ideological or organizational, that enabled Jesuits and Franciscans to continue their conversionary work despite repeated disappointments.

[17]Neill, *Missions*, p. 224.

Lacking the resources either for mass conversion or for dogged persistence in evangelism, Protestants in the colonizing era were even more inclined than Catholics were toward attempts to educate or reform. The eventual stereotyping of the Americans as the supreme civilizers or activists (as opposed to evangelists) in the world mission enterprise stemmed from these pre-Revolutionary realities as well as from conditions of the nineteenth century. Since the civilizing efforts were frequently as disappointing as the evangelizing ones, however, colonial experience also contributed to an important countermovement. By the mid-nineteenth century, powerful voices reminiscent of the Propaganda two centuries earlier would question the achievements of the civilizing approach and would revive a "Gospel only" ideal for missions.

That ancient ideal was not entirely forgotten even in the colonial period. Congregational and other Protestant missionaries repeatedly voiced the heartfelt aspiration to preach an unadulterated, culture-free Gospel. One of the special contributions of Count Nicolaus Ludwig von Zinzendorf, the great leader of the Moravians, lay in his forceful and repeated warnings to his followers to free themselves from all provincialisms, doctrinal as well as cultural. God, said Zinzendorf, has created different peoples with differing gifts. Missionaries should allow each society "to stick to its own language and ways," and should not attempt "to remould other peoples according to [the Europeans'] own pattern." Well aware that this sort of restraint is difficult, perhaps impossible, the Count urged a long-range strategy that would later be called self-propagation or indigenization. If the Europeans could not leave their cultural baggage at home, they could at least resolve to make their visit short, and move on. Still better, they could train others to continue the evangelizing process. "It would be much better," Zinzendorf wrote, "if there were men of their own nation among the Hottentots and other heathen, who could take care of their own people; for, as soon as we send people there, the heathen remain for ever subject to the Europeans."[18]

Such admonitions received something more than lip service when Baptists as well as Moravians refused to set high educational qualifications for native communicants; or when Quakers, in striking agreement with Zinzendorf, placed the emphasis in missions on serving and example rather than on the urging either of European behavior or of right doctrine. And among the Congregationalists, Presbyterians, and others whose method was doctrinal and intellectual, the evangelical awakenings of the eighteenth century revitalized the sense that the

[18]Quoted in Baudert, "Zinzendorf's Thought," p. 395.

missionary must, above all, spur that "turning of the heart" that defines conversion. David Brainerd, who gained the largest posthumous reputation of all apostles to the Indians, would be celebrated more for his archetypal heart religion than for any appreciable success in either conversion or education. The ideal of the primacy of evangelism, against whatever odds, remained very much alive throughout the colonial period.

Yet Zinzendorf's followers departed from his prescriptions, while Brainerd, finding the language of the Delawares "defective," made little effort to do without English and for all his heroism betrayed a good deal of squeamishness about actually living with those whom he called filthy and indolent savages.[19] Whatever the status of the civilizing component in the original form of a missionary venture—and usually there was some such commitment, overt or unconscious—experience tended to expand and elaborate it.

In the attitudes of John Eliot, who was active from the 1640s to the 1680s, one finds more appreciation for Indian personality, life, and culture than missionaries of Brainerd's sort displayed. Yet Eliot, like the missionaries of New France and like most of his own Puritan colleagues, found it "absolutely necessary to carry on civility with religion." In pursuit of civility Eliot with astonishing energy organized his "praying Indians" into fourteen towns in which they were to learn to divest themselves of their native culture—to become both good Puritans and good Englishmen. Behind such plans, of course, lay the standard insistence upon Christianity as the only true religion. Indians along with everyone else were warned on pain of death against the "blasphemous" denial of the Christian God. (Though there is no evidence that Eliot called for the death penalty against anyone, we also do not find him denouncing the law that provided for it.) Such strictures implied, however, not only that the Indians would forsake their powwows, or priest-medicine men, but that they must adopt a settled existence—cut their hair, learn to read, and learn trades.[20]

The religious requirements laid upon the Indians—for example, that they meet the Puritans' standards for church membership—were so unbending that Eliot and his Puritan colleagues have been charged with the sort of implicit racism that many find and deplore in modern intelligence tests. Not until 1652, six years after Eliot began preaching to the Indians in their own language, were the first laborious examinations begun so that a few natives might become communicants. The church of "praying Indians" at Natick, which included a large number

---

[19]Bowden, *Indians and Missions,* pp. 152–55; Edwards, *Memoirs of Brainerd,* pp. 336–38; Pettit, Introduction, pp. 14, 21, 58–59.

[20]Winslow, *Eliot,* p. 131; Salisbury, "Red Puritans," pp. 27–54.

of converts but only about a dozen communicant members, was not finally established until 1660.

To dismiss this cautious approach as racism or even as condescension is scarcely just, since Eliot's intentions can be read in the opposite way. The councillors in their ignorance of twentieth-century social science ("no anthropologists being present," as one historian notes) imagined that in pressing equally high standards for Englishman and Indian they were treating the latter with dignity and something like equality. But certainly the catechetical and other requirements were shot through with demands for both literacy and "civility" conceived in English terms. Eliot, indeed, set the tone at the outset, telling inquiring Indians in the 1640s that they could not think of forming a church until they had first "come up into civil Cohabitation, Government, and Labor."[21]

Concrete and lasting results—whether in the form of Indians socialized and converted, or in the form of increased missionary activity— were no more impressive in Eliot's case than in Brainerd's. Even before the Indian revolt of 1675 called King Philip's War had, in Henry Bowden's words, "destroyed much of what Eliot had tried to nurture in these isolated Christian communities," the fourteen praying towns had contained only 1,100 Indians. Of these, 119 were baptized Christians and only 74 were full communicants. The figures for Plymouth Colony and for Martha's Vineyard were similar, and were to be similarly diminished in the last quarter of the century. No more than twelve Congregational ministers became actively engaged in Indian missions during the seventeenth century.[22]

What Eliot did contribute to the inspiring of later generations, along with an example of hard work and devotion,[23] was a set of techniques that, as mission leaders came to believe, might work better in overseas settings than they had among the natives in North America. These included the transcribing of native languages, a venture to which Eliot had made undeniable contributions. But more often they were techniques for conveying the English language and culture. Eliot, the early Moravians, and others before about 1670 had "found it necessary" to civilize. Among the devoted workers of the later colonial era one rarely meets even their degree of original insistence on the imparting of a pure Gospel without European embodiment. The matter seemed to have been settled. By the eighteenth century Cotton Mather's view had

---

[21]Winslow, *Eliot,* pp. 148–57.

[22]Bowden, *Indians and Missions,* pp. 130–31, 113.

[23]At least one modern observer questions how much can be called devotion, how much was opportunism and window-dressing. Jennings, *Invasion of America,* pp. 238–42.

become the most common one: "The best thing we can do for our Indians is to Anglicise them."[24]

This does not mean that differences in approach were unimportant. Virtually all mission work suffered from cultural arrogance, and from obliviousness to the strength of Indian spirituality (or, better, a blank refusal to believe such a thing existed). Yet the differences among whites with respect to cultural awareness and spiritual sensitivity could be astonishing. One cannot, for example, simply lump together the missionaries who disdained actual contact with native Americans and those who spent a lifetime living and working with them.

Of the 309 Atlantic-coast agents of the (Anglican) Society for the Propagation of the Gospel in the eighteenth century, not one lived among the Indians. Such worthies are, justifiably, not so well remembered today, and certainly did not serve so well as missionary models for the nineteenth century, as the Mayhews and Sargeants in New England, David Zeisberger and the brothers Brainerd in the Middle Colonies, and such insistent promoters of Indian education as Eleazar Wheelock in New Hampshire and Samuel Kirkland in New York. Even within the latter group one finds significant variations in technique and emphasis: the Mayhews (over several generations) and Samuel Kirkland displayed unusual sensitivity to the integrity of Indian folkways; Zeisberger was outstanding in learning, teaching, and recording Indian languages, and in conforming his personal style to that of the people he served; Wheelock maintained a strong concern for indigenization, holding that Christianity would succeed among the Indians to the extent that Indians themselves became its preachers and purveyors; while David Brainerd, especially as interpreted by his friend Jonathan Edwards, provided a model of personal piety and self-sacrifice under radically adverse conditions.[25]

Amidst all this variation, the venerable commitment to preach "Christ only" seemed to have been locked away in some back drawer of white consciousness. That the missionary, in the above list, who was later considered most inspiring was the unhappy and largely ineffectual Brainerd may seem both strange and sad. Edwards even as he embroidered the biography found it necessary to criticize his friend's reclusiveness and excessive introspection; and one modern historian finds it remark-

---

[24]In a letter of 1710 "copied out" by Samuel Sewall, in Massachusetts Historical Society, *Collections* (6th series, no. 1, 1886), 401.

[25]Bowden, *Indians and Missions,* pp. 135, 112, and chap. 5; L. C. M. Hare, *Thomas Mayhew, Patriarch to the Indians, 1593–1682* (New York: Appleton, 1932), p. 104. Axtell finds Wheelock too dictatorial to delegate authority to anyone, Indian or white. *Invasion Within,* pp. 204–15.

able that Brainerd "contributed anything at all."[26] Brainerd's suffering, the piety with which he responded to it, and Edwards's publicizing, do constitute vital parts of the explanation. Another part, I think, lies in the fact that Brainerd's career recapitulated the whole cycle of missionary efforts to save Indians from themselves and their white tormentors; and by the same token prefigured what was most frustrating, as well as much that was most heroic, in the later foreign-mission experience. Brainerd, more than the others, represented an enterprise that repeatedly launched its efforts in prayerful determination to preach Christ only, then fell back on preparatory techniques that, whatever their other benefits, also produced few conversions.

Brainerd, who had been expelled from Yale in 1742 because of tactless utterances arising out of his zeal for the new revivalism, went to work that same year for the Scottish mission agency that was working in the Middle Colonies. After a period of self-preoccupation so intense that his Indian charges and their problems figured as little more than intrusions, the young missionary developed a genuine, even compulsive, dedication to the work of conversion: "Last year," he wrote in 1744, "I longed to be prepared for a world of glory, and speedily to depart out of this world; but of late all my concern almost is for the conversion of the Heathen; and for that end I long to live." He had also, however, acquired an especially dreary estimate of Indian personality and culture. The Indians were so "brutishly stupid and ignorant of divine things" that Brainerd in his journal acknowledged a fear that "there is no God, or if there be, he is not able to convert the Indians, before they have more knowledge, etc."

Brainerd showed himself willing in the face of defeat to persevere for the glory of God and the sake of his own salvation: "God . . . was pleased to support my sinking soul, amidst all my sorrows; so that I never entertained any thought of quitting my business among the poor Indians; but was comforted, to think, that death would ere long set me free from these distresses." Yet, continually discouraged about lack of results, he returned regularly to white settlements for relief and "planning"; he pursued a fitful quest for more propitious settings and better methods. When his charges, in any given place, did not respond to his ministrations, Brainerd took this as further evidence of the Indians' deficiencies, and usually of their wickedness.[27]

By his own report at least, Brainerd returned gentle and reasonable answers to the Indians' "frivolous and impertinent questions." Asked "why I desired the Indians to become *Christians,* seeing the Christians

[26]Bowden, *Indians and Missions,* p. 154. For data on Brainerd's later reputation, see Conforti, "Edwards's Most Popular Work."

[27]Edwards, *Memoirs of Brainerd,* pp. 154, 342, 157, 145.

were so much worse than the Indians" and were more adept at lying, stealing and drinking, Brainerd assured his questioners that the whites they referred to were the bad whites. He and those who sent him, he explained, were good whites who would never steal Indian land. The Indians then asked, plaintively, "Why did not *these good people* send you to teach us before, while we had our lands down by the seaside." Brainerd at such points found his patience and spirit tried, and he complained in frustration that "the poor creatures [imagined] that I should be much beholden to them, in case they should hearken to Christianity . . . insinuating that this was a favour they could not now be so good as to shew me, seeing they had received so many injuries from the *white* people."[28]

The Indians also feared that the missionaries had been commissioned "to draw them together, under a pretence of kindness to them, that they may have an opportunity to make slaves of them, as they do of the poor negroes." In this as in other Indian hesitations Brainerd could see both merit and unreasonableness. While never a defender of "bad whites," he complained of the Indians as "some of the most jealous people living, and extremely averse to a state of servitude." They seemed to have "no sentiments of generosity, benevolence, and goodness," and thus could not imagine that others might be moved by kindly sentiments in dealing with them.[29]

With respect to the spiritual and theological matters that Brainerd and his admirers cared most about, it is difficult to say which participant in such exchanges was the more befuddled. The Indians, however, as Brainerd reported them, seem to have made the greater effort to understand, and to have applied a clearer, less encumbered intelligence to the difficulties in the way of mutual comprehension. With the same show of catholicity that Hennepin had found so maddening, Indians repeatedly assured Brainerd that his God was perfectly satisfactory. The problem, they said, was that Brainerd's was quite obviously a different God from the one who had made them. There are probably three deities, they explained, who created the white, red, and black people respectively. They suggested, moreover, by way of accounting for the puzzling deficiencies of the English, that the God who created the Indians must have been observing and profiting from the errors of the God who had made the whites. "It is certain," Brainerd wrote incredulously, "that they look upon themselves, and their method of living, which, they say, their God expressly prescribed for them, [as] vastly preferable to the white people, and their method." By the same token, although the natives thought the Christian heaven sounded excellent, they preferred

[28]Ibid., pp. 344, 174.
[29]Ibid., pp. 342–44.

to go to the one reserved for Indians. Brainerd reported that they regularly, in rebuffing the offer of Christianity, expressed a wish to "live as their fathers lived, and to go to their fathers when they die."[30]

Brainerd could not understand how people well known to be spiritually and intellectually vacuous could manage to have an answer for everything. (The Devil's energetic workings might, he suspected, provide some explanation.) When one presented the miracles of Christ and his apostles as proof of the truth of Christianity, the Indians countered with miracles allegedly wrought in early times among the Indians, "which Satan makes them believe were so." At the same time, he wrote, defects of language and of intellectual equipment made and kept the Indians "either wholly ignorant of, or extremely confused in their notions about" major points of Christian doctrine. Most such points were so simple that no rational creature could fail to grasp them; but there were simply no Indian words for "Lord, Saviour, salvation . . . justification, adoption, sanctification . . . with scores of the like importance." Though the Indians showed the strongest attachment to their own "fabulous" notions and to their "frantic and ridiculous kind of worship," their language obviously lacked terms to "express and convey ideas of spiritual things."[31]

In ethical matters Brainerd again found the Indians full of ideas yet ultimately obtuse. When he pressed an "ancient, but intelligent" Indian about the afterlife, the latter explained that souls go southward after death, and that in those regions the good are happy while the souls of bad folks are miserable. The Indian having then defined bad folks as those who lie, steal, mistreat aged parents, quarrel with neighbors, and are in general a plague to humankind, Brainerd reflected with astonishment that "not a word was said about [sinners'] neglect of divine worship, and their badness in that respect." He could explain such ethical lapses only by concluding that Indians cannot grasp divine truths. There is, he said, "no foundation in their minds to begin upon."[32]

Modern readers may wonder, at such points, whether Yale College in officially expelling Brainerd for rudeness may actually have sought to rid itself of one of its dimmer scholars. But Brainerd's attitudes concerning Indian capacities were the rule rather than the exception. To berate him for his seemingly ardent misperceptions is, as Frank Shuffelton remarks in relation to Brainerd's Puritan predecessors,[33] to condemn him for being a man of his century—and, also, one must add,

[30]Ibid., pp. 345, 178.
[31]Ibid., pp. 178, 344, 351–52.
[32]Ibid., pp. 346–47, 352.
[33]Shuffelton, "Indian Devils," p. 116.

for being a man whom many nineteenth-century Christians could accept as the ideal missionary.

AGAINST THE GRAIN: THE QUAKERS AND ROGER WILLIAMS

The colonial experience, however, presented a few alternative models that would also be honored in the theory and practice of foreign missions. As already suggested, different understandings of the Indians' spirituality and capacities, and of the appropriate means for their conversion, are evident in a number of Moravian and Puritan instances. Such differences appear most sharply, however, in Quaker ideology and in the highly individual approach expounded and practiced by Roger Williams in Rhode Island.

Quakers, far from agreeing with Brainerd that the Indian personality lacked foundations for spirituality, were predisposed (and often, one suspects, quite determined) to find such foundations. The Quaker working among the Indians fully expected to "bring proof, as from a controlled experiment, that the Inner Light operated as Friends claimed it did in all men, even among savages isolated from all earthly means of learning divine truths."[34] So Brainerd's contemporary John Woolman was using an established Quaker vocabulary when he explained that "a concern arose to spend some time with the Indians, that I might feel and understand their life and the spirit they live in, if haply I might receive some instruction from them, or they might be in any degree helped forward by my following the leadings of truth among them." Though Woolman was less tortured than Brainerd was by the sense of his own unworthiness, he was more able to respect the religious knowledge and sensibilities of unconverted Indians, and even to view their condition as superior to his own: "This day, though I had the same dangerous wilderness between me and home, I was inwardly joyful that the Lord had strengthened me to come on this visit, and had manifested a fatherly care over me in my poor lowly condition, when, in my own eyes, I appeared inferior to many among the Indians."[35]

In line with this attitude of humility, and with the Quaker style generally, the means to the long-range goal of conversion were most likely to include education, the pursuit of peace and economic justice, and a type of personal witness that might or might not involve preaching. The Quakers' impressions about Indian receptivity were, moreover, likely to be different from those of the Puritan and other Calvinist

[34]Sydney V. James, *A People Among Peoples: Quaker Benevolence in Eighteenth-Century America* (Cambridge, Mass.: Harvard University Press, 1963), p. 93.
[35]Woolman, *Journal,* pp. 142, 153.

John Eliot as model for nineteenth-century missions. This three-foot statue, completed in 1889 and later destroyed, was one of six fashioned by the popular sculptor John Rogers. Courtesy of the New-York Historical Society, New York.

David Brainerd in later depiction. The caption quotes Brainerd's diary: "There is no rest but in God!" From a biography of about 1900: Jesse Page, *David Brainerd: The Apostle to the North American Indians* (New York: Fleming H. Revell, n.d.), frontispiece.

evangelists. George Fox, the sect's most eminent leader, reported during his American journey of the 1670s that the Indians had been kind and attentive as he set forth a message not noticeably milder than Brainerd's. He had instructed them

> that God made all things in six dayes, and made but one man and a woman and how that God did drowne the old world, because of their wickednesse, and soe alonge to Christ, and how that hee did dye for all and for their sinns, and did inligh- ten them, and if they did doe evill hee would burne them, and if they did well, they should not bee burned.

"Blessed be the Lord," the enthusiastic Fox exulted after one of these sessions. "His truth doth spreade." A later Quaker writer, however, who doubted "how much the untutored natives profited by this doctrine," recorded that attempts to preach it were "happily succeeded by the teaching of industrial arts."[36]

William Penn's plea, some forty years later, for more work to en- lighten the savages was, as Sydney James reports, "politely ignored." Though the hope of drawing the Indians into Christian fellowship persisted, and at some points showed encouraging results, the story of Quaker missions in the colonial period is one of a declining commitment and meager results.[37] Quakers of Woolman's prominence can be seen, nonetheless, as offering alternative models of some importance.[38]

The same surely could be said of Roger Williams, the best known of those who dissented from Puritan orthodoxy and an explicit op- ponent of that orthodoxy's stance toward missions. If John Eliot and others were apostles *to* the Indians, Williams can aptly be called an apostle *among* them.[39] His exemplification of what some twentieth- century theorists have called "Christian presence" was partly a matter of personal style but also stemmed from practical considerations—cal- culations as to what would work—and from theological conviction.

In practical terms, Williams questioned whether even the best, most linguistically competent missionaries could convert Indians to a Chris-

---

[36]Fox, *Journal*, 2: 236, 229; Kelsey, *Friends and Indians*, p. 21.

[37]James, *People Among Peoples*, p. 102.

[38]Woolman was more widely identified in the nineteenth century as a prophet of antislavery than as a model for missionaries. (See John G. Whittier's Introduction to the 1871 edition of the *Journal* [Boston: Houghton].) But the images bore strongly on each other, especially in view of the widespread appreciation for Quaker modes of dealing with the Indians.

[39]Garrett, *Williams*, p. 130.

tianity presented as doctrines and propositions. He would have been surprised not by Brainerd's lack of success along this line, a century later, but by Brainerd's having expected anything else. His great contemporary John Eliot, he reported, had been misunderstood when he promised an old Indian a suit of clothes; and Williams feared the natives "would farre more hardly understand Mr. Eliots preaching of the garment of Righteousnesse Christ Jesus." If they became converts, this might easily be for the wrong reasons. Believing readily in more than one God, they would opt for the English one, who seemed to offer superior material benefits. Especially suspect from Williams's point of view were the wholesale, seemingly impressive conversions of tribes or villages. These were all too likely to reflect conversion "from one false worship to another."[40]

A more serious complication lay in the painful fact that Indians, though sinners like everyone else, were "far short of European sinners." Christians were the "onely people of God," and the Indians were barbarians; yet surely it was improper and foolish to reserve the name of "heathen" for the latter. What people were guilty of misusing God's material benefits? Not the Indians, "for they have them not." Nor had Indians sinned "against the Gospell light (which shines not amongst them) as the men of Europe do." Even if Indians had been worse sinners than the white men, Williams insisted, they still would not be any farther from the great ocean of God's mercy than those who were seeking to convert them. If anything, he said, Indians were closer to the fount of grace than the "unchristian Christians" currently running to and fro in Massachusetts Bay.[41]

Finally—and this was the central point theologically—those seeking to convert the Indians were unsuitable for such a task because at best they were pastors and not apostles. Ministers of Christ, said Williams, are called only to preach and prophesy in their own assemblies. If unsaved persons, of whatever sort, come into those assemblies, "*God* will graciously more or lesse vouchsafe to *catch* them if he intends to save them." But it was improper and unscriptural for purported missionaries to go out "to convert *sinners* . . . without such a powerful *call* from *Christ,* as the twelve and the seventy had: or without such suitable *gifts* as the first *Ministry* was furnished with." Williams said he could not presume to act apostolically himself, and he had no faith "in the *Actings* and *Ministrings* of others."[42]

---

[40]Williams, *Writings*, 4: 373–74; 1: 83; 7: 37.
[41]Ibid., 7: 32–35.
[42]Ibid., 7: 176.

MISSIONS AND MILLENNIUM

Roger Williams found support for his restrained attitudes toward missions in biblical prophecies concerning the end-time. He doubted whether there could be "any great *Conversion* of the *Nations* before the downfall of *Antichrist*." While humanity awaited and strove toward the consummation of all things, he could commend only "the pious *Endeavors* of any (professing *Ministry* or not) to doe good to the *Soules* of all Men as We have *opportunitie*."[43] His willingness to go only that far distinguished Williams, not merely from most contemporaries, but from later spokesmen who would read the millennial drama as an urgent summons to conversionary activity. This more positive linkage between millennium and mission, especially as expounded by Cotton Mather and Jonathan Edwards in the course of the eighteenth century, would predominate in mission thinking after 1800.

Though Edwards for a time ministered to Indians at Stockbridge, Massachusetts, neither he nor Mather could be influential as models of missionary dedication. What they did provide was, first of all, a broadgauged ideal, formed in close conversation with European brethren, of evangelistic efforts arising out of a "concert of prayer" among Christian people. As spokesmen for the North American element in this partnership, both Mather and Edwards offered millennial scenarios in which the New World was depicted as God's staging area. The saints who had taken refuge there were seen, just as they had been in the preceding century, as especially chosen and obligated to carry out God's errand. The native Americans, though sometimes cast with Moslems as instruments of Satan and thus scheduled for suppression, figured in most millennial thinking as akin to the Jews. This meant that, according to Scripture, they must and would be converted before the return of Christ. Mather, indeed, gave some credence to the possibility that the native Americans *were* Jews—descendants, that is, of the Lost Tribes of Israel.

It is probably fortunate that Mather could not provide a personal model for later missionary emulation. He was, to put it charitably, not at his best when expressing Christian solicitude for God's less favored children. Unlike most of the active missionaries, and in sharp contrast to Woolman or Williams, Mather seemed to have no vocabulary for the Indians except that of belittlement, condescension, and invective. In his mind they were lying, lazy, insubordinate creatures who habitually deceived and threatened their long-suffering English benefactors. Since he also viewed the religion of these "nations of wretches" as "the most explicit form of *devil-worship*," Mather, like Brainerd some forty years

---

[43]Ibid., 4: 371.

later, could discern no spiritual foundations to build upon. Even "to humanize these miserable animals, and in any measure to . . . civilize them, were a work of no little difficulty"; to induce them to accept the religion graciously offered by their benefactors was nearly impossible. On some occasions, he thought, when Indians had requited fair treatment with barbarous responses, it would have been *the most unexceptionable piece of justice in the world for to extinguish*" the offending savages.[44]

Yet, because humankind were in all likelihood living in the last days, Christians must pursue this seemingly futile work, this "burden which is likely to make even the shoulders of angels bow and flinch." God's plan for the close of history was to be fulfilled, and the Devil's scheme thwarted, by the conversion of the heathen nations. Mather cautioned that God alone could know whether the time had actually arrived for the pouring out of the Holy Spirit and the coming of the Kingdom. "I believe, however, that it is at hand." The Church was close to her fulfillment, and one of the great tasks of her true servants was to reach out to those, like the Indian peoples of America, whom the Devil had astutely hidden away so that the biblical prophecies could not be carried out.[45]

Two other elements in this rationale for missions made it especially comprehensive and also explicitly "prophetic" of the missionary enthusiasms that would flourish after the founding of the American commonwealth. One of these was a sense of American exceptionalism that was to become especially strong in the early years of the nineteenth century. The other was the sort of zeal for a reunited Protestantism, and for a simple Gospel not divided on sectarian lines, that in the twentieth century would be called ecumenism.

Mather, whose magnum opus celebrated "the *Wonders* of the CHRISTIAN RELIGION, flying from the Depravations of *Europe,* to the *American Strand,*" did more than any other colonial author to lay the foundations for a formula in which God's mission and America's would, by and large, not demand an either/or decision. And in his correspondence, through the early years of the eighteenth century, with German Pietists who were initiating the Protestant missionary venture in Asia, he linked the sense of American chosenness to the ecumenical theme. America, he assured August Hermann Francke, was not the realm of outer darkness into which, in the parable, the unworthy servant is cast. Though haughty European theologians had thought otherwise, America was a region, he told Francke, where the saving light of the

---

[44]Mather, *Magnalia,* 2: 552; *India Christiana,* p. 29; *Magnalia,* 1: 215.
[45]Benz, "Pietist Sources," pp. 42, 50, 48–49.

Gospel had come to shine, and where "true and original Christianity" was flourishing. It was the land where, beyond all others, essential Christianity could be practiced and propagated—removed as the New World was from the sectarian factions and hatreds of the Old. America, besides being the continent where many of the heathen had been sequestered, was a place where one could recover the very Gospel that must be preached to them: the simple Christian message, the *evangelium aeternum*.[46]

Jonathan Edwards, a preeminent preacher and the leading theologian of the evangelical awakening in the mid-eighteenth century, enlarged this vision in several respects. Like Mather, he contributed to missionary idealism more through his writings than through personal example. But Edwards did serve as a missionary, and one whose theology, like that of Roger Williams, induced a moderated sense of the moral distinctions between Europeans and Indians. His ministry to Indian and white congregations in western Massachusetts, through most of the 1750s, was marked neither by great success nor by extraordinary personal sacrifice; the outstanding product of those years was his treatise on the *Freedom of the Will*. But he earned applause for taking over a poorly designed mission, managing skillfully its schools as well as its churches, and earning the affection both of Indians and of whites. Because of those modest achievements, but more because of his enormous reputation as a leader of the new evangelicalism, it was Edwards's ideas about world evangelization that (along with those emanating from British and German evangelical sources) would have the most powerful and palpable influence in the century following.[47]

Edwards's understanding of the missionary task, like Mather's, stressed both the need for Christian unity and the claims of Protestant America as God's instrument for the fulfillment of biblical prophecies. But his prognosis was distinctive in ways that made Edwards's thinking especially congenial to that of the nineteenth century. In particular, his version of the final dramas of history came close to what is usually called postmillennialism.

Though Edwards's various millennial expressions were not always consistent, during the halcyon days of the Great Awakening he placed himself on record as expecting a glorious career for humanity before Christ's return. " 'Tis probable," he wrote, that in a number of respects "the world shall be more like Heaven" in that preparatory time. Though he foresaw that people would then be more occupied with spiritual

[46]Mather, *Magnalia*, 1: 25; Benz, "Pietist Sources," pp. 32–33.
[47]Chaney, *Birth of Missions*, pp. 293, 57–70; Winslow, *Edwards*, pp. 268–92; Rooy, *Theology of Missions*, pp. 292–93.

employments, still some very mundane developments would make this possible: "There will be so many contrivances and inventions to facilitate . . . [people's] necessary secular business that they shall have more time for more noble exercise." Edwards in fact predicted something like the partially realized global village of the twentieth century. The people of the future, he wrote, "will have better contrivances for assisting one another through the whole earth by more expedite, easy, and safe communication between distant regions than now. The . . . mariner's compass is a thing discovered by God to the world to that end. . . . And so the country about the poles need no longer be hid to us, but the whole earth may be as one community, one body in Christ."[48]

America's role in the unfolding drama was reasonably clear. Over and over again, as he defended the New England revivals against those who thought them spurious or devilish, Edwards insisted not merely that the revivals were genuine but that they confirmed God's intention to redeem the world through this youngest and perhaps least of his peoples. That the millennium would begin soon with the conversion of multitudes from every nation, was virtually certain; that the revivals constituted "the dawning, or at least the prelude" for this process was not unlikely. Many things, for example those biblical passages that seemed to allude to the geography of the New World, made it on the whole "probable that this work will begin in America."[49]

Edwards's rather cheery predictions for improvement in the human situation before Christ's return have been seen, rightly, as signaling a new departure in Calvinist thinking.[50] These "postmillennial" ideas, not unique even when Edwards expressed them, were to become much more common in the next two generations. Samuel Hopkins, an Edwards disciple who was harsher on some Calvinistic points than his mentor had been, also outdid the latter in describing the facilities and enjoyments in store for a redeemed human race. The missionary thinking of the revolutionary and immediate postrevolutionary generations, while it embraced the usual gamut of motives, increasingly featured the kind of worldly anticipation that had marked Edwards's new departure.

In doing so, it gave added visibility and respectability to the civilizing impulse. Education and other preparatory techniques were less likely,

---

[48]*The Philosophy of Jonathan Edwards from His Private Notebooks,* Harvey G. Townsend, ed. (Eugene: University of Oregon Press, 1955), pp. 207–8.

[49]Jonathan Edwards, "Some Thoughts concerning the Present Revivals," in *The Great Awakening,* C. C. Goen, ed. (New Haven: Yale University Press, 1972), pp. 353–58; Stein, Editor's Introduction, pp. 28, 15–29.

[50]Goen, "New Departure," pp. 25–40.

by the revolutionary period, to be embraced by default, less likely to be resorted to because barbarous natives were greeting the pure salvific Word with stares and laughter. "Civilization" came to be urged, instead, within a thoroughly affirmative depiction of the millennial role assigned to a Protestant society and culture. While this tendency to make a virtue out of what had been a mere necessity should not be overdramatized, the growth of a postmillennial enthusiasm that affected all mission activities was at least as dramatic as the parallel rise of revolutionary consciousness.

The resulting "American" mission ideologies are best seen, not as superseding or submerging the biblical imperatives, but as intensifying them. The essential errand, and the bedrock reality, remained a demand laid upon the church rather than upon Americans or even Protestants. Yet within Christendom, Protestants had regularly seen themselves as exceptional to the point of constituting the only true church. The course of American prenational development, from Puritan migrations through intercolonial wars, had further narrowed and intensified this exceptionalism in the crucible of radical Protestantism and within Anglo-Saxon cultural forms. By the revolutionary era, it seemed to Americans that the task to be carried out for God, while still to be shared with other Protestants and especially with the better sort of Englishmen (the Evangelicals), seemed quite evidently to be assigned to the Americans above all others. Those who worried about such matters at all, and who preached or wrote about them, seldom felt any essential tension between the glory of God and what poets of the revolutionary generation celebrated as "The Rising Glory of America."[51]

---

[51]This was the title of a commencement poem by Philip Freneau and H. H. Brackenridge for the College of New Jersey (Princeton) in 1771.

CHAPTER 2

New Nation, New Errand

If the Church . . . is to rise from this day forth, where is it more likely to arise than in the United States, the most favored spot on this continent which was discovered, as I may say, by the light of the Reformation?

Edward Dorr Griffin, 1813

Any presentation of American mission ideology in the context of early national history must start by acknowledging that in the beginning the foreign mission interests, however grandiose their proclamations, constituted a tiny minority. A traditional view, that Americans turned inward after the second war with England, seems generally accurate. The confidence about reforming Europe and saving the world, so evident in the formal and popular expression of the revolutionary period, gave way to zeal for nation-building; the expansionism promoted as our "manifest destiny" tended to be continental, not worldwide. The Monroe Doctrine of 1823, even as it offered rationales for future hemispheric imperialism, addressed Europe in tones more of resigned disapproval than of any disposition to renovate or reform.

In that setting, the dispatch of a few dozen missionaries to lands beyond Europe does not suggest a groundswell of confidence that God's American agents were going to evangelize the world. The most impressive sending organization, the American Board of Commissioners for Foreign Missions, operated outside the denominational structures; and despite the forming of "boards" with denominational titles, missions for some sixty years would not be taken to the bosom of organized Protestantism. Clearly this was not a majority movement, nor even a broadly popular one.

The concrete signs and effects of a missionary impulse were, nonetheless, far from negligible. Promoters, though they fretted about the thinness of support for their venture, also boasted about the size of their budgets and the numbers of their workers and converts. As a modern scholar has remarked in chronicling Protestant voluntary activity, the "benevolent societies," taken all together, came off rather well if one compared their expenditures with what the Federal Government was spending on roads and canals. And though most of these voluntary associations devoted themselves to domestic enterprises, several of the largest were engaged in foreign missions; among the thirteen leading organizations in 1828, the American Board stood second in income, just below the American Bible Society.[1]

The early foreign mission societies represented internationalist impulses not only in their concern for people in exotic lands but also in their strong sense of connection with coworkers abroad. Like the antislavery, peace, prison-reform and other movements, the mission organizations maintained strong ties and active correspondence with their European (overwhelmingly this meant British) counterparts. Over and over again in the promotional literature and embarkation sermons, the obligations of a general Anglo-American community were stressed along with those of Protestantism at large, and almost as much as those of the specially favored Americans. The Anglo-American connection, which over the years would generate both the greatest triumphs of the missionary movement and some of its more retrograde tendencies, was clearly visible in the earliest activities and hagiography of the movement.

The original expressions of American foreign mission idealism reflected the push and pull of sentiments that were sometimes hard to reconcile. The optimistic expansiveness of world conquerors struggled against the despair occasioned by inadequate support at home. Enthusiasm about American responsibility and leadership was tempered by broader alliances and deeper commitments. Though a civilizing conception of missions was in vogue, uneasiness and vacillation on that point were also apparent.

But when it came to the issue that has perhaps been most troubling, in retrospect, both to apologists and to critics—that of nationalist motivation versus religious motivation—little debate arose because most contemporaries saw no need for a choice. Christian obligation and American obligation were fundamentally harmonious. The mission advocacy, in other words, involved the same profound interweaving of religious and political symbols that historians have consistently found in the social and literary mind of the early Republic.

Those who thought and acted on behalf of missions were the keepers of a newly relighted and somewhat sputtering flame. To insist that the flame's ignition was purely religious, or that it was merely a matter of national identity or expansiveness, would be to miss the point that is probably most vital for an understanding of American efforts, then and

---

[1]The figures for those organizations were $143,000 and $114,000. The third-ranked, the American Tract Society, had an income of $69,000. *Christian Almanac for New England* (Boston: Lincoln and Edwards, 1830), p. 31. The comparison with expenditures for internal improvements appears in Foster, *Errand of Mercy,* p. 121.

later, to redeem the world. The national and the religious impulses were fundamentally not separable. Operating, in their profound interdependence, more as presuppositions than as propositions, neither could be a mask for the other, nor be reduced to the other.

If somehow deprived of either of these components, the flame of American participation in missions would, for the time, have gone out.

HOME BASE AND FOREIGN FOOTHOLDS

The American Board of Commissioners for Foreign Missions (ABCFM) deserves the special attention that has always been accorded to it. Founded in 1810, it was the first and for a half-century the largest agency to send workers abroad. It was also, in its combination of breadth with provincialism, an epitome of the enterprise at large.

Though a federative organization that served the needs of denominations outside New England, the ABCFM was heavily dominated by Massachusetts Congregationalists. While its leaders accepted a more than regional responsibility, they spoke and wrote as heirs of the Puritans. And though the organization sent its small band of missionaries to a number of fields, its concentration of personnel and publicity on a very few of them—notably on the Sandwich Islands, or Hawaii—had the effect of sharpening the definition of the entire movement for the purposes both of promotion and of caricature.

The influence of New England and the centrality of the ABCFM are suggested in some overall statistics. About two dozen American agencies for evangelism and Bible distribution were founded between 1810 and 1870. From imperfect data we can calculate that 2,000 Americans served overseas, in that time, as missionaries, lay assistants, workers, and wives (who were not yet listed as missionaries).[2] But five of the sending agencies—the ABCFM; the boards representing Northern branches of the Baptists, Presbyterians, and Methodists; and the Southern Methodists—accounted for 80 percent of the activity. And the persisting dominance of the ABCFM within this leading group is suggested by the figures for the early 1850s when, as the agent for Presbyterian and Reformed bodies as well as for the Congregationalists, the Board was sponsoring 40 percent of all missionary personnel. At the end of the 1860s this was still the most formidable organization in numbers of workers and, by quite a margin, in wealth. The Baptists, neighbors on Beacon Hill and soul mates in both rhetoric and strategy, had been

[2]My sources for these and the immediately following estimates included Bliss, *Concise History,* esp. pp. 307–11; Newcomb, *Cyclopedia of Missions;* Anderson, *Memorial Volume;* Anderson, *Foreign Missions,* esp. p. 342; and Warneck, *Outline.*

second in founding date (1814) and for some years were second in most other respects. The Congregationalist and Baptist pluralities, through these formative years, ensured that a New England heritage was being implanted as well as (sometimes egregiously) proclaimed.

About 10 percent of the total "foreign mission" personnel, during the first half-century, served the American Indians. For the rest, the two most frequented areas of the world were the Levant or Middle East, and the region that included Burma, Ceylon, and the Indian subcontinent. The American Board sent large and roughly equal numbers to these two areas; while the Baptists concentrated heavily on Burma and India. The ABCFM up to 1860 sent one-fifth of its personnel to Hawaii and Micronesia, one-eighth to the East Asian fields that rose in importance after 1830, and just over one-tenth to Africa.

As for other groups active in this period, the "Old School" Presbyterians (who did not work through the American Board) sent missionaries to West Africa and India; the Reformed Presbyterians (Covenanters) to the West Indies and Syria; the Methodists to Liberia, South America, and China; the Episcopalians to China, Liberia, and Greece; the Lutherans to India and Liberia; the Disciples of Christ to Turkey, India, China, the West Indies, and Europe; and the United Brethren to West Africa. When Japan was opened to the West, the Episcopalians, Presbyterians, and Dutch Reformed were immediately on the scene.

Mission Apologetics

The many-layered rationale by which the promoters sought to inspirit embarking missionaires and draw public support involved biblical, humanitarian, and "national" arguments in about equal measure. The biblical and humanitarian justifications were normally stated first, not merely because they were putatively fundamental, or because one usually argues from the general to the specific, but most importantly because the entire scheme of reasoning was profoundly historical. It proceeded from God's creation of the world and its peoples through the revelation in Christ, the first appearance of missions in the apostolic church, and the long ages of missionary neglect; only then focusing on the present age, in which the true intent of the Reformation had found expression in America and, for the great majority of spokesmen, in New England.

An "Address to the Christian Public" in November 1811 placed the ABCFM's earliest activities in the context of two justifications for missions: the oneness of humanity and the instructions of Christ. Having determined to send envoys to a distant and little-known region called the "Birman Empire" (Burma), and foreseeing the objection that Christians ought to expend their resources closer to home, the Board's spokesmen pressed the theme of universality. Burma was admittedly distant but, they asked, "is it not composed of our brethren, descended from the same common parents, involved in the consequences of the same fatal apostasy from God, and inhabiting the same world, to every creature in which the Savior has directed that his Gospel should be preached?" Heathen at home and heathen halfway around the world, they argued, have the same claim to attention "so long as the means of access to them are in our power." Surely the common parentage of humankind signifies the equal worth of all souls in the sight and creative purposes of God. Similarly, the divine response to humanity's Fall and consequent sinful condition is an offer of salvation that makes no distinctions among persons. Leonard Woods of Andover Seminary listed, as one of the six leading motives for missions, the plenteousness of Christ's provision for the salvation of all mankind: his sacrifice means that all who believe can be saved.[3]

An important corollary was the inadequacy of all other religions as responses to the human condition. Woods was typical in contrasting Judaism and Christianity as, respectively, exclusive and expansive religions. (Late in the century, when scholars could claim at least rudimentary knowledge of other world religions, the same contrast would be drawn with nearly all of them except Islam and some forms of Buddhism.) The point was that these exclusive or reticent faiths had ruled themselves out of contention. Their failure to express a sense of universal responsibility and aspiration could be taken as acknowledging Christianity's right of conquest even in their own homelands. Or at least—and this may be a fairer statement of what most spokesmen had in mind—one could safely judge these other religions to be incapable of progressing beyond tribalism. Their votaries, already half aware of this, would eventually acknowledge it fully and with joy embrace the broader faith.

As all this implied, non-Christian religions were confidently assumed to be ill suited, not merely for general adoption, but even for meeting the needs of their own adherents. Samuel Worcester, a founder of the American Board, in 1815 attempted "a Christian survey of the Pagan world." Asserting the utter worthlessness of the morality and the wisdom of other religions, he concluded that, without exception, those outside Christianity

[3]ABCFM, *Minutes of the Second Annual Meeting,* p. 25 (bound in *First Ten Annual Reports* [Boston: Crocker and Brewster, 1834]); Woods, *Newell Ordination,* pp. 10–13.

have no good hope. . . . Their gods cannot save them; their
wise men will not, cannot direct their feet into the way of
peace; their religion does not satisfy the heart or the life; does
not bring them to the blood which cleanseth from sin,—does
not shew them a redeeming God, does not fit them for the
mansions of immortal light and purity,—does not dissipate the
darkness which heavily broods over them, thickening into the
blackness of eternal night![4]

Any notion about relative virtues in other religions, therefore, could
be nothing more than "an impious dream of infidelity." Spokesmen for
missions admitted readily that "Christendom itself presents scenes for
pious exertion, which for ignorance and misery are in heathen regions
scarcely exceeded." Critics thought such acknowledgments devastating,
but the proponents saw no contradiction at all; Christianity had faltered
in Europe or America only where misinterpreted or mixed with "vain
superstitions"—in places, that is, where evangelistic efforts were needed
as much as they were needed in Burma or Hawaii. Pagan conditions,
moreover, were vastly worse than those in the apostate regions of Christendom. In his very religion, not just in his irreligion or apostasy, the
non-Christian indulged in practices that were "absurd, sanguinary, and
obscene."[5]

This kind of invective betrayed ignorance (or studied obliviousness)
even to what the Jesuits and other Westerners had learned about Eastern
religions; and it was scarcely suggestive of compassion or human understanding in those who voiced it. Yet compassion was central to the
response people like Worcester were proposing. Unlike Jonathan Edwards's auditors in Enfield, Connecticut, distant heathen were generally
not regarded as sinners in the hands of an angry God; they were seen
as piteously lost souls in the thrall of the Devil and his ingenious systems.
Even "the greater glory of God" had receded to the background as an
argument for missions,[6] while benevolence and compassion had assumed leading places. In Leonard Woods's ordination sermon for the
missionaries going to Burma and India, no motive resembling "Gloria
Dei" was mentioned; and even obedience to Christ's Great Commission
appeared rather far down the list. Woods instead began his catalogue
of reasons for missions with more than two pages detailing the Christian's capacity "to feel for his fellow creatures," to yearn for their tem-

---

[4]Worcester, *Paul on Mars Hill,* p. 26.

[5]Ibid., p. 27; Richard Furman, "Address," in *Proceedings of the Baptist Convention for
Missionary Purposes* (Philadelphia: The Convention, 1814), p. 40.

[6]Beaver, "Missionary Motivation," pp. 113–51; see esp. pp. 139–47.

poral comfort and their prospect of "immortal happiness in the world to come." The plight of the heathen must evoke the Christian's "tenderest affections." The relevant attribute of God, Woods insisted, is his love for his creatures, not his demand for glorification or even obedience.[7]

Obedience occupied a central place, however, in the second cluster of pro-mission arguments. Spokesmen commonly interpreted both the biblical commands and the apostolic example as calling for what Samuel Hopkins was ingeniously depicting, within a stern Calvinist system, as "disinterested benevolence."

This conception, which could serve as a rationale for religious activism of all kinds, again was grounded not upon terror but upon divine and human compassion. Adoniram Judson, a Congregationalist-turned-Baptist and the most celebrated of the first generation of foreign missionaries, preached duty and obedience in voluntaristic and very personal terms. One is reminded of the hymn, "How gentle God's commands! How kind his precepts are!" Judson thought that simple admonitions to do one's duty, or to obey the Great Commission, were usually cold and inappropriate. The idea, instead, is that in exercising benevolence one is responding to the benevolence of God. And obedience to Jesus' explicit commands should be motivated not by terror or even by the stern requirements of conscience but by the opportunity, as Judson put it, of "pleasing Christ." In 1846, Judson advised the students at Waterville College (later Colby) in Maine that "if any of you enter the Gospel ministry in this or other lands, let not your object be so much to 'do your duty,' or even to 'save souls,' though these should have a place in your motives, as to *please the Lord Jesus*. Let this be your ruling motive."[8]

Such formulas reflect the conscious rejection of hard-core Calvinism that also appeared in revivalism and the emerging liberal movement. The revitalized convenant under which the foreign mission errand was being conducted did bear traces of the old contracting parties: a God who is angry with infidels and his own backsliding people, and an elect who own the covenant in fear and repentance. But the predominating tone is quite different, both more affirmative and more ebullient. The parties to the renewed covenant are a God of yearning compassion and an elect people, already blessed, who are bound to act out of gratitude more than out of a need for repentance or expiation. To understand that difference is to appreciate more fully both the exuberance and the completely convinced self-righteousness that pervaded the new sense of religious and national mission.

[7]Woods, *Newell Ordination*, pp. 9–11, 14.
[8]Quoted in Judson, *Adoniram Judson*, p. 473.

"Let your object be to please the Lord Jesus." Adoniram Judson arrested as a subversive person, Burma, 1824. From Thomas Smith and John O. Choules, *The Origin and History of Missions*, 2 vols. (Boston: Gould, Kendall, and Lincoln, 1837), 2: frontispiece.

"Hopkinsian" ways of stating the motives for world improvement were highly influential. At Andover Seminary, where most of the earliest participants in the foreign mission movement were trained, Samuel Hopkins's "consistent Calvinism" was so pervasive and to some so oppressive that in 1809 the original professor of Sacred Literature had resigned in protest, whereupon the Hopkinsian influence had become even stronger.[9] Yet the term Consistent Calvinism seemed in some ways a misnomer, or even a joke, since Hopkins had managed to make the theology of Jonathan Edwards both more harsh and more optimistic. He had discouraged, more firmly than Edwards had, the sinner's hope of promoting his or her own salvation; yet he had also framed a charter for reform activism, and had himself behaved as a reformer.

The explanation lay in an inner logic that linked Calvinist determinism to exactly the kind of self-sacrificing human effort the missionary and reform movements called for. Hopkins in his role as super-Edwardsean insisted that humans can do nothing to effect their own

[9]Elsbree, *Missionary Spirit,* p. 99.

regeneration. But he went on to argue that they must therefore work and act benevolently without hope of salvation or reward. The converted person "will be a friend to God, and must be pleased with [God's] infinitely benevolent character, though he see not the least evidence, and has not a thought, that God loves him and designs to save him." Whether the professing and hopeful Christian is really on the way to salvation or to damnation, he rejoices "independent of his own personal interest," knowing that his actions are small recompense for all God has done for him and for the world. *Et voilà:* the road to personal assurance—to the modicum of assurance available to humans—leads directly through the precincts of social reform and public betterment! Though the redeemed person will actually hold a higher sense of his own needs than the unredeemed sinner can, yet "he is disposed to give up and renounce all [self-interest] so far as it is inconsistent with the public interest, and as is necessary to promote the greatest common good."[10]

THE LANGUAGE OF SPIRITUAL EXPANSIONISM

These various arguments for foreign missions converged in a charter and battle plan for Christianity's final conquest of the world. At this point the language of tenderness and compassion could be drowned out by that of militance—even of ruthlessness. The Reverend Heman Humphrey, pastor of the Congregational Church in Pittsfield, Massachusetts, in 1819 delivered the ordination sermon for Hiram Bingham and Asa Thurston, leaders of the first party of missionaries to the Sandwich Islands. Humphrey preached on "The Promised Land," using a text from the thirteenth chapter of Joshua to proclaim that for the modern church, as for the Israelites, "there remaineth yet very much land to be possessed." In this as in nearly all the manifestoes of this period, the element of "Jeremiad" or thundering rebuke was mainly retrospective. Present company were not berated; it was the forefathers who had failed to press onward and obtain the promise that the present age must now see fulfilled. The church, after the initial successes of the apostolic age, had stopped short and, like the Israelites before them, had neglected to complete the conquest of the world.

The Israelites had faltered, Humphrey warned, because their courage had "failed them in the midst of the most brilliant success." Though God had promised that they should possess the fertile lands of the Philistines, and the coasts held by the Sidonians and Amorites, and the

[10]Samuel Hopkins, *Works,* 3 vols. (Boston: Doctrinal Tract and Book Society, 1852), 1: 389, 395–96.

hill country around Mount Lebanon; though he had devoted "several other nations . . . to utter destruction"; the people sat down "ingloriously contented with present acquisitions." Such a state of things "was neither safe, nor honorable to those who had been brought thither through so many perils, and encouraged to push their conquests by so many promises." The Israelites had had to be chastised severely and *ordered* to possess the land.

In the same way, the church had sat itself down through "thirteen whole centuries of strange and criminal apathy" and the still more astonishing eras of "Protestant remissness, since the glorious reformation." Only in the present age, the preceding twenty-five years, had a new forward movement begun. Lest anyone consider the Old Testament analogy tenuous, Humphrey assured his hearers that it was exact in all respects save one: the weapons of the modern Israelites must be spiritual ones. Otherwise, the text admitted of "an easy, and I think a legitimate application to the present comparative state of the church and the world":

> As the nation of Israel was then *militant,* so is the church now.
> As the land of Canaan belonged to Israel, in virtue of a divine
> grant, so does the world belong to the church; and as God's
> chosen people still had much to do, before they could come
> into full and quiet possession of the land, so has the church a
> great work to accomplish, in subduing the world "to the obedi-
> ence of Christ."

As one follows the Old Testament parallels through Humphrey's long sermon, it is clear enough that the modern Israel he has in mind is not New England, or America, or even Christendom. It is the church. Though he several times refers to the special advantages and duties of "our American Israel," and clearly would be capable of expanding those references, the sermon is a forceful reminder that the plea for foreign missions could be stated comprehensively without allusion to a national mission. As John A. Andrew concludes, in a study of the very missionaries Humphrey was addressing, "the empire they sought to establish was the kingdom of God; that it was also American seemed only providential."[11]

"Only providential." But this of course was the nodal point; here the missions of church and of nation converged and blended. God's placement of America, and of New England, at the threshold of the

[11]Humphrey, *Promised Land,* esp., pp. 4–5, 15; Andrew, *Christian Commonwealth,* p. 170.

ther date, while others were content to leave the matter vague.
arly everyone agreed it would happen within two centuries.[12]
st millennialists, whether they located the new society on earth
ehow in the heavens, described the coming perfections, as Ed-
had, in terms that were highly familiar to earthlings. Samuel
ns's *Treatise on the Millennium,* published in 1793, showed once
low a supposedly harsh Consistent Calvinism could, in the end,
t the hopeful spirit of the times. Or even support it in the
ing: Hopkins, reversing the order found in the jeremiad and
ther forms of pastoral discourse, gave the good news first, and
en—after nearly one hundred pages describing millennial con-
—gave the bad news concerning the years of calamity, wicked-
d suffering that must precede this glorious time.

kins believed the true reign of Christ would begin at the end
wentieth century. The preceding time would be filled not only
sasters and struggles but also with signal triumphs over Ro-
, "Mohammedanism," and all other forms of infidelity. Writing
ment when European society, in particular, seemed poised be-
lissful hopes and new calamities, Hopkins depicted this time
and waiting in words that anticipate Percy Bysshe Shelley's "If
omes, can spring be far behind?" (though they also make one
God did not assign the writing of Romantic poetry to New
divines):

e winter in the natural world is preparatory to the spring
ummer . . . and the former is necessary to introduce the
and in the best manner to prepare for it: So in the moral
, or the church of Christ, what precedes the Millennium
he winter, while the way is preparing for the summer, and
t takes place has reference to that happy season.[13]

active promoter of evangelistic work among the Indians, and
missions to Africa, Hopkins frequently expounded the role of
ionary movement in the unfolding millennial drama. But a
or at least more cantankerous) Calvinist, Edward Dorr Griffin,
nore vivid connections between the glowing enthusiasm for
and a firm, conservative biblical framework. Griffin, white-
gigantic, and eloquent, preached a Calvinism so harsh that
College and several successive congregations ruled him objec-
before he found his true vocation, that of a forceful college
who rescued the nearly extinct Williams College and subdued

Goodell Ordination, pp. 17, 21.
ns, *Millennium,* p. 83.

millennial age was therefore central to sti
tions. The general and more transcendin
are justified at any time, why they ought
since Christ's ascension—deserve to be s
specific, local questions—Why now, afte
activity? Why here, in this small corner
planations that made up in drama and
might lose by their ostensibly second-or

To begin with, the insistence upon a s
helped spell out the meaning of obedi
Christians must be obedient to the dicta
the manifest divine plan for the develo
Jonathan Edwards in 1740 had though
the world's final redemption would b
missionaries and their supporters, seve
plained their enterprise within the sa
breathtaking expectation. (Whether, wi
America's spectacular part in it, the p
supported in the same way is quite anc

To say that millennial belief was so
that everyone read the biblical proph
notoriously not the case. Premillennial
along with other cataclysmic events,
history; while the postmillennial schen
thousand-year period. But our biblical
been told they must choose between tl
which were not invented until the l
various possible ways of ordering tl
Christ's spiritual or bodily return. The
plicated point was that virtually all Ch
in history to be near. The Presbyteri
the matter as follows in 1822:

> That there is a time coming, whei
> tre of rebellion against God, and
> ing which is the natural offspring
> restored to the reign of truth, anc
> blessedness, is, if I am not deceiv
> pectation of all who bear the chri
> vation! Happy world!

Some, as Miller added, believed the
the door," while others thought it tc

or anc
But n

Mo
or son
wards
Hopki
again
suppo
beginn
many
only th
ditions
ness, a

Hop
of the
with d
manisn
at a m
tween
of trial
winter
gratefu
Englanc

As th
and s
latter
worlc
is as
all th

As ar
of black
the miss
stricter
offered
missions
maned,
Harvard
tionable
presiden

[12]Miller,
[13]Hopki

its unruly students. Yet beginning with a famous missionary sermon in 1805, *The Kingdom of Christ,* he repeatedly proclaimed the place of Christian missions in a triumphant, highly optimistic picture of human and sacred history. In one of those discourses he suggested that the founding of British mission societies in the 1790s, together with the cycle of American revivals that began soon after, had initiated the "heavenly showers of grace" foretold in biblical prophecy. "May we not then yield ourselves to the confidence," he continued, "that Zion has seen her darkest hour, and that her light will henceforth continue to shine with increasing brightness to the perfect day?"[14]

Even allowing for a certain amount of cheerleading on the part of those responsible for awakening potential givers, the overwhelming enthusiasm of the early promoters is important to recognize. Missionary spokesmen might, after all, have aroused support by stressing human wickedness, social and international chaos, a coming Judgment, and the immediate need to save as many brands from the burning as possible; in other words, by preaching jeremiads and taking a consistently premillennial stance. Instead, their enthusiasm for human spiritual and social renovation rolled through their "addresses to the Christian public" like great breakers on a windy shore, suppressing and absorbing the smaller waves of worldly pessimism or of concern about the exact sequence of millennial events. Though Christians of their own generation, according to the ABCFM leaders, had seen "most astonishing and unparalleled displays of human wickedness," they had also beheld

> innumerable trophies of divine grace. From nations betrayed, enslaved, weltering in their blood, and shrouded in a starless night of infidelity and profligacy, their attention has been turned with transport to the light which has encircled the dwellings of the faithful, and to the rising glories of the Sun of Righteousness. Their ears, for a long time stunned by the outcries, blasphemies, and unutterable confusion of a wicked world suffering the vengeance of God from the hands of cruel men, have found a happy relief in hearing the glad sounds of salvation reverberating through heathen lands, and in listening to the songs of converted idolators.[15]

No one who claimed to rely on the biblical prophecies could be entirely cavalier about the great and devastating battle of Armageddon— Satan's last stand—that must be fought before the final return of Christ and the Last Judgment. But even at that point the residents of Protestant

[14]Griffin, *Sermon in Sandwich,* pp. 31–33.
[15]ABCFM, *Second Meeting,* pp. 49–50.

lands need not be too apprehensive: Samuel Miller thought it possible that the final conflagration would cause more misery in "the old Latin Earth" than in lands where true Christianity had triumphed. The battle "must rage with peculiar violence on the site of that Empire of persecution and blood, over which Satan, for so many ages, reigned." He prayed, at any rate, "that our beloved Country, which has so little of *the blood of the saints* in its skirts, may be in a great measure exempted from the horrors of that awful scene!" However that might be, Christians should not be deterred by apprehensions about those events. For one thing, "*the Lord of hosts is with us.*" For another, even within a Calvinist framework the devoted and united effort of Christians could mean that "THE CONFLICT SHALL BE MADE SHORTER STILL!"[16]

While it was not common to come right out and propose an American exemption from Armageddon, it was quite usual to draw bold inferences from what seemed the plain fact of a favored status. The Americans, in fulfilling their covenanted obligations, would be expressing gratitude for blessings already conferred; but also, quite simply, acknowledging that God had chosen as his instrumentality this little knot of the world's population. Edward Dorr Griffin offered a classic statement of the formula according to which the Deity pursued his most ambitious cosmic purposes by winnowing the galaxies and civilizations and depositing the choice grain somewhere between Cape Cod and the east end of Boston Common. In 1805, Griffin had averred that, while there might be life in other worlds, earth is undoubtedly God's chosen planet. In the later sermon he narrowed this down:

> If the Church, now chiefly confined to two countries [the United States and her current enemy, Great Britain], is to rise from this day forth, where is it more likely to rise than in the United States, the most favoured spot on this continent which was discovered, as I may say, by the light of the Reformation? And if in the United States, where rather than in New England? And if in New England, where rather than in Massachusetts, which has been blessed by the prayers of so long a succession of godly ancestors? And, if in Massachusetts, on what ground rather than this . . .?[17]

[16]Miller, *Goodell Ordination,* pp. 28–29.

[17]Griffin, *Kingdom,* p. 11; *Sermon in Sandwich,* p. 33. Others of course had very different ideas about where the launching would occur. Alexander Campbell some years later predicted that "the last great conflict . . . seems to be reserved for a theatre somewhere in the New World: most probably it will be found in the great valley of the Mississippi." From a baccalaureate address (Bethany College) of 1847, in *Popular Lectures and Addresses* (Nashville: Harbinger Book Club [1861?]).

"On what ground rather than this?" Edward Dorr Griffin, who shared with many others a conviction that the millennium would commence in or near Boston. From *The Semi-Centennial Celebration of the Park Street Church* (Boston: Henry Hoyt, 1861), frontispiece.

New England had also been blessed with relative affluence, and the promoters referred to this constantly, both in order to reinforce the theme of special obligation and to underline the connection between godliness and a happy, successful civilization. The American Board in its 1811 "Address to the Christian Public" stressed that, of all the nations on earth, only England and New England had the resources to pursue foreign missions; and American wealth was more accessible than England's. "Our public burdens are light compared with those of England, and there is among us wealth sufficient, abundantly sufficient, to employ all the instruments which will be offered to our hands." And that thought gave occasion for observing that no nation could hope to be similarly prosperous and happy without Christianity. "Of all our social and civil enjoyments, scarcely one is worthy to be mentioned, which is not derived directly, or indirectly, from this holy religion."[18]

The reality of this abundance undercut a common objection: that the churches ought to concentrate on domestic obligations. We have the human and material resources for both tasks, the spokesmen insisted. Besides, all souls being of infinite value in God's sight, he is equally concerned to save Bostonians and "Birmans." But there were still other responses to this query, and some of them remind us that the terms "civilization" and "wilderness" could stand for gradations, as well as for a simple polarity.

New Englanders, like most others, were able to assume both an equality of souls before God and an inequality in the actual distribution of divine favors; and this inequality could be observed among Christian peoples. Bostonians have been chided excessively, over the centuries, for imagining everything south and west of Connecticut to be a howling wilderness; but such caricatures have been inspired by some very real assumptions, at least among a New England *literati*, about what defines a high civilization. It did not occur to the Reverend Mr. Griffin that the millennium might begin in Virginia or New York or South Carolina; these areas had been blessed with worldly resources but not—not really—with a "godly ancestry" and therefore not with a true and exemplary civilization. And beyond these semicivilized Eastern regions lay the real American wilderness, inhabited largely by peoples whom the mission boards as well as the War Department regarded as "foreign."

The distinction between "home" and "foreign" missions had scarcely been formulated; and if one admitted an obligation to convert the native Americans, then it was a short step, or even no step at all, to admitting a responsibility for heathen everywhere. As the Baptist Board of Foreign Missions explained in their first annual report, "foreign missions are in reality only domestic missions extended,—the sound which has been uttered on the frontiers of a country, going out into all lands."[19] Within the terms of this godly form of noblesse oblige, those from whom the most is expected can also anticipate, if they are faithful, a continued blessing and recompense. Here was additional ammunition against those

[18]ABCFM, *Second Meeting*, pp. 29, 28.
[19]Baptist Board of Foreign Missions, *First Annual Report* (Philadelphia: William Fry, 1815), pp. 6–7.

who thought the churches' resources, however abundant, should be spent at home.

To argue for missions as beneficial to the home churches was to adopt a line of reasoning that could and did get out of hand, and not just among New Englanders or Americans. In one form it was an innocuous debating point, a mild rebuke to those who pled domestic obligations but really preferred to do nothing at all, either at home or abroad. But it could also take more questionable forms. As soon as spokesmen argued, as they frequently did, that foreign missions were essential as an invigoration and positive benefit to the home churches, they could find themselves assigning primary importance not to compassion and benevolence but to the needs and the supposed internal logic of Christianity.

So long as most Westerners could take for granted the benefits of Christianity and civilization to foreign peoples, claims that missions improved the health of the home churches would offend only those who disliked missions for other reasons. Later, however, when Christianity's superiority, unalloyed benefits, and "right of conquest" had all become more problematic, the movement would be widely criticized for retaining such arguments in its rhetoric or implying them in its activities.

So far as one did stress the presumed benefits to New England churches, and to the people in them, this provided increased leverage for an appeal to the "stay-at-homes." Along with obligations to God and the heathen, and concern for the vitality of the church, those soliciting funds stressed every Christian's duty to support the people who had been adventurous and devoted enough to go abroad. The self-giving of the missionaries was frequently alluded to; and while church-people were not condemned out of hand for staying behind, promoters were not above shaming them into some degree of like sacrifice.

This again could take dubious forms. Despite the record of many centuries in which Christianity admittedly had not been a missionary religion, spokesmen frequently implied, or asserted outright, that opponents of missions were not truly Christian. And they could be strident in their language. Leonard Woods remarked that it was "absurd" for a real Christian to oppose missions. Edward Dorr Griffin made any holding back tantamount to a denial of the sovereignty of God. And the Reverend Joel Hawes carried the indictment a step further: "To be indifferent . . . or to stand still, and refuse to act, is rebellion. To possess wealth, and talents, and influence, and not employ them in advancing the cause of Christ, is disobedience which God will punish."[20]

[20]Woods, *Death of Worcester*, p. 24; Griffin, *Kingdom*, p. 24; Hawes, in Andrew, *Christian Commonwealth*, p. 135.

LEGACIES

Ideas, as Sir Lewis Namier wrote, "outlive the conditions which gave them birth, and words outlast ideas." The passionate rhetoric of the early spokesmen for foreign missions, representing the deepest kind of commitment to the Christian task as it appeared in that time and place, injected itself into the hymns, the slogans, the prayers, and the loyalties of the continuing movement. Much of it, even so, would change with the times or at least would be amenable to questioning by those who thought differently about the meaning of Christianity or the obligations of believers. But Professor Andrew is not wrong, merely somewhat premature, when he suggests that as early as the 1820s "foreign missions had become the new orthodoxy." This meant, on the one hand, that the pioneering missionaries and their spokesmen had given lasting embodiment to ideals of compassion, service, human rights, and self-sacrifice that have not been thought ludicrous, nor even seriously questioned (though methods, of course, have been) in later phases of American world outreach. Such words and ideas, outliving the conditions of the revolutionary era, have been reappropriated in some form by every generation from that time until the days of the Peace Corps, foreign aid, and—in mainline Christianity—a mission outlook featuring service, personal witness, and collaboration with other religions.[21]

Certain words or ideas that became deeply imbedded during this period—that became a part of the orthodoxy—were destined to encounter more opposition as they persisted into later eras. One of these was a belief that expansion is part of the definition of Christianity; and that, in consequence, the Christian who raises questions about conversionist foreign missions is somehow not a genuine believer. Another was the militant description of Christian objectives in the terminology of empire and of world conquest. A third, ultimately the most troubling to both internal and external critics, was a providentialism that, by taking the "opening" of the non-Western world as God's warrant for Christian expansion, helped forge a fundamental link between missions and imperialism.

The term "imperialism" was not invented until the 1850s, and even then it connoted a "colonialism" that Americans, generally oblivious to the colonialism involved in their conquest and management of the native Americans, were inordinately proud of having avoided. Often, therefore, we have pictured late-nineteenth-century imperialists like the Reverend Josiah Strong as the first important spokesmen for a linked religious

[21]L. B. Namier, *England in the Age of the American Revolution* (London, Macmillan, 1930), p. 4; Andrew, *Christian Commonwealth*, p. 135.

and cultural conquest of the world. But that presumed relationship had been equally important to the millennial enthusiasts of the earlier part of the century; and it had been proclaimed in that era by figures more towering than Josiah Strong would be. To Nathaniel Emmons, who ranked next to Hopkins as prime developer of the Edwardsean system, and who was president of the Massachusetts Missionary Society, Americans in 1800 already seemed a chosen people whom God would never forsake "if our present enterprising spirit continues to operate." If all goes well, he continued,

> we shall in a very short time have the possession and dominion of this whole western world. It seems to be the design of Providence to diminish other nations, and to increase and strengthen ours. . . . Hence there is great reason to believe that God is about to transfer the empire of the world from Europe to America, where he has planted his peculiar people. . . . This is probably the last peculiar people which he means to form, and the last great empire which he means to erect, before the kingdoms of this world are absorbed into the kingdom of Christ.[22]

That sort of effusion was not generally deplored either in 1800 or fifty years later. Contemporaries did, however, question a number of the elements in this religious-political idealism, and in the ways it was being applied. Such objections were voiced within the missionary movement as well as among skeptics or outsiders. What is most revealing, and perhaps most admirable, is that these hesitations arose almost as much out of successful missionary experience as from its resounding failures.

[22]Emmons, "God Never Forsakes His People," pp. 179–80.

CHAPTER 3

Christ, Not Culture

We are not commanded to teach schools in order to undermine paganism.
. . . If this is our duty, the command must be found in another gospel; it is
not found in the gospel of Jesus Christ.

Francis Wayland, 1853

The Deity who had provided "innumerable trophies" of his approval
as the mission enterprise began seemed in the ensuing years to be
sending more complex messages. Between 1810 and 1850 the foreign
mission movement experienced spectacular success in the Sandwich
Islands (Hawaii); depressing failures among the American Indian tribes;
mixed results in India, Ceylon, and other fields. And, curiously, even
where "the songs of converted idolators" rang loud and clear, notes of
warning and correction seemed almost equally compelling. In either
context, whether of failure or of success, the warnings bore most directly
upon those "civilizing" programs that had seemed so natural to the
founding generation and so sure of fulfillment.

The Hawaiian venture, in particular, seemed almost a case of divine
entrapment, an instance in which an efficient triumph revealed, just as
efficiently, the perils of missionary success. To a society already in process
of overthrowing its ancient idols, God had sent the bright-eyed representatives of a republican experiment that thought of itself as the new
order of the ages. He had seemingly prepared the way by providing
Hawaiian royalty and leadership with every sort of motive for collaboration with the missionaries and for conversion to Christianity; and
he had sent a massive revival of religion, in the 1840s, to ensure a more
general triumph for evangelical Christianity. He had pitted the missionaries and their native supporters against the Western commercial
interests, not in the usual ambivalent ways, but over such brutally clear-
cut issues as sailors' access to prostitutes, and he had awarded signal
victories in such matters to the men and women of God.

And yet after all that, the Deity, who had arranged so many advantages and awarded such great success, could be seen as displeased—as
if he were saying, with T. S. Eliot's cruel and laconic character, "That
is not what I meant at all. That is not it, at all."

If the rebuke—or, less dramatically, the admonition to rethink missionary assumptions—seemed an untoward response to success, changes in policy were also more difficult to effect when things seemingly had gone so well. When a mission failed, one closed it down, at the same time closing down much of the controversy surrounding it and clearing the way, perhaps, for a hazy or elliptical remembrance in the history books. But when missionaries to Hawaii triumphed so thoroughly among chiefs and people that they were asked to help govern the country, changes in strategy were hard to effect. When English-language schools in India were thriving, but arguably for the wrong reasons and with dubious results for evangelism, the agony and contentions could, and did, continue for decades.

These instances—the successful conversion of the Hawaiian peoples and the sturdy development of educational work in India—constituted exhibits B and C for those who, by the mid-nineteenth century, were demanding a shift from civilizing to evangelizing. Exhibit A was the bitter experience with missions to the native Americans.

"LITTLE ELSE THAN DISAPPOINTMENT": LESSONS FROM THE AMERICAN-INDIAN MISSIONS

As a recent interpreter of the ABCFM remarks, "the question of the precedence of civilization or Christianization which plagued all the missions of the Board came to its crisis in the Indian work."[1]

Native American ventures were carried out in two quite distinct stages. In the first, beginning in 1817, the Board established missions and schools among the four principal tribes of the Old Southwest—the Cherokees, Choctaws, Chickasaws, and Creeks—and expanded across the Mississippi to take on work among the Osage Indians of Missouri. In the second stage, after fighting and losing the heartrending struggle against President Jackson's Indian removal policy, the Board and its missionaries in the 1830s followed these wards westward, and also began work with the Ojibwa, Pawnee, Nez Percé, Flathead, Sioux, and Abenaki.

One notes in the pronouncements concerning all these efforts a certain grimness and hesitancy that contrasts with the millennial confidence surrounding the promotion of overseas missions. Not only was it easier to project sweeping triumphs in distant and relatively unknown lands; nearly everyone knew how regularly, in the past, determined outreach toward the Indians had been thwarted by an even more determined white expansiveness and rapacity. The Board took heart from

[1]Phillips, *Protestant America*, p. 65.

the colonial examples, however romanticized, of John Eliot, the May-hews, and David Brainerd; and from the government's current support for missionary projects in education and husbandry. The first phase of activity, moreover, brought some heartening results: by 1830, the Board sponsored thirty-three mission stations, claimed nine hundred Indian converts, and taught one thousand students in its schools. Missionary efforts to create written alphabets had produced in some tribes literacy rates as high as 50 percent.[2] Yet the tone even of the early advocacy and rhetoric was restrained. After the removal it reflected, by and large, little more than dogged determination.

In the first phase of the Board's Indian work this sober outlook contributed to a marked emphasis on assimilation. The pattern of as-similative ideas was not unusual. It presumed that the white man's civilization would inevitably supersede that of less developed cultures, and that those who did not appropriate the best features of this civi-lization would be victimized or even destroyed by its worst features. The work of civilizing, therefore, was more than an adjunct to con-version; it was a matter of practical necessity, indeed of the Indians' physical survival.

A rationale of this sort has cropped up, throughout missionary his-tory, whenever the movement or its agents have found themselves in tension with the military or commercial components of imperialism. Much later, one would find spokesmen (whether or not they still equated Westernization and civilization) taking a "Westernize to survive" line in reference even to more developed and militarily impressive societies such as that of the Japanese. Westernization would be seen (often by native regimes as well as by the mission interests) as mandatory—the only alternative to stagnation. The problem, from a missionary per-spective, would be to tame the Westernizing process and control its effects.

In the case of the Indian missions, directed as these were toward people who (despite removals) must continue to live in close propin-quity with the American majority culture, the desire to succor and protect the natives implied something more than a strong educational commitment, more even than a process of community-building in New England modes. Concretely, this desire led to acts of civil disobedience by missionaries who resisted the government's removal policy, and pro-voked the imprisonment of some of them by the state of Georgia. In

[2]ABCFM, *Annual Report,* 7 (1816): 134–35; 20 (1829): 97; 21 (1830): 104; Bliss, *Encyclopedia of Missions,* 1: 459–60; Strong, *American Board,* p. 40. For the ventures of all the major boards in the half-century following the adoption of the Constitution, the most satisfactory account is McLoughlin, *Cherokees and Missionaries.*

at least one crucial episode, it also produced a championing of racial intermarriage in defiance of community sentiment.

Despite the usual ambivalences, the civilizing objective of mission work had been clearly enunciated. American Board instructions and reports, in fact, often mentioned the civilizing functions first, as though, for the moment at least, settled schools and communities were truly the controlling vision. Samuel Worcester described the Board's objectives as "civilizing and christianizing," in that order. The plan, as he explained in 1816, was to provide for "the instruction of the rising generation in common school learning, in the useful arts of life, and in Christianity," with the aim of making "the whole tribe English in their language, civilized in their habits, and Christian in their religion." At this early date it was thought that the language of instruction and general usage must be English, partly because the Indians could learn to read in that language more easily than in their own, but even more because "assimilated in language, they will more readily become assimilated in habits and manners to their white neighbors; intercourse will be easy and the advantages to them incalculable." If increased intermarriage with whites also followed, Jedidiah Morse explained several years later, that would be all to the good: "They would then be literally of one blood with us, merged in the nation, and saved from extinction."[3]

With this last part of the assimilationist vision many contemporaries of course roundly disagreed; so the mission directors shortly had opportunity to show whether or not they were serious. The Board, in order to train and socialize potential native leaders from the various mission fields, established a school for them in Cornwall, Connecticut. When two of the students—one of whom was the Cherokee leader Elias Boudinot—married white women, the resulting furor attested to the problems a consistent assimilationism would face. Community sentiment, in this case led by the Reverend Lyman Beecher and the school's board of directors, supported most plans to civilize, socialize, and protect Indians, but not if this meant treating them as equals.

The ABCFM's Prudential Committee (as its executive body was called) took a less firm public stand than might have been desired. Privately, however, the Committee reprimanded the school directors, ordered that there must be no interference with the marriages, and insisted "that Boudinot, should he visit Cornwall, will be treated as becomes a Christian and civilized community to receive a youth educated among themselves and professing a faith in the Gospel of our common salvation." Jeremiah Evarts, who by then had succeeded the

[3]ABCFM, *Annual Report*, 7: 135–36; Phillips, *Protestant America*, p. 65

"Merged in the nation, and saved from extinction." The mission school for Indians at Cornwall, Connecticut. From Ralph H. Gabriel, *Elias Boudinot, Cherokee, and His America* (Norman: University of Oklahoma Press, 1941), facing p. 54. By permission.

deceased Samuel Worcester as corresponding secretary of the Board, proved to be even more stalwart than Worcester in defending inter-marriage. "How does it appear to be the will of God," he asked the school agents in 1825, "that individuals of different tribes and nations should not intermarry?"

> Is there anything in the Bible, that asserts or implies, that man and wife be precisely of the same complexion? . . . Does it not tend strongly to irritate the young men, who have been edu-cated at Cornwall, not only in the Cherokee nation, but wher-

ever else they live, will it not strike their minds as equivalent to a declaration that their people are doomed to perpetual inferiority; and that every attempt to rise to an equality with the whites is impudent and criminal?[4]

The Cornwall school closed two years later, in part because of the demoralizing effects of this dispute but also because of milder challenges to the assimilationist approach. The school had continued to do well; it enrolled seventeen students when the decision was made to close it; its value in advertising the missionary cause and acquainting provincial New Englanders with talented Asian and American Indian youth was reasonably clear. But, as the Prudential Committee reported to the Board, equivalent institutions were now available in the students' own homelands. Where these were not available, or in cases justifying more advanced training, nonwhite and foreign youths might better be placed in American colleges, not sequestered and placed on show in a separate institution.

Two other reasons for the closing pointed to future changes in missionary policy. The first was that too many of the students either had sickened and died, having failed to surmount climatic and cultural dislocation, or else had experienced crippling problems of readjustment in returning to their own societies. Boarding schools, as the ABCFM concluded several years later, could induce "a very undesirable feeling of dependence on the part of the scholars and adult Indians."[5] Educators and governments later understood and could prepare for this difficulty, even if they were still far from able to solve it. In the 1820s, after a number of years in which promoters and the public had made matinee idols of young converts like the Hawaiian Henry Obookiah (who died before he could return to his homeland), the evidence was shockingly instructive.

Not all the inducements to changes in policy were so negative as this one. The retreat from civilizing also reflected a growing preoccupation, as the new revivalism of Charles G. Finney swept much of the country, with individual conversions. "Let it be your great object at all times," the Committee instructed a missionary to the Cherokees in 1832, "to convince the Indians of their depravity and guilt and of their perishing need of an interest in the great atonement in Christ. . . . Expostulate with sinners with a warmth and constraining energy which cannot be resisted." Along with this, reduced reliance on English and English instruction owed a great deal to the success of missionary and

---

[4]Quoted in Phillips, *Protestant America,* pp. 68, 67.
[5]ABCFM, *Annual Report,* 23 (1832): 164.

native linguists in producing alphabets for the various spoken languages. George Guess (or Sequoya) and Elias Boudinot became famous for this in the American Indian missions, Hiram Bingham in those to the Sandwich Islands; but the contributors were legion and their results impressive. New missionaries to the Ojibwa were told in 1832 to consider the acquisition of the native language "indispensable to your extensive and highest usefulness."[6]

Brooding over all the instructions, nonetheless, was a querulous, grudging tone that seemed to be telling devoted workers: "Good luck to you, but we're not sure anything will work, and not sure how far we can support you." The ostensible message was that missionaries must learn the native languages because reliance on interpreters was expensive and embarrassing, and because any attempt "to introduce the English language . . . especially without boarding schools, is vain." The Board conceded the need for small day schools, and even for some instruction in English "till books in the native language can be prepared." Just below the surface, but plain enough, was evidence that the authorities had become reluctant about spending money on elaborate institutions of any kind. If boarding schools (as opposed to day schools) were continued at all, this should not be "at the expense of the Board."

The new outlook rejected other forms of "large secular establishment" in similar terms: sending out farmers and "mechanicks" (i.e., craftsmen) to teach and demonstrate the arts of white civilization had proved costly, troublesome, and not especially fruitful. Someone, perhaps the government, might continue to make such efforts, but they were not to be prescribed in the operating instructions of the missionaries. A few years' experience had damaged even the more moderate expectations that tribes of contented Indians, under missionary tutelage, would turn to praying and farming like Anglo-Saxons, building white frame houses, and writing instruments of government rooted in Magna Carta.

The Board seemed to be announcing, along with their narrowed Indian program, a measurable shift of resources from Indian to overseas missions. The envoys to the Ojibwa, even before they had a chance to try their talents, were told candidly that the Indian work thus far had cost more and produced less "than any other missions of the Board." If the new recruits failed to come up with solutions that the secretaries and Prudential Committee confessed themselves unable to find, the Board's resources would have to be directed to more promising fields.

How are the numerous tribes throughout the continent to be evangelized? The Committee have thought on this subject with

[6]Ibid., pp. 167, 165.

much anxiety. . . . Considering the claims of other heathen nations, with a vastly more dense population, more accessible, and where the means of subsistence are far cheaper . . . the Committee would not feel justified in carrying their operations among the Indians to a far greater extent, unless some less expensive plan can be devised.[7]

Rarely have mission boards been so ready to acknowledge their own bewilderment, or missionaries been dispatched with such restrained enthusiasm. And results bore out the apprehensions. Continued Indian removals—forced and voluntary—along with the ever-increasing pressures of white settlement and acquisitiveness, created nearly impossible conditions for missionaries, even though their good will and stabilizing potentialities were more needed than before. While the Board continued some efforts among the Indians until the 1880s, a number of the new missions were closed within a few years. Others, such as the Osage mission, in ten years made no converts at all. The Committee in 1838 reported "little else than disappointment." Anyone acquainted with the usual self-congratulatory language of annual reports, from the home office of any organization, will recognize how desperate the outlook must have seemed.[8]

HAWAII AND THE PERILS OF SUCCESS

The Board secretaries, in these dealings, could sound much like parents who try to invigorate one sibling by citing the successes of another. Of all the ostensibly successful siblings whom they could hold up as examples, the Hawaiian or Sandwich Island mission was the most startling and celebrated. Certainly it was the venture that best realized early visions of entire tribes and nations entering the Kingdom on something like the urgent millennial schedule. As a cynical Unitarian observer remarked, when anyone dared to suggest that failure in some mission field raised doubts about the divine intention, the blasphemer would customarily be "referred to the Sandwich Islands."[9]

The American Board's first contingent, consisting of two missionaries, five assistants, three native teachers, and seven "females," set out for Hawaii in 1819. There they were introduced to a process of rapid social change in which Westerners, up to that time, had served mainly as agents of disruption. Europeans had introduced intoxicants, new diseases, and untraditional modes of labor, all of which had figured in

[7]Ibid., pp. 165, 164.
[8]ABCFM, *Annual Report*, 29 (1838): 138.
[9]Quoted in Phillips, *Protestant America*, p. 97.

a serious physical depletion of the native population. From the first, the young, enthusiastic American missionaries, effectively led by the Reverend Hiram Bingham, struck native leaders as offering something far better.

Conversion of influential chiefs to Christianity did not begin until 1825, and conversions in the general population were not massive for a decade after that. But the missionaries, at first accepted on probation, were very soon invited to stay, to call for reinforcements, and to establish the schools that were the staple of all beginning enterprises. New contingents began arriving in 1822, and then were supplemented regularly until the mission, at its high point in 1837, numbered ninety Americans together with several hundred native workers. By then the Hawaiian kingdom had a constitution that proscribed any laws "at variance with the word of the Lord Jehovah"; and the church, after a wave of revivals in the late 1830s that again seemed to demonstrate divine approval, could count over 18,000 actual communicants within a population of 100,000.[10]

Yet in the Hawaiian nearly as much as the native American case, directors at home came to feel that events had eluded their control. Once again it was the civilizing responsibilities, so confidently assumed, that seemed to frustrate or confuse the overall effort. The American Indian missions were being defeated by a particularly vicious form of the westward march of empire. The Hawaiian mission, a textbook case of successful evangelization, provoked criticism and reform when emissaries who had been told to avoid political and other secular involvements found it impossible to do so.

The difficulty, easily seen in hindsight, was that this set of missionaries, along with most others, had been given two sets of instructions that, though perhaps compatible in theory, tended to collide in practice. Like the young woman who asked her mother's permission to swim, they had been told, "Yes, but don't go near the water." In official instructions and other excited documents the Hawaii missionaries had been advised to "aim at nothing short of covering those Islands with fruitful fields, and pleasant dwellings, and schools and churches." They were to raise an entire people "to an elevated state of Christian Civilization." But the men and women of God had also been told to devote themselves "expressly and solely" to saving their "long lost fellow beings." Especially after the earliest years of the mission, they were repeatedly warned against "all interference with the local and political views of

---

[10]ABCFM, *Annual Report*, 28 (1837): 96; Hawaiian Mission Children's Society, *Jubilee Celebration* (Honolulu: *Daily Bulletin*, 1887), pp. 115, 116.

the people," or with the "private and transient interests of chiefs and rulers."[11]

Was the Board trying to have it both ways? Perhaps so; but only in the sense that ready identification of religious with societal values led its directors, especially at the outset, to imagine that evangelization would serve, without added political effort, to produce the broad social results they envisaged. Over the long run, the mixed signals were just as much a matter of responsiveness to experience. The Board seems to have realized, early on, that in the spectacular Hawaiian venture it had committed itself to holding a tiger by the tail. Or rather two tigers: a mission that, welcomed by political leaders, had become politicized; and a leader, Hiram Bingham, whose personal attractiveness and force had helped bring about that result.

Novelistic and other depictions of South Seas missionaries, like the emotions of that unfortunate actress described by Dorothy Parker, have "run the gamut from A to B." Only Calvinists and proto-fundamentalists need apply; and it is obligatory that male missionaries be either lusty hypocrites or cadaverous, preferably impotent, zealots. Nothing else will do if one is to make the most of Puritan intrusions in a steamy Paradise. In James Michener's *Hawaii* (which avoids some of the worst stereotypes), the first leader of the missionaries is Abner Hale, a "thin, sallow-faced . . . emaciated . . . stringy-haired, pasty-faced" fellow who shows "obvious tendencies toward identifying him-self with God." Michener's fledgling missionary leader is a weak and repressed youth who is so intent on his pedantic theological studies that his "rowdy and . . . worldly" Yale classmates cannot pry him from his desk, and who therefore nearly misses the stirring lecture that will propel him, gulping and weeping, to a missionary career.

In real life, on the other hand, the remarkable and problematic career of the Hawaiian mission was very possibly determined by the fact that none of the missionaries seems to have fit such an image. Sam Whitney, a Yale man "more inclined to bodily than to mental exertion," was indeed "long-faced and solemn" compared with his pretty wife. Among the others—for example, the "robust, broad-shouldered" Thurston or the farmer Chamberlain with his "firm look of command" and "features that seem about to break into a smile"—neither a Michener nor a Somerset Maugham protagonist comes into focus. One is reminded, instead, of the David Treadups and Eric Liddells of 1980s fiction, the rowers and runners who by then were being called upon to convey the

[11]"Instructions," appended to Humphrey, *Promised Land,* pp. ix, ii; Phillips, *Protestant America,* p. 115.

moral athleticism of the missionary venture. The story of Thurston's gaining a Hawaiian challenger's respect by throwing him over a high sea-wall may be apocryphal; but his election at Yale to the honorable post of Class Bully—leader of Gown against Town—is part of the record.[12]

As for confusing oneself with God: that part of the Michener fantasy may be apt. Bingham was handsome, self-confident, intelligent, "courageous to the point of belligerency . . . admirably qualified to be the guiding force in a pioneer enterprise."[13] The Hawaiian king and chiefs trusted him as a counselor. His colleagues—including Thurston, who had equal credentials for leadership of the party—also respected and followed Bingham, but with a growing irritation and concern about his imperious manner and about the way in which his interpretation of the "civilizing" responsibilities of the mission had led all of them into ever deeper and more complex involvement in the secular affairs of the Hawaiian society.

Officials in Boston shared these worries about their star mission and its leader, so much so that when Bingham came home in 1840 they refused to reappoint him to the Islands. Both before and after that episode, the Board's response to every Sandwich Island triumph combined praise and support with appeals or demands for restraint. In the mid-20s, for example, the American missionaries were influencing the Hawaiian authorities to crack down both on prostitution and on Catholicism. Bingham and his colleagues managed thereby to stir criticism not only among the commercial and shipping interests but among Western consular and military functionaries. The Prudential Committee in 1826 therefore reiterated its warning against "all interference and intermeddling with the political affairs and party concerns of the nation or people."[14]

The response of the missionaries, in turn, restated the historic civilizing formula—with its historic loophole. They agreed that they ought not to interfere in political or secular matters *except* where issues of religion and sound morals were involved. The self-restraints they had in mind were specific: they promised not to meddle in the choice of rulers, in the levying of taxes, in trade and land dealings, or in the government of the islands. Given the missionaries' assumptions about

[12]Michener, *Hawaii*, pp. 114ff.; Smith, *Yankees in Paradise*, pp. 28–30; *Biographical Sketches of the Members of the Class of 1816 of Yale College* (New Haven: T. J. Stafford 1867), pp. 57–60. David Treadup is the principal character in John Hersey's *The Call*. *Chariots of Fire*, one of the most popular films of the 1980s, was based upon the athletic career of Eric Liddell, who was later a missionary in China.

[13]Bradley, *Hawaii*, p. 129.

[14]Quoted in Andrew, *Christian Commonwealth*, p. 159.

"Courageous to the point of belligerency": Hiram Bingham. From his auto-
biography, *A Residence of Twenty-One Years in the Sandwich Islands* (Hartford:
Hezekiah Huntington, 1847), frontispiece.

the nature of a Christian society, however, such disclaimers left considerable running room. They were renouncing responsibility only for
those "customs and usages of the country that are not in direct varience
[sic] with the spirit and precepts of the Gospel."[15]

[15]Ibid. For a further account of Bingham's Hawaiian career, see the early chapters of
Miller, *Fathers and Sons*.

The "robust, broad-shouldered" Thurstons. From the Rev. and Mrs. O. H. Gulick, *The Pilgrims of Hawaii* (New York: Fleming H. Revell, 1918), facing p. 168. By permission.

The growing, ambitious, socially involved Hawaiian enterprise aroused outside criticism, as well as praise and satisfaction, on a number of issues. Yet external attacks centered on the same questions that were bothering the home office: questions relating to cultural imposition and its consequences.

The novelist Herman Melville was the most celebrated of the external critics and the one who probably, even after Mark Twain's more explosive attack a half-century later, did the most to fix an adverse image of missionaries in literature and the public mind. The accuracy of Melville's observations, in the novels *Typee* and *Omoo,* is often questionable; as a biographer remarks, many of the Hawaiian references "do not carry the conviction of an eyewitness's testimony." But Melville spent four years in the region, including probably seven months in the Sandwich Islands, and "read up every account of the South Seas he could lay his hands on." Thus, fully accurate or not, his views both reflected and augmented negative images that were probably, at this time, as prevalent among the reading public as was enthusiasm for missions.

In Melville's view the missionaries, in Hawaii as throughout the South Seas, had participated all too willingly in the destruction of a once-happy people. The context for this indictment was a depiction of life among the Typees that was romantic to the point of self-parody:

There seemed to be no cares, griefs, troubles, or vexations in all Typee. The hours tripped by as gaily as the laughing couples down a country lane. . . . No foreclosures of mortgages, no protested notes, no bills payable. . . . Here you would see a parcel of children frolicking together the livelong day, and no quarrelling, no contention among them. . . . As for the warriors, they maintained a tranquil dignity of demeanor . . .

The modern reader guffaws (as did many contemporaries, whether or not they liked missionaries). But in spite of what Charles Anderson calls "Rousseauistic overplus," Melville was guilty less of inaccuracy than of a certain disingenuousness, a failure to tell the whole story. He probably knew, nearly as well as anthropologists know now, that South Seas existence had rigidities of its own; that to a great extent the tranquil, ostensibly rule-free conditions represented marriage customs and social arrangements imbedded in elaborate systems of tabus and prescriptions. But he could become forgetful on such a point because he was intent on contrasting the pristine island cultures—cannibalism and all—with the diseased and decimated remnants to which he thought they had been reduced after a half-century of "civilization."[16]

Melville also genuinely believed that Polynesian society at its worst might not be more wicked than his own. That some islanders were cannibals, as he conceded somewhat flippantly, was "very true; and a rather bad trait in their character, it must be allowed." But the English practice, not long since, of beheading, disemboweling, and quartering honest "traitors" was just as bad, and "the fiend-like skill we display in the invention of all manner of death-dealing engines" was palpably worse. Such social customs were enough "to distinguish the white civilised man as the most ferocious animal on the face of the earth." Melville thought that "so far as the relative wickedness of the parties is concerned, four or five Marquesan islanders sent to the United States as missionaries might be quite as useful as an equal number of Americans dispatched to the islands."

The point about missionaries was not that they sometimes behaved as badly as other Westerners. Their undertaking, as Melville allowed, was "in itself but human; and subject, like everything else, to errors and abuses." His more profound and telling complaint was that, with a mainly adverse Western impact in plain view (one could not, for

[16]Anderson, *Melville in the South Seas,* pp. 328, 7, chap. 7; Melville, *Typee,* pp. 168–69. The anthropologists, in continuing to react to moral repressiveness in Western societies, have not always avoided Melville's misreadings. See Derek Freeman, *Margaret Mead and Samoa: The Making and Unmaking of an Anthropological Myth* (Cambridge, Mass.: Harvard University Press, 1983).

example, deny the depletion and horror resulting from venereal disease), the missionaries were placing most of their emphasis on the wrong kind of salvation. Like the tea-drinking philanthropists at home who backed them and who credited their overblown reports, the missionaries failed to show any real concern about physical suffering, degradation, and Western misdeeds. Instead, they exulted ("Behold the glorious result!") that the abominations of paganism had given way to the pure rites of Christian worship. Thus, as Melville remarked with a turn of phrase that has played especially well in the history books, "the small remnant of the natives [have] been civilised into draught horses, and evangelised into beasts of burden." The marauding Westerners had invaded a garden and transformed it into a moral wilderness.

Melville asserted unequivocal support of "the cause of missions in the abstract." No Christian, he said, "could possibly be opposed" to that. He took pains to acknowledge that others besides the missionaries were responsible for the sad state of the islanders, and even conceded that certain island peoples were better off with the missionaries than without them. Ought the godly messengers to leave, therefore, or stay? Melville's answer seemed to be that they might stay, on the understanding that they were to become more pious and to live less ostentatiously. Above all, they should correct the "collective mismanagement" that allowed them to baptize people under swaying palm trees "whilst the miserable natives are committing all sorts of immoralities around them."[17]

Since the missionaries not only considered conversions the sine qua non for improved morality but had been especially criticized when they did attack vices more directly, they could be excused for thinking Melville's advice confusing. Elizabeth Elkins Sanders of Salem, Massachusetts—philanthropist, polemicist, and inveterate critic of missions—offered a more coherent program. Should the missionaries get out? Yes, she wrote, in the sense that they should get out of the business of converting the natives—at least until such time as their own compatriots showed the marks of conversion. While awaiting that perhaps unlikely development, they should offer service and sacrificial love, restricting any proselytizing activities to the conversion of Westerners. The biblical admonition to preach the Gospel to every creature was all very well, said Sanders; but other Gospel injunctions concerning motes and beams, and those that advise the Christian to "let your light shine before men that they may see your good works" are both "prior, and preparative." In practice, "all attempts to improve the natives will be abortive while

[17]Melville, *Typee*, pp. 166–67, 264–67; *Omoo*, p. 228; *Typee*, p. 267.

. . . visitors and foreign residents are so debased, and so ignorant of their duties."[18]

It seems clear that, though the Hawaii missionaries enjoyed enough public adulation to keep their spirits up, they were being offered a Hobson's choice by their critics, even by such logical ones as Elizabeth Sanders. They would be accused of meddling if they acted as moral and social reformers, and pilloried for insensitivity and irrelevance if they did not. If they concentrated on "the infamous proceedings of the officers and crews of foreign ships," they would please Mrs. Sanders and offend others. If they adopted a less adversarial approach towards other Westerners, they would be typed as co-opted chaplains to the Europeans.

The romantic alternative—that of reversing most Hawaiian social change since Captain Cook—was scarcely attainable, while the idea of leaving the Western cultural invasion to operate without some idealistic component was not necessarily attractive even to the critics. In that perspective, the changes in policy that mission directors proposed and partially implemented in the mid-nineteenth century can be seen as "trimming" responses to impossible dilemmas. But they also drew upon the long tradition of concern about cultural imposition. The most force-ful attempt at redirection, led by the ABCFM's senior secretary, Rufus Anderson, called for missionaries to withdraw as soon as possible from civilizing functions that Anderson thought were not biblically based and that should never have been assumed. Eventually, once native churches had been established, a given mission must close down entirely.

RUFUS ANDERSON AND THE NEW MISSION POLICY

If Anderson had his way, the difficulties in applying the Great Com-mission would be met by what can be called, without pejorative intent, the Great Compromise. Between the extremes of complete aloofness from the expansionist process and permanent commitment to it, the Andersonians proposed a stance resembling (not by accident) the me-diating ideal later proclaimed when the United States acquired overseas colonies. One goes in, imposing values and making available (though, Anderson would say, not imposing) a model for the society. But one then gets out, for practical reasons but also because the model itself, influenced heavily by democratic and congregational ideologies, dictates that churches and peoples must be self-governing.

[18]Sanders, *Tour Around Hawaii,* pp. 23–24.

The campaign to reverse the civilizing emphasis in missions, while especially associated with Anderson's name, was neither wholly American nor the work of a single board or leader. Henry Venn, a revered figure in nineteenth-century British missions, had been especially remembered for his championing of autonomous and self-supporting native churches. Closer to home, Francis Wayland and other influential Baptists supported both that line of argument and also Anderson's disapproval of civilizing endeavors and the use of English in teaching. Yet without question it was the ABCFM, under the leadership of its longtime senior secretary, that developed the most wide-ranging rationale for these revisions, and that succeeded at least temporarily in applying the rationale.

Anderson, the outstanding American organizer and theorist of foreign missions in the nineteenth century, had observed the early successes and failures at close range. Having been exposed by his father to Hopkinsian ideas, and then strongly affected by the ordination service in 1812 for the first band of foreign missionaries, Anderson went to work for the Board while still a student of Andover Seminary. In the mid-1820s he applied for overseas service, but was instead kept in Boston as assistant secretary. In 1832, after impressing the Prudential Committee by his work both at home and in a Near Eastern tour of inspection, he was chosen as one of three "secretaries for correspondence." Technically that designation did not change, but Anderson became first among equals, known informally but regularly as the senior secretary.

Anderson's career as an innovator in missions was marked by calm persistence and persuasiveness in the face of constant opposition. His physical makeup helped to shape Anderson's career and also, perhaps, to ensure that opponents would underestimate him. When he first aspired to the mission field, and for some years thereafter, he was a frail consumptive, "peculiarly slender and delicate, one whom the practiced eye would select for early decline."[19] He was the sort of person whom mission boards, despite popular impressions to the contrary, did not ordinarily select to send overseas. Both of Anderson's parents, and both younger brothers, did in fact die of tuberculosis; but Rufus regained robust health, worked strenuously as an executive to age seventy, and persevered as an author until his death at age eighty-four.

Anderson said the longevity resulted from "a good home and a high aim." One suspects it was also a matter of even temperament and the sort of moderation that kept him, as a policymaker, "behind the rash, but in advance of the hesitating." He seemed to welcome criticism or

[19]Thompson, *Rufus Anderson,* pp. 37–38.

opposition, and showed repeatedly that he could be responsive to it. To his detractors, that simply meant he was cagey, and was confident about fundamentally getting his own way. The rhetoric of more friendly commentators ran to phrases about "judicial cast of mind," "avoidance of needless offense," "the wisest man in America," and even—from an Indian convert—"just like Jesus Christ."[20]

Anderson's program for missions, clarified early in his career and then maintained with stubborn consistency over forty years, was built upon two massive convictions. One of these, the expected triumph of Christian religion and civilization, represented the conventional wisdom of his time and required little argument—merely occasional incantation at the expected level of militancy. "The kingdom of our blessed Lord," he admonished young ministers,

> evidently has no national boundaries. "The field is the world"; and the Redeemer will not be "satisfied with the travail of his soul," until his kingdom become coextensive with the earth. . . . Were universal conquest the leading object of our nation, then every student in our military and naval schools would regard the field of his duty as in some sense coextensive with the world. . . . And are not candidates for the gospel ministry in training for the world?[21]

The millennial framework, moreover, was still in place, even though Anderson and his colleagues of mid-century gave proportionately less attention to it than their predecessors had. Anderson's *Memorial Volume,* commemorating the first fifty years of the ABCFM, used the following apocalyptic language to explain "the political ascendency of Protestant Christianity":

> Every war in Asia, for the past half-century, has been fulfilling the prophecy, that the valleys shall be exalted, and the mountains and hills made low, the crooked made straight, and the rough places plain. The apocalyptic angel has hold upon "the dragon, that old serpent, which is the Devil and Satan." The great anti-Christian powers are acting under mighty restraints. . . . And these providential influences are more and more evidently preparing the way for Christ's progress, with his gospel, through the unevangelized nations.[22]

[20]Ibid., pp. 38, 16–19, 41.
[21]Anderson, *Foreign Missions,* pp. 249–50.
[22]Anderson, *Memorial Volume,* p. 388.

The other and more distinctive conviction informing Anderson's program was a thoroughgoing trust in the working of the Holy Spirit. His lifelong campaign against the imposition of Western cultural and religious patterns, and in favor of independent native churches, bespoke no appreciable sympathy for foreign peoples or cultures; it rested on an insistence that the Gospel, once implanted, can be relied upon to foster true religion, sound learning, and a complete Christian civilization—all in forms that will meet biblical standards and fulfill the needs of a given people.

From these fundamental principles, and out of history and current experience, Anderson drew a number of distinctive guidelines for the prosecution of missions in the modern world. The missionary, first of all, is a planter only. What will appear in the harvest, indeed whether or not there will be a harvest, is up to God. It is, consequently, not the missionary's business to export or advocate either his own forms of civilization or the peculiarities of doctrine and church organization that form the integument of his own faith. Since some "secular" auxiliaries are nonetheless necessary, the missionary movement must distinguish between those that are urgently required (medical missions, for example) and others that are intrusive or are simply not important to the work of evangelization (such as missions to teach farming and craftsmanship).

Where a given secular activity, such as education, does bear upon evangelization and the training of ministers, one must again distinguish carefully, according to Anderson, between forms of the activity that promote evangelization and others that do not. Above all, to use English with the unconverted, or to spend time teaching them English, will generally alienate natives from their own people and culture, and will not result in a substantial number of genuine conversions. Teaching the unconverted, in their own language, was certainly in order; and he was also content to have converts receive some of their advanced education in English. But these were practical concessions. Anderson thought the missionary movement's substantial and central commitment to education, in India and elsewhere, was a vast mistake.

The final chapter in this new rule-book for missions (or one might say the final exam, the real test of sincerity and determination) could have been entitled "Letting Go." It involved three stages or processes, each one of which was an occasion for tension between determined executives and their committed workers in the field. The requirement in the first of these stages was that the missionaries train and ordain native ministers and then—this generally was more troublesome—give them actual responsibility. In the second stage, the churches of the people and of the missionaries, if not already separate, should become so in the interest of autonomy for the natives and a correct, efficient use of Western help. The point was that the missionary should never be the "minister" of a native church. In his preaching function, Anderson pointed out, the mission worker is an itinerant. In his managing functions, whatever these may be in a given case, he should not interpose his authority in an established native congregation.

Anderson did not fail entirely to foresee the danger in this second prescription, a danger that the churches or religious entities it fostered would, in the nature of things, be not only separate but unequal; and that missionaries who declined to be pastors for the flocks would instead be bishops for the native pastors. But such anomalies would be temporary and bearable because of stage three in the process of devolution. This last prescription was the simplest to state, if not to accomplish. It was, of course: Missionary, go home! or at the least: Missionary, move on![23]

Anderson's modern-sounding ideas, and indeed the totality of his contributions and career, must be kept in perspective. His programs for delimiting local mission functions and the overall operation could be interpreted as nothing more than streamlining—a precursor of modern time-and-motion studies rather than of modern cultural sensitivity. If it is, the resemblance of his rationale for "indigenization" to that of, say, the World Council of Churches in the mid-twentieth century will seem largely coincidental. One should also bear in mind that Anderson was a large fish in what was still a small pond. Not only was the foreign mission enterprise a modest one; competing attempts to formulate a full-scale theory were almost nonexistent.[24]

That last caveat also means, however, that Anderson deserves to be seen as dominating his age, the more so because this ideologue was a forceful and well-placed administrator who put ideas to the test. Having developed a fairly subtle and unsentimental critique of the relations between missions and civilization, he was able almost singlehandedly to place it in operation in several areas of the world. He was also adept at using the results of practical application—including his own failures and successes—in the further elaboration of theory.

The best illustration of this dialogic process lies in the development of Anderson's distinctive argument concerning, as we might phrase it,

[23]This summary of Anderson's guidelines for missions is drawn from all of his writing and policy, but concise statements appear in chapters 6 through 8 of his *Foreign Missions,* and in an ordination sermon of 1845 on "The Theory of Missions to the Heathen" that is reprinted in Beaver, *To Advance the Gospel,* pp. 73–88.

[24]Forman, "Mission Theory," p. 80.

"the disadvantages of a superior civilization." He agreed with most contemporaries about the ultimacy and God-given brilliance of Western civilization. Those excellencies had made the missionary movement possible, and the evident superiority of Christian culture assured that something very like it would emerge automatically wherever the seed of the Gospel might be implanted. But this excellence and high development were also responsible for the wrong turn that early foreign missions had taken.

Anderson's 1845 sermon on "The Theory of Missions to the Heathen," which is the short-form manifesto for his entire program, begins with the paradoxical assertion that the modern age is both the easiest and the hardest time for missions. Along with numerous other gifts, "the civilization which the gospel has conferred upon our New England is the highest and best, in a religious point of view, that the world has yet seen." But this very perfection is "a formidable hindrance" to the establishing of purely spiritual missions. The problem, according to Anderson, is that we are conditioned to identify Christianity with "the blessings of education, industry, civil liberty, family government, social order, the means of a respectable livelihood, and a well-ordered community. Hence *our* idea of piety," he warned, and "*our* idea of the propagation of the gospel," are clothed in social and doctrinal forms that we mistakenly associate with the Gospel itself. And this cultural bias is most marked in those, like the New Englanders, "whose privilege it is to dwell upon the heights of Zion." The result is that missions try to mix their "sublime spiritual object" with the more dubious aim of "reorganizing, by various direct means . . . the structure of that social system, of which the converts form a part."[25]

Anderson usually referred to first-century Christianity for the models that deserved to be imitated. For instructive counterexamples he alluded to the failures, successes, and mixed experiences of the Board itself. "Farmers and mechanics," he recalled in 1869, had been sent to the American Indians and to the Hawaiians. "The honest aim in sending these secular helpers was to aid the preaching missionaries." But the Board had quickly seen its mistake. "A simpler, cheaper, more effectual means of civilizing the savage, was the gospel alone." To illustrate the dangers in a seemingly harmless emphasis on English instruction, he cited experience among the Syrians and the Choctaws. The effect on Syrian students had been "on the whole . . . to make them foreign in their manners, foreign in their habits, foreign in their sympathies; in other words, to denationalize them." Among the Choctaws one could witness the next step: the English-educated pupils (here he quoted a

[25]Anderson, "Missions to the Heathen," pp. 73–74.

"A more effectual means of civilizing was the gospel alone." Rufus Anderson, senior secretary of the ABCFM. Courtesy of Harvard College Library.

Board missionary, Dr. Kingsbury) had "regarded themselves as elevated above their parents, and the mass of their people, and [become] vain in their imaginations, and their foolish hearts were darkened." With some exceptions, Anderson concluded, "those who acquired the most knowledge of the English language seemed the farthest from embracing the gospel."[26]

[26]Anderson, *Foreign Missions,* pp. 97–99.

Though these arguments against civilizing motives and functions encountered immediate opposition (to be discussed at some length in the next chapter), and were largely defeated in the longer cycle of nineteenth-century missions, Anderson also enjoyed both support and success during his half-century of influence. The preeminent directors of Baptist missions, Francis Wayland and Solomon Peck, though they failed to carry their organizations with them as well as Anderson did, were eloquent in seconding his program. Wayland, who was a minister and moral philosopher, and the longtime president of Brown University (1827–55), insisted that the appeal of the Gospel can and must be made directly, without the mediation of education or any sort of civilizing:

> The son of God has left us no directions for civilizing the heathen, and then Christianizing them. We are not commanded to teach schools in order to undermine paganism, and then, on its ruins, to build up Christianity. If this is our duty, the command must be found in another gospel; it is not found in the gospel of Jesus Christ.[27]

Even more crucial than such external support was the steady and nearly-unanimous backing of the Prudential Committee and of the Board itself, although Anderson's power and persuasiveness undoubtedly helped create that supportive situation. The secretary's success in applying his principles, in any case, took both affirmative and negative forms. He induced the Board to send an increasing proportion of preaching missionaries to the field, and to emphasize evangelization in its instructions to both new and older workers. Negatively, he put an end to some functions and modified others. Whereas in the earliest missions auxiliary workers had outnumbered preachers, by 1842 preachers outnumbered these other functionaries by nearly two to one; and by 1852 there were no farmers or mechanics in the missions. During the same period, particularly in the wake of a highly controversial tour of inspection that Anderson led in 1854–55, a number of missionary schools were closed, aborted, or forced to continue without Board sponsorship; while many more schools were induced to alter their commitment to English-language instruction.

The story of the Anderson deputation of 1854–55, besides its interest as a minor cause célèbre, displays in microcosm the range of issues that have tortured the missionary movement throughout most of its history. The Prudential Committee instructed Anderson and his colleague Augustus Thompson to place before the missions in India, Ceylon, Syria, and Turkey a set of polite but loaded queries about their

[27]Wayland, *Apostolic Ministry*, p. 19.

operations. By posing questions on the order of "Would it not be well to stop beating your wife?" Anderson and Thompson were to discover to what extent "the oral preaching of the Gospel is actually the leading object and work of the missions." They were to inquire whether or not the missions were "ready" to terminate the sort of educational effort that regards schooling as preparatory to conversion, or that uses English as the principal language of instruction. They were to ask why the missions were finding it so difficult to ordain native pastors and to induce natives to build their own churches. The Board wondered why mission printing presses could not seem to restrict themselves to publications in the vernacular, and why missionaries found it necessary to focus their efforts on the upper classes. Once on the scene in India, Anderson and Thompson also inquired whether it was really advisable to accept educational grants from governments since, as Anderson reminded the Ceylon missionaries, "ours is an exclusively evangelical work and no alliance with secular powers can be otherwise than injurious."[28]

Missionaries in the various stations surely recognized that these were more than innocent inquiries. But whether they did or not, many either welcomed Anderson's overtures or were persuaded by them. The deputation succeeded, according to Anderson's biographer, "because these missionaries were willing, for whatever reasons, to satisfy the Prudential Committee's desire to turn theory into practice." The Mahratta mission was typical in averring that the deputies from Boston had "given us new ideas of the best mode of gathering and organizing churches, placing native pastors over them and preparing them speedily to be self-governing." It was the local missionaries, not Anderson or the Board directly, who halted plans for a new English high school at Bombay. It was they who ordained native pastors, closed boarding schools, suspended a seminary in Ceylon until it could be reorganized for vernacular instruction, and in general carried out a surprising number of those reforms that the Board and its secretary quite obviously desired.[29]

But some doubtless would have joined with special fervor in the benediction the Mahratta missionaries added to their report: "May the Great Head of the Church prosper them on their way." Second thoughts overtook others after the formidable Anderson had embarked, and after it became evident that his preferred policies might actually be implemented. Back home, moreover, Anderson had to battle challenges within the Board that in turn led to distortions in the public press: the *New York Times* complained that the secretary had closed the missionary schools and had restricted missionaries to "sermonizing or lecturing";

[28]Schneider, "Senior Secretary," pp. 153–54.
[29]Ibid., pp. 165, 156–57.

at most, the paper said, South India teachers would be allowed to train a few theologically disposed young men to preach in Tamil. While Anderson's actual, more moderate, aims for the limiting of educational functions were implemented to a remarkable extent, within twenty years the tide would be flowing visibly in the other direction.[30]

Getting missionaries to close their schools was less difficult, however, than edging them toward the most wrenching adjustment of all: closing the mission. Since any reneging at that stage could discredit the sincerity of the entire indigenizing effort, Anderson fretted, expatiated, and worked more in the interest of establishing strong native churches than in the pursuit of any other goal. "In our undue estimate of the influence of civilization as an auxiliary to the gospel," he wrote in a typical passage, "we have been slow to believe that native churches . . . could stand without foreign aid." In India, it had taken some forty years of prodding from the Board, followed by the prodding of the deputation, before one native pastor had finally been ordained in 1854. The record was similar in the missions to the American Indians, the Hawaiians, and nearly everyone else. Native preachers had been trained, but the missionaries on the scene, as Anderson lamented, had been egregiously unwilling to grant them pastoral responsibilities: "Hence the prolonged existence of mission churches with their centre and seat at the residence of the missionary," and entire church memberships retained unnecessarily "under the pastoral supervision of the missionary himself."[31]

Here again the Hawaiian experience, in dramatizing the surprises and perils that came with success, epitomized the larger missionary movement during its "great century." The Hawaiian missionaries, with some willingness, much ambivalence, and a certain amount of kicking and screaming, were induced between 1839 and 1863 to turn their churches and facilities over to "native" control. On occasion, amidst the constant pleas to missionaries to stay out of politics, the Board had cut official ties with those who accepted positions with the Hawaiian government. And at the end of the era, the Board formally ceded control and properties to the Hawaiian Evangelical Association.[32] Yet the scenario thus gloriously completed was shot through with ironies.

Keeping the missionaries out of native Hawaiian churches theoretically promoted autonomy but actually perpetuated subordination. Turning the mission over to the natives was excellent except that by the 1850s the missionaries and their children were becoming Hawaiian

[30]Ibid., pp. 178–221; and chapter 4, below.

[31]Anderson, *Foreign Missions*, pp. 101–2.

[32]See Anderson, *Sandwich Islands*, esp. chapters 28 and 33; Phillips, *Protestant America*, p. 118.

citizens; the Evangelical Association that eventually took control not only retained ties to the Board but also initially, to Anderson's horror, was composed entirely of American-born members. To a great extent, moreover, divestiture of Board properties after 1848 meant sale of this property to Board missionaries, or to former missionaries who had resigned in order to work for local churches or agencies.[33] Politically, an American missionary community almost uniformly zealous for Hawaiian autonomy contributed ideas, personnel, advice, and in effect entire constitutions to a Westernizing process that, with help from East Asian migrations, thoroughly suppressed Hawaiian culture.

Looking back in the 1870s, Anderson introduced his book on the Sandwich Island mission by calling the whole experience "peculiar" and "very instructive." But it is safe to say that few contemporaries matched Anderson in their willingness to be instructed. The missionaries at one point defended themselves (very properly, as later scholarship has shown) against charges that they were engaged in economic exploitation. But even in doing so they placed themselves a step or two behind Anderson by reflecting their age's obliviousness concerning cultural and religious forms of imperialism. "We seek," as the missionaries declared in a stunning aphorism, "not *theirs* but *them.*"[34]

Anderson himself, with just a touch of "I told you so," finessed that distinction by insisting that the officious and persisting involvement with Hawaiian affairs had not aligned "them" even with the Declaration of Independence. The Westerners' maddening paternalism and their stubborn insistence on "civilizing" had perverted the process of civilization as surely as it had confused the goals of evangelization. The political goal, supposedly, had been an independent Hawaii; but Anderson saw that Western withdrawal was at least as grudging in the political culture as in religious life.

The effects of a pervasive paternalism in both spheres were sometimes hard to define, but to Anderson they were perfectly clear; and his observations of the 1870s throw light on America's strange and tortured imperialist involvements of twenty years later. Anderson recalled that when the Prudential Committee in 1853 "ventured upon a somewhat jubilant announcement, that the Sandwich Islands had been Christianized," the news had "awakened no apparent interest" in the Board as a whole. The Board had sensed correctly, he said, that the Hawaiians had not been Christianized—only missionized. "The island churches were

---

[33]Phillips, *Protestant America,* p. 127; Hawaiian Evangelical Association, *Proceedings for 1863* (Boston: T. R. Marvin and Son, 1864), p. 89.

[34]Anderson, *Sandwich Islands,* p. viii; Smith, *Yankees,* pp. 323–29; Andrew, *Christian Commonwealth,* p. 162 (italics added).

in their primitive condition as late as 1863." Though the Hawaiians had gained an official independence from the Westerners in both church and state, "the important discovery had scarcely then been made, that self-governed, self-reliant churches are hardly a possibility among the heathen, without pastors of the same race." And if the churches were not autonomous, the government could not be: "Churches formed as those at the Islands had been, and so much under the direction of the missionaries as they were, could do comparatively little to educate the nation for self-government in its civil departments."[35]

Anderson may not have been what his friend and cobelligerent Wayland called him—"the wisest man in America"—but his understanding of the subtler forms of cultural imposition makes him worthy of more notice than he has yet received. Some of his insights into the deeper meanings of autonomy would not be widely appropriated, among self-absorbed Westerners of the twentieth century, until the points were underlined in the colonial societies by civil disobedience or revolutionary violence. "As a missionary society, and as a mission," Anderson wrote in 1847, "we cannot proceed on the assumption, however plausibly stated, that the Saxon is to supersede the native races."[36] An entire "paradigm shift" lay between the scattered statements of such admonitions in the nineteenth century and their acceptance by any appreciable number of Anglo-Americans.

In other communications of the late 1840s Anderson had spelled out, for missionaries and other Americans who would continue not to listen, the cautionary lesson of the Hawaiian experience: actions and forms of beneficence that are innocent in themselves can destroy pride and initiative in one culture while strengthening, in the other, all the self-fulfilling expectations about their own singular capacity to direct society's affairs:

> What I fear is, that the foreign members of [the Hawaiian] government will imperceptibly be so multiplied, that the young chiefs now in school, will never be able to rise to consideration and influence. . . . [Foreigners] deem themselves more competent to fill the offices than the natives, and would fain believe that the natives are incompetent to fill them. . . . [Natives] cannot, indeed, perform the duties as well as foreigners, *if the duties must be performed just as they are in foreign courts and governments;* but at the same time, it is better for the islanders,

[35]Anderson, *Sandwich Islands,* pp. 170–71.

[36]Anderson to the Sandwich Island Mission, 1846, quoted in Phillips, *Protestant America,* p. 126. In an interesting slip, the reference is misdated, in this source, as "1947."

and it is essential to the continuance of their institutions as a nation, that the offices should be filled by natives. Better have the duties performed imperfectly, than not be done by them.[37]

Anderson's outbursts on civil government are especially credible in that it would be difficult to attribute them to any narrow concern for strictly missionary conquest. In another sense, however, all his advocacies, including those relating to civil government, subserved the goal of Christian conquest of the world. Anderson's broader social and political prescriptions, at the end of his career, in fact brought the movement's original "civilizing" enthusiasm full circle. His thought had reflected the shifts from full-blown benevolent paternalism, through the corrective insistence on an evangel freed from Western doctrinal and cultural forms, to the only kind of "Christian civilization" that he believed could be genuine—the kind that grows entirely in and from a native soil.

The Kingdom of God is a seed. The missionary is a planter. The missionary plants the seed. The missionary leaves. Yankee go home! Anderson pled again and again, sometimes almost embarrassed to keep haranguing good people who for decades had failed to appoint a single native pastor. "I feel bound to call your attention to the subject," he wrote to the Sandwich mission in 1846,

> because I believe that if the churches are officered by foreigners, the offices of the government will continue to have foreign occupants. Nothing will save the native government but a native ministry placed over the native churches.[38]

The next generation, aloft with a vision not unlike that of 1810, dealt with Anderson by generally not mentioning him.[39] ("We do not repudiate our ancestors," said the philosopher Santayana, "we pleasantly bid them goodbye.") The temptation, especially if one is trying not to exaggerate Anderson's importance, is to portray his minority report as "filed and forgotten" from about 1880 to 1920. But that would also

[37]Ibid., pp. 126, 125. Italics in original.

[38]Ibid., p. 126.

[39]Mission apologists after 1880 wrote entire histories of the movement without acknowledging the leader of the ABCFM. As late as the 1940s, K. S. Latourette brushed Anderson aside as an executive of "positive convictions" whose views of education were at odds with prevailing opinion and "not permanently pursued." The Presbyterian and ecumenical leader Robert E. Speer, who did appreciate Anderson's importance, honored his campaigning for indigenous churches but underplayed his convictions about education and civilization. See Dennis, *Missions After a Century;* Latourette, *Expansion of Christianity,* 6: 161; Speer, *Missionary Leadership,* chap. 6.

be a distortion. The anticivilizing theories of Anderson, Wayland, and others were forced underground during that later period; yet, anchored as they were in a pure-Gospel tradition long antedating these nineteenth-century figures, they would re-emerge. Other emphases, such as the stress on native churches and pastorates, would continue steadily (whether the name of Anderson was invoked or not) to have champions among mission executives and, in daily practice, among the tens of thousands of missionaries. Much of this championing might seem like lip service and window dressing; "letting go" was not exactly a watchword in 1900 or 1920. But mission ideology on its cultural side had usually been a dialogue rather than a monologue, and that feature would still be evident in a subsequent era that on the whole repudiated Anderson.

CHAPTER 4

A Moral Equivalent for Imperialism

There is a false imperialism which is abhorrent to Christianity, and there is a true imperialism which is inherent in it.

Robert E. Speer, 1933

The renewed strength and acceptability of civilizing ideals at the end of the nineteenth century owed a great deal to the sheer momentum that missions attained in that period. By 1900 the sixteen American missionary societies of the 1860s had swelled to about ninety. That kind of spectacular growth encouraged "the impatient generation" (as Valentin Rabe calls them) to hope for the evangelization of the entire world in their own time. Rabe is also correct, almost certainly, in concluding that missions nonetheless remained "the preoccupation of a minority of even Protestant church members." But the members of that minority were zealous, growing in number, confident, and articulate; and far more than in the past they seemed to have the support of United States presidents and others in high secular places. While actual broad-based support at home seems to have been nearly as fragile or evanescent as many of the results abroad, there is ground for saying, as some historians have, that the American public in this era "took missions to their hearts."[1]

During the same period, "evangelization" became a more and more inclusive term. It came to encompass both evangelism and, with little if any apology, all the "civilizing" functions that Rufus Anderson had tried to suppress. Since the latter were forms of endeavor for which "results abroad" were neither fragile nor evanescent—were in fact quite spectacular—the broadened definition of evangelization was in large part the recognition of a fait accompli. What made "the evangelization of the world in this generation" something more than a glorious day-

[1]Rabe, *Home Base*, pp. 5, 51. For one of the many illustrations of a sharply increased mission enthusiasm that was "unable to sustain its appeal to a massive constituency," see Patricia Hill's account of the women's missionary societies, *The World Their Household*, p. 3 and passim. The final quote is Charles Forman's, in an unpublished comment on a draft of this book, October 1985. The Speer epigraph is from his *Finality of Jesus Christ* (New York: Fleming H. Revell, 1933), p. 372.

dream were not the statistics for conversions but the truly impressive statistics for mission schools and hospitals and social services.

Leaders like Robert E. Speer, however, who were unwilling to stand on merely quantitative justifications for mission policy, argued that emphases had changed because times and human needs had changed. Such spokesmen were not advocates of what would later be called situation ethics, yet they seemed to agree with James Russell Lowell: "New occasions teach new duties, Time makes ancient good uncouth." Speer explained that in the early days of the movement, when Christians were "adjusting and readjusting in their minds" the relation between evangelism and the social statement of the Gospel, Rufus Anderson "had felt called upon to discriminate between missions and civilization." Speer, despite his almost unique appreciation for Anderson, and despite his own zeal for evangelism, thought that Anderson's sharp separation was no longer appropriate.[2]

Of all the new occasions that taught new mission duties, the most urgent and pervasive was the rapid advance of the new imperialism, the end-of-century surge of Western economic, political, and cultural expansion into the non-Western world. While missionary attitudes toward imperialism ran the gamut from wholesale enthusiasm to condemnation, and varied with particular locales and embodiments, the most common response voiced two assertions: that imperialism was an inexorable force, and that this force must somehow be tamed. Mission theorists viewed Western expansionism in the way the philosopher William James wanted this same generation to think of patriotism and national loyalty; that is, as a mode of human action whose incidental benefits could be retained only if some traditional ways of gaining the benefits were rejected. Just as James sought to replace war with other vehicles for loyalty, competitiveness, and animal spirits, American missionary thinkers, by and large, wished to displace the evil or dubious forms of expansionism—those involving exploitation or colonization—in favor of the "fine spiritual imperialism" that their own movement aimed to represent.[3]

In the resulting conception of themselves as chaplains and tamers of Western expansion (their professed primary role as evangelists for Christ did not change) the Americans maintained the potent mix of universal

[2]Lowell's poem, "The Present Crisis" (1844), provided the words for the hymn "Once to Every Man and Nation" (1896); Speer, *Missionary Leadership,* p. 266.

[3]William James, *The Moral Equivalent of War* (New York: American Association for International Conciliation, 1910); Carver, "Baptists and World Missions," p. 327. Cf. Hunter, *Gospel of Gentility,* pp. 7–8. For an especially forceful plea for missions as a necessary moral equivalent and corrective, see Henry C. King, *Moral and Religious Challenge,* pp. 343–84.

and particularistic impulses that had invigorated their movement initially, and that by now was deeply ingrained. As Christians they felt called and fitted to spiritualize a powerful force in secular development. As Americans, gloriously free from the colonial and other impediments of old Europe, they felt entirely comfortable in the role of spiritual directorship that history seemed to be thrusting upon them.

The steady growth, in both absolute and proportional terms, of American contributions to the worldwide movement lent plausibility to the renewed sense of national spiritual vocation. Certainly it appeared that where others were dispatching civil servants, American society was commissioning religious workers. When Anderson compiled statistics in 1869, the American and Continental mission contingents were each about half the size of the then-dominant British force. Yet in 1900, Americans outnumbered Continentals by two to one. By 1910 they had also passed the British in financing, in number of missionaries, and in several other departments.[4]

American leaders, meanwhile, achieved prominence at an even greater rate; and here again the "moral equivalent" notion gained concrete expression. Though no one can say with certainty that under another system the Andersons and Speers (or, earlier, the Binghams) of the missionary movement would have been viceroys or colonial functionaries, it is entirely plausible that they would have been, along with scores or hundreds of second-echelon leaders. As it was, John R. Mott and others, opting for religious rather than any sort of political roles, declined even to accept diplomatic posts.

The flooding of the world mission leadership with these articulate and confident Americans helped in turn to produce an impression, especially among increasingly alarmed Continental mission leaders, that Americans (with the connivance of their British friends) were refashioning the common enterprise on the model of their own activistic religion and their civilizing forms of outreach. In actual fact the Americans were deploying their resources—whether evangelistic missions or hospitals, ordained persons or laypersons—in much the same proportions as were the Germans or Scandinavians. By such criteria Americans were no more activistic than most others. What was happening, however, in a time when civilizing ventures were booming and conversionary ones lagging, was that Americans were doing more of everything. And this included, quite definitely, the talking and defending. Amid the general Western enthusiasm for conquering the world, once and forever,

[4]Anderson, *Foreign Missions,* pp. 342–45; Dennis, *Centennial Survey,* pp. 9–48; Dennis et al., *World Atlas,* pp. 81–102.

Ivy League recruiters for the mission army: Robert E. Speer and John R. Mott at Northfield, Massachusetts, 1900. Courtesy of Yale Divinity School Library.

on behalf of "Christian civilization," Americans were proclaiming this intention with a louder voice and a loftier idealism than even their very righteous British cousins.[5]

[5]Andrew Walls believes the British in this period were losing their enthusiasm for "civilizing missions," and were conceding to colonial bureaucrats the same functions that American missionaries were gladly assuming. Andrew F. Walls, "British Missions," pp. 159–66.

The increasing American dominance owed something, as well, to the fact that these leaders spoke with remarkable unanimity across the theological spectrum. The gospel of Christian civilization, in its American phrasings, flourished among the theological liberals and Social Gospelers who applied their energies to foreign missions; but it also made its appearance among devotees of a new and growing premillennialism that showed little enthusiasm for the Social Gospel, and none at all for liberal theology. In view of the bitter falling-out that was to come after 1920 between liberal Protestants and their biblically-conservative brethren, the extent of this earlier collaboration is striking. Opposing forces could collaborate because the principal common enterprise, converting the world to Christ, seemed more compelling than any differences; but also because they shared a vision of the essential rightness of Western civilization and the near-inevitability of its triumph.

THERMIDOR: RESISTANCE TO THE ANDERSON POLICIES

The renewed enthusiasm to export Christian civilization had been prefigured well before the end of the century as various missionaries had voiced opposition to the policies of the American Board and the Baptist leaders. Resistance to the indigenous-church idea and to the Andersonian constraints on education had especially shown the shape of the future.

One of the major forces opposing independent native churches was denominationalism (or as Andersonians would have said, "sectarianism"); and a growing denominational consciousness was central to late nineteenth-century development. Though unitive impulses persisted, and provided something of a counterforce, denominations after 1850 were operating with new vigor in sponsoring mission personnel, managing mission stations and institutions, and organizing native churches. The various church bodies became markedly less willing to leave foreign missions to pandenominational or nondenominational associations. Increasingly, mite boxes for the cause were passed with collection plates, so that congregants could support First Church's man in China or Central Church's woman in Persia. The pressures both to prosecute missions "our way" and to keep "our missionaries" where they were, mounted commensurately.

Between 1857 and 1870, the three denominational bodies associated with the Congregationalists in the ABCFM—the Reformed Dutch (as the denomination was then known), the German Reformed, and the New School Presbyterian—all withdrew and placed their missions directly under their own boards. The case of the Reformed Dutch separation showed rather clearly what forces were at work: resentment against "outside" control by the ABCFM and its strong-minded secretary; growing denominational self-consciousness; practical considerations of money-raising and of smooth relations between the denomination and its own missionaries; and, most portentously, a willingness or even eagerness to have native churches replicate the ones at home.

Some of the Reformed Dutch missionaries agreed from the start with Anderson's wish that denominational forms not be imposed on individual churches. Even after leaving the ABCFM, those at Amoy, in China, resisted all pressures to organize the native congregations into a Reformed classis, or synod. But the Arcot (India) mission, under Dr. Henry M. Scudder and his brothers, clashed with Anderson over the issue, accusing the secretary of "ecclesiastical aggressions." When the Reformed Dutch withdrawal occurred, that kind of animosity was masked by expressions of gratitude, or of simple readiness to assume independent responsibility. But one passage in the valedictory report to the ABCFM of the Reformed Dutch officials identified the changes in church organization that had helped cause the tensions in the first place. "It is not to be concealed," said this voice of the new denominationalism, "that there is a growing disinclination for what have been called voluntary associations, and a tendency to ecclesiastical responsibility." Moving closer to the marrow, the report spoke of a growing conviction that questions relating to ministers and missionaries should be decided "by ecclesiastical action, where [such workers] have the right of appeal, and not by committees."[6]

Those who were solicitous about a missionary's right of appeal could also, of course, be concerned about the welfare of native churches; but in either case they used denominational language and criteria to beat down the Andersonian formulas. When the New School Presbyterians debated this issue in 1859, the Reverend Daniel Poor characterized the American Board's allegedly "independent" churches as "mongrel organizations, subject to the Episcopal supervision of the Prudential Committee." That became a common, however muddled, accusation: that Anderson's undenominational native churches were really Congregational churches in disguise, and that Anderson wanted to rule over these churches as archbishop, if not as pope.

In any case, why not allow non-Congregationalists to organize the natives in the ways *they* thought best? "If the Presbyterian polity is good for us," the Reverend John Jenkins insisted, "it is good for our churches

---

[6]This and the following two paragraphs draw upon Schneider, "Senior Secretary," chap. 7.

abroad." And when the Reformed Dutch, several years later, found themselves forcing synodical organization on unwilling missionaries, a denominational official put this sentiment more eloquently. "Deep down in the heart of the Church," Talbot Chambers explained, "lies the conviction that our missionaries, who carry to the heathen the doctrine of Christ as we have received it, must also carry the order of Christ as we have received it. . . . The substantive elements of our polity must be reproduced in the mission churches."

Restraint about dictating polity to native churches had usually been linked to the longer-range commitment to get the missionaries out of the churches they had formed and, if possible, out of the country. As Anderson had discovered in Hawaii, and as Speer and others observed regretfully in the later period, no other policy was more redolent of good intentions, nor more likely to produce ingenious reasons why missionaries should stay just a little longer. In the absence of Anderson's acute sense of the dangers of paternalism, even those who championed autonomy in principle found it inapt in particular situations. Miron Winslow argued that though one must trust the vessels of grace chosen by the Holy Spirit, some vessels—in this case the Euro-American ones—were likely to be more trustworthy than others. Before leaving Indian converts on their own, Winslow wrote, one must consider such intractable realities as "the weakness of the Hindu character, and the peculiar temptations in every Hindu church to retain heathen customs and Hindu caste."[7]

In the bitterly contested matter of missionary schools, Anderson's opponents further sharpened the contours of positions that would prevail at the end of the century. Royal Wilder, furious with Anderson after the latter refused in 1857 to return him to India, attacked the Board's educational policies with special vigor. Their prejudice against schools in which the vernacular language was not "the grand medium of instruction," and against those serving other purposes besides evangelism, had meant the closing of numerous institutions on which "the blessing of God has rested." In one mission, Wilder asserted, "more than *five hundred* children and youth, who were daily enjoying faithful instruction in the saving truths of the Gospel, were 'turned out into the great and terrible wilderness of the heathen world,' by order of the Deputation."[8]

Miron Winslow, whose school at Madras had been spared (unlike Wilder's at Kolapur), reached the same conclusion by a different route.

[7]Winslow, *Hints*, p. 209.
[8]Wilder, *Mission Schools*, pp. 16–17.

Winslow acknowledged most of the difficulties that had induced the Board to send a deputation and to take drastic action. With respect to boarding schools, for example, he seemed to agree that nothing failed like success. The better the school, Winslow lamented, the more crowded it was with students who were determined not to become Christians. Under the so-called hothouse system, the youth "were isolated from their heathen friends and idolatrous festivals, and lived together under the missionary's eye." Short-range results had been good, especially with very young pupils; long-range effects had been "less practical . . . than we had expected." Yet Winslow insisted that the Anderson policies were, by and large, ill-conceived. The schools Anderson had berated—open to the unconverted, utilizing some unconverted teachers—on balance had been worthwhile. And instruction in English, at least in the high schools, was necessary for such purposes as the development of a learned ministry.[9]

Cyrus Hamlin, head of the school and seminary at Bebek, Turkey, before he broke with the Board over language policy, expressed his dissent in the same modulated way. The Baptists in India, Hamlin said, had tried the allegedly apostolic method ("no education at all") and the results had suggested why the apostolic church had not withstood the paganizing influences of Constantinian Rome. The Baptist experiment had proved disastrous. In one supposedly Christianized community after another, Hamlin reported, most children had grown up "without being able to read one sentence in the word of God." The Baptists had at length felt compelled to establish a system of education.

Hamlin thought that when able and earnest people had tried to pursue missionary objectives without teaching English, the results had been equally sad. Just as "no society, no body of men, no theorists" had been able to resist the growing nineteenth-century insistence on education, most experts had come to acknowledge the need for "linguistic study" in education. And wherever a large proportion of missionaries and educators were Anglo-Saxon, English was bound to be the medium; the wide diffusion of English by commerce and colonization made its pedagogical use inevitable. "Its rich stores of Christian thought, science, and philosophy" meant that it was "destined to form a band of sympathy and intercourse among the nations, beyond any other language." The stars in their nineteenth-century courses, he seemed to believe, fought against any reluctance to export the English language.[10]

[9]Winslow, *Hints*, pp. 126–90.
[10]Hamlin, *Among the Turks*, pp. 275–82.

Royal Wilder's persuasiveness in the same cause was undermined by his vendetta against the senior secretary; yet his arguments made clear some of the assumptions supporting that civilizing emphasis that the next generation would, less belligerently, take for granted. In his apologia for educational missions and his own performance, Royal Wilder built a bridge across the chasm that had opened between meager conversionary results and a soaring confidence in the evangelization of the world. To a very great extent, this bridge consisted of faith not in the power of a "pure Gospel" but in that of a Gospel-centered civilization.

Wilder's 400 pages of enthusiasm for *Mission Schools in India* began with the admission that the missionary effort over seventy years had produced a Christian contingent in that land of some 30,000 persons—one hundredth of 1 percent of the population. But it closed with an assertion that twenty-five years later would take its place as the "watchword" of missions: "I verily believe the Church of Christ is able to evangelize the heathen world in one short generation." In between one finds not merely an extended celebration of missionary schools but a plea for Christian civilization that, however curiously, was only made stronger by Wilder's insistence that civilizing is not the main objective.

Wilder wrote that "civil and social benefits . . . in comparison with the spiritual results, are as time to eternity, earth to heaven." The point, however, was that the civilizing strategy was a sine qua non for spiritual results. This seemed a far cry from St. Paul's desire to "know nothing" among a foreign people except for the knowledge of Christ and the Cross. But Wilder in 1860 joined the tendency to question whether the apostolic Church deserved its reputation for missionary success: "We are constrained to feel that the triumphs of the Gospel in the achievements of modern missions eclipse all that is recorded of Apostolic times."[11]

By the era, some forty years later, that has usually been considered the golden day for missionary expansion, apostolic or Andersonian models seemed even less plausible. Speer in 1900 estimated 1.5 million converts in the missionized areas. About 800,000 more had been converted by 1910. These statistics could be made to sound impressive, and promoters did that when appealing for support at home. But as Speer,

---

[11]Wilder, *Mission Schools,* pp. 14, 420, 13. Though A. T. Pierson, Wilder's successor as editor of the *Missionary Review,* is usually thought to have originated the controversial watchword ("The Evangelization of the World in This Generation"), Wilder seems to have said it first.

Mott, and most other leaders were painfully aware, the country-by-country conversion figures were meager indeed when set against total populations. K. S. Latourette lamented, toward the end of this period of extraordinary overall growth, that "in none of the major areas to which missionaries have gone do the younger churches include more than one percent of the population. In some limited areas the proportion is much larger. In most lands it is smaller."[12]

When challenged to explain how such results could portend the evangelization of the world in one, or even in many, generations, spokesmen responded earnestly that "evangelization" had never carried the implication of huge numbers of converts.[13] But they also were likely at that point to "refer the questioner to the Sandwich Islands"—to change the subject and talk about successes. Speer in 1902, remarking that he disliked "enumerations" anyway and would offer a few only "to be rid of them once and for all," claimed a total of 558 missionary societies (American and European), 7,319 mission stations, 14,364 churches, 94 colleges and universities, 20,458 schools, 379 hospitals, 782 dispensaries, 152 publishing houses, 452 translations of the Bible, and "sixty-four ships belonging exclusively to Christ." The missionary movement, worldwide, then employed 18,682 missionaries and 79,396 native workers, and claimed income of more than twenty million dollars a year.[14]

These are the figures, surely, that can lead one to understand the sense of momentum and of divine inevitability that gripped the souls of this generation, and that enabled perfectly sane people to talk of speedy world evangelization. The fact that by this time the number of schools exceeded the number of missionaries (as well as the number of churches) could be taken as heartening proof that in some respects indigenization was taking hold; more directly it attested to the dimensions of the civilizing effort. The hundred-odd colleges and 1,200 medical institutions might seem less impressive than the number of schools; but the point for contemporaries was that these in particular seemed to have come out of nowhere in a mere thirty years. Speer, exaggerating only slightly, recalled that as recently as the 1870s there had been "no great conspicuous institutions such as hospitals and colleges."[15]

[12]Speer, *Principles and Practice*, p. 501; Dennis, *Centennial Survey*, p. 263; Dennis et al., *World Atlas*, p. 83; Mott, *Evangelization*, p. 102; Mott, "Tasks of Tomorrow," p. 264; Latourette, *Missions Tomorrow*, pp. 94–95.

[13]Mott, *Evangelization*, pp. 7–10. For a representative indication that the leaders nonetheless cared a great deal about conversion statistics, present and prospective, see ibid., chap. 5.

[14]Speer, *Principles and Practice*, pp. 501–2; Dennis, *Centennial Survey*, p. 263.

[15]Speer, "A Few Comparisons," p. 7.

"Peace Corps types before the Peace Corps." Newly appointed ABCFM missionaries, 1915, as photographed for the publication of the Congregational Women's Board of Missions, *Life and Light* (July 1915): facing p. 297. Courtesy of the United Church Board for World Ministries. (Accompanying identifications indicate that only four of the women pictured here were spouses; the rest were going out as unmarried missionaries. The percentage of women appointed by the ABCFM in 1915—63%—was almost as high as what the picture suggests.)

This flourishing of auxiliary institutions involved a strengthening of lay participation that in turn owed something to the augmented function and status of women. Between 1868 and 1910 the proportion of laypersons in the missionary force (American and European) rose from 52 percent to 70 percent. Since women dominated the lay cohort at both dates, this proportional change reflected an increased female presence. By 1910, a statistically typical group of 100 missionaries would comprise thirty ordained men, twelve laymen engaged in nonmedical work, five physicians (including one woman and one of the ordained men), and fifty-five women.[16]

Although many laypersons, female as well as male, would have regarded their work as a form of direct evangelism, such a consideration would be more than counterbalanced by the fact that large numbers of

[16]Anderson, *Foreign Missions,* p. 346; *Missionary Review* 9 (November 1886): 552–53; Bliss, *Encyclopedia,* 2: 626–30; Dennis et al., *World Atlas,* pp. 86–102.

ordained persons ran schools or YMCAs, preaching seldom or not at all. By any reckoning, the preponderance of those "teachers, farmers and mechanics" whom Anderson had wished to leave at home had become more striking than in Anderson's early years. And women, while still clearly subordinate in the missionary hierarchies, had gained greatly in practical influence. Changes in nomenclature—from (at most) "assistant missionary" to "missionary"—told only part of the story. A providentialist might say, in fact, that a deity who did not wish missionaries to build schools and emphasize social service would surely have induced missionary directors either to leave the women at home or to let them preach.[17]

The ABCFM and other boards had indeed shown hesitation, for at least a half-century, about sending out single women. But from the beginning they had placed considerable, not always healthy, pressure upon male aspirants to find themselves wives before setting out; the scurrying-about of Hiram Bingham and his impatient young colleagues before their embarkation has always been a staple in the legend of the Hawaiian venture. These chosen companions in general had been, like their husbands, among the most spirited and highly educated persons of their time; and many, given the opportunity and social approval, would gladly have preached. As it was, they gladly taught, counseled, organized, and engaged in various forms of social service. By 1910, when the numbers of married and unmarried women at most stations were about equal, all were normally called missionaries. But in the mainline and in many of the minority or sectarian groups, they were not ordained or licensed to preach.

One tendency of the time—a somewhat ironic one, in view of these realities—was a celebration of the "layman's" role, in missions and elsewhere. John R. Mott, Sherwood Eddy, and other leaders in the missionary and student movements had not attended theological seminaries. Others, such as Robert E. Speer and Robert Wilder, had attended seminaries, or even taken divinity degrees, but had eschewed ordination. This lay emphasis, though it became something of a fetish, marked a genuine affirmation, not merely of an abstract "priesthood of all believers," but of the specific lay activities that in the mission field fell conspicuously to women workers.

PROTESTANT LIBERALISM AND MISSIONS

The newer mission theories that, by the end of the century, had restored respectability to civilizing objectives did not come with theological

---

[17]The literature on women's participation, in the field and at the home base, is now considerable. See especially Beaver, *Women in World Mission*, and Hill, *World Their Household*.

labels attached to them. Confidence in the technology, education, and other modalities of Western culture was too pervasive for that. A healthy majority both of missionaries and of mission administrators, moreover, sought to minimize theological distinctions and are therefore difficult to classify clearly as "liberal" or "conservative." Yet theological tendencies did strongly influence what was said and done in missions. The idea of civilizing missions received powerful support, direct and indirect, from the rapidly growing liberal movement in Protestant theology, while the "pure Gospel" tradition was more regularly kept in view by those who considered themselves conservative evangelicals.

Protestant liberalism affirmed God's indwelling in nature and humanity, took a relatively hopeful view of human prospects, and could envision "world evangelization" in the broadest postmillennial terms. Yet the theologically revisionist or negative elements in the liberal gospel were probably just as important, over the long run, in supporting a civilizing or social-service emphasis in missions. Liberals, for example, simply lacked enthusiasm for direct evangelism, whether at home or overseas.

The liberal movement that had been spreading in the churches since mid-century had usually stood in an adversary relation to revivalism, sometimes opposing it wholesale, more often criticizing excesses or particular methods. While liberals who supported missions were unlikely to call preaching unimportant, or to deny that personal conversion was the real aim of the enterprise, their critics were surely right in charging that zeal for personal evangelism was lessened insofar as one hoped, as liberals characteristically did, to bring people and societies to Christ by environmental influences and a kind of spiritual osmosis. Detractors of liberalism were also justified in thinking that the new principles, even if put to work in the cause of direct evangelism, lacked two other important elements: a concern for doctrinal specificity and a sense of urgency.

Liberals (though they were not alone in this) characteristically voiced an aversion to formal or detailed creeds. George Angier Gordon, minister at Old South Church (Congregational) in Boston, expressed such an aversion directly in relation to missions, advising the ABCFM in 1895 that "we are not under obligation to export our entire body of belief," and that "there is no particular call for our church polity, our special theology, or the traditions of our Christian life. These are not wanted; if sent, they would prove unsuitable."[18]

William Newton Clarke, the liberals' leading systematic theologian and an enthusiast for foreign missions, extended the injunction to in-

[18]Gordon, "Gospel," pp. 99–100.

clude social or cultural "creeds" as well as ecclesiastical ones. Reviving the idea of the missionary as one who merely plants a seed and moves on, Clarke opposed exporting specific Western modes even for the purposes of social amelioration. Though missionaries must obviously respond to social need and injustice when confronted with them, on the whole they should rely on the power of Christianity as a revolutionary force. "The Christian life, when once it has entered among the people, will wage its own battle."[19]

Had all liberals been as consistent as Clarke was, their avoidance of doctrinal specificity would not have contributed to a "civilizing" ideology. But most of them, caring less than Clarke did for consistency, or else caring more for social reform, minimized religious doctrine without becoming at all shy about promoting Western education, technology, and secular ideas. In general, therefore, disparagement of doctrine helped open the way for enterprises of social salvation.

The tendency to deemphasize creeds (or in the liberals' own view to reduce them to essentials) went beyond mere antisectarianism and became a distinctive, notably ethical conception of what is basic to Christianity. This was a theologically affirmative stance, one buttressed at every point by scriptural references to Christ as teacher, healer, and savior. Yet it was also a point at which lack of urgency could fairly be ascribed to the liberal position. American liberals in missions carried forward an idea given currency by the mid-century theologian Horace Bushnell: salvation is a gradual process in which environmental influences play a major role. Liberals neither expected an imminent end of the world nor believed all those untouched by the Gospel would go straight to Hell. As a result, their conception of the core of Christianity, of the simple message to which everything else can be reduced, was substantially different from that of conservative evangelicals. For the latter, the central message had to be expressed in the language of radical conversion—"believe and be saved"—while for liberal theologians the key idea was that "the Kingdom of God is within you." George Gordon wrote that the essential Gospel is an immanent or indwelling force, "the living, loving God, moving with ineffable power in the living, loving Christ."[20]

It followed that liberals, with a good deal of support from the kind of conservative who had been nurtured in a calm and painstaking pietism, were either uncomfortable with slogans about evangelizing the world in one generation or else simply reinterpreted such objectives in

[19]Clarke, *Missions,* pp. 72–74.
[20]Gordon, "Gospel," p. 99.

their own fashion. Clarke doubted whether even "the simplest form of faith in Christ" could be announced, let alone made effectual, in a short span of decades. "It is quite impossible," he wrote, "that within the lifetime of a generation Christ should become intelligently known by all men." The cautious "Andover liberals" of the 1880s, sharing such doubts, had devised a theological compromise under which the unreached millions might hope for a future probation, a posthumous opportunity to hear and accept the Gospel. Twenty years later, liberals in general felt little urgency even about concocting that kind of solution. And this relaxed attitude toward evangelism owed a good deal, in turn, to the liberals' steadily lessening sense of the danger and iniquity in non-Christian religious systems.[21]

On the surface, the typical liberal stance concerning world religions retained much of the traditional militancy. Clarke insisted that the attitude of Christianity "is not one of compromise, but of conflict and of conquest," and that Christianity proposes "to displace the other religions." Gordon justified interfaith collaboration on the ground that Christianity will always show itself superior to anything "these natives have to offer." And American spokesmen for the World's Parliament of Religions, held at Chicago in 1893, defended that project as a Christian missionary venture, not merely as an exercise in interreligious understanding. Dr. Barrows, who had organized the great meeting, assured the "good men [who] have criticised the Parliament mercilessly" that delegates from all faiths had joined daily in reciting the Lord's Prayer. "The Parliament," he boasted, had "ended at Calvary."[22]

Anomalies of that sort—inviting venerable Buddhist leaders to Chicago to recite the Lord's Prayer—are less mysterious if one recognizes how far the appreciation of other cultures had had to come just to reach the level of condescension liberals had attained by the 1890s. Invective had declined. There was some willingness to listen, or even to learn. But this cautious new catholicity was obliged to protect its flanks against a traditional rhetoric that still regularly vilified "heathen" religions and cultures on the basis of ex parte evidence, circular reasoning, and, too often, substantial and stubborn ignorance. Against that background, liberal concessions were indeed sufficient to erode not just the urgency Christians felt about evangelism but also that belief in Christian uniqueness that the orthodox considered a prerequisite for any evangelism at all.

[21]Clarke, *Missions,* pp. 73–74. For a more extended discussion of the Andover stance, see, Williams, *Andover Liberals,* chap. 4 and passim.

[22]Clarke, *Missions,* p. 107; Gordon, "Gospel," p. 101; Barrows, *World's Parliament,* pp. 1560, 1578.

Gordon and Clarke, while insisting that Christianity is ultimately incomparable, also made full use of the biblical notion that Christianity goes forth to fulfill rather than to destroy. Though Clarke stressed conflict and displacement, he saw this as one system completing the partial virtues of another. Gordon, despite his Anglo-Saxon condescension, urged that the Christian "dreams of dominion" must more and more rest on the foundations of the native religions. Jesus, Gordon said, "must prove Himself a better ruler to Japan, a nobler Confucius to China, a diviner Gautama to India; the whole sacred past must reappear in Him transfigured and carried utterly beyond itself. . . . He must come as the consummation of the ideals of every nation under heaven."[23]

The mixed signals coming out of the World's Parliament of Religions followed the same pattern. Had most of the Christian speakers at Chicago voiced the intransigence of one Professor Wilkinson, of the University of Chicago, the representatives of other faiths undoubtedly would have left on the next steamer. (Some said as much.) Wilkinson, while allowing that individuals might be saved without having accepted the Gospel, found he could offer no hope or solace to non-Christian religions, either primitive or advanced. To the question whether any kind of non-Christian belief could be called "a true religion, only not perfect," Wilkinson answered that "Christianity says No." The attitude of Christianity toward religions other than itself, he added, "is an attitude of universal, absolute, eternal, unappeasable hostility." But within the Parliament at least, that kind of bravado was rare. Swami Vivekananda, the Hindu leader who later founded the Vedanta Society in the United States, spoke of such "jarring notes" as having "by their striking contrast, made the general harmony the sweeter." If any at the conference, Vivekananda said, hoped that unity among religions would come "by the triumph of any one of these religions and the destruction of the others, to him I say, 'Brother, yours is an impossible hope.' . . . I pity him from the bottom of my heart."[24]

It is clear, nonetheless, that world unity on Christian terms was exactly what many delegates had in mind, or else projected subconsciously. The World's Parliament resembled an Olympics competition to which all are invited but in which the host country rather expects to win the gold medals. If Vivekananda (who may have been playing his own little game) really was unaware of that, he was going to learn about it in the course of his later struggles to establish an exotic faith in the West.

[23]Clarke, *Missions,* pp. 117–21; Gordon, "Gospel," p. 103.
[24]In Barrows, *World's Parliament,* pp. 1249, 170–71.

Yet many of the 1890s unquestionably had moved, not merely beyond unappeasable hostility, but even beyond Gordon's acknowledgment of "partial truths" that are to be grandly completed by the religion of the Westerners. A number of the Christian speakers at Chicago expressed a hope for actual collaboration among religions. A few made bold to propose—as would be done more memorably in a celebrated "Laymen's Report on Missions" forty years later—that the real struggle in the world is not between Christians and others but between spiritual forces and material or demonic ones. The Reverend George T. Candlin, a British missionary in China, linked the ecumenical urges within Christianity to an emerging respect for competing faiths: "By the new pathway of comparative religion, men are finding their way to the belief in the common possession of a spiritual nature on the part of all the members of the human family," and to a "dawning consciousness of the Saviour's care for all the spiritual [sic] in all climes and ages."

Candlin's demand that Christianity approach the non-Christian world "in a spirit of love and not of antagonism" could have seemed a merely pious and ambiguous expression had he not also berated the "confusion of thought" that kept Christians from recognizing the vital and inalienable role other religions play in their own cultures. Christian apologists, he complained, had consistently tried to make the "heathen" religions responsible for the worst in non-Western societies, while automatically giving Christianity credit for all that is best in Christendom. Invidious contrasts of that sort, he argued, are indefensible even on Christian theological grounds. "The true root of sin always and everywhere is irreligion. Religion wherever we find it makes its appeal to the human conscience . . . and makes a stand, effective or ineffective, against evil."[25]

Although liberalism conspicuously, in these several ways, opened a back gate to activist and "serving" approaches to missions, it also seemed clear by the late 1890s that a front entrance had been thrown open, and that evangelicals as well as liberals were driving enthusiastically into the mission compounds with the coach-and-four of a civilizing ideology. Robert E. Speer in 1902 summarized one of James Dennis's ponderous volumes on *Christian Missions and Social Progress* by exulting that socially oriented missions had "promoted temperance, opposed the liquor and opium traffics . . . checked gambling, established higher standards of personal purity, cultivated industry and frugality [and] elevated woman." Missions had restrained "polygamy, concubinage, adultery and child-

[25]Ibid., pp. 1181, 1185–87.

marriage and infanticide." They had stood against the slave trade, "abolished cannibalism and human sacrifice and cruelty, organized famine relief, improved husbandry and agriculture, introduced Western medicines and medical science, founded leper asylums and colonies, promoted cleanliness and sanitation, and checked war."[26]

Dennis's three-volume work on missions and reform, published between 1897 and 1906, was itself a monument to the social enthusiasm. Its premise was that although "the evangelistic aim is still first . . . a new significance has been given to missions as a factor in the social regeneration of the world." The author's brief for social missions was so nearly unequivocal that his nods to evangelism could be interpreted as backhanded or merely ritualistic. He patronized traditional evangelists by remarking that "God often uses men of one special aim, with a somewhat contracted although vivid and intense conception of their mission, to accomplish through them a work of larger and grander scope than they realize." Arguing that the preoccupation with evangelism had been largely responsible for the "tardy progress of missions in the past," he cited the views of the activist Grace Kimball that this distorted emphasis had implied "a separation of the soul from its God-given earthly conditions; a snatching of the brand, not a putting out of the fires for the benefit of brands at large; a jealous care for the individual, not supplemented by an equal care for the society of which he is a member . . . a hopeless condemnation and fleeing as from the doomed Sodom." Dennis held that social missions, by contrast, deserved the appreciation of "every lover of humanity [and] every student of social science," and also of those who considered themselves revolutionaries.[27]

Surely Dennis was right in suggesting that persons of reforming spirit and worldwide concern could respect the aims of this international Social Gospel. Yet his own magnificent effort to promote and celebrate that movement became quickly dated and virtually forgotten.[28] While the scanting of personal evangelism made his book less than useful to conservatives, his equally strong tendency to belittle foreign cultures and religions was soon to be regarded by liberals as bad form (whether or not those who ceased to voice belittling attitudes would genuinely recant them). Not only did Dennis's book give no quarter in the battle with non-Christian religions; its cataloguing of missions' social achievements rested on a base of blindly ethnocentric disapproval of exotic

[26]Speer, *Principles and Practice,* pp. 419–20.
[27]Dennis, *Missions,* 1:23, 47, 48n, 43–46.
[28]Latourette's three-volume work of the 1940s (*The Great Century*) neglected to mention, in either text or bibliography, Dennis's three volumes of a half-century earlier.

cultures. Though in some respects the most thoroughly progressive statement of missionary ideology in its generation, Dennis's book was among the most regressive from the viewpoint of anyone who hoped to disentangle missionary purposes from those of an implicit cultural imperialism.

At the World's Parliament of Religions, an Indian speaker had asked a large audience how many had read *The Life of Buddha,* and had expressed amazement when only five hands were raised. Dr. Barrows's reaction had been that the question was somewhat unfair since hundreds of the delegates, as he remarked innocently, would have read Sir Edwin Arnold's *Light of Asia.* Dennis, similarly, could see nothing wrong with relying exclusively upon Western observers for the data that supported his detailed condemnations of alien social systems and his assessment of improved conditions after the missionaries' arrival. Since, as he said, the inner life of distant peoples can be understood only through "close contact and long observation," Dennis had employed the newest social-science techniques and sent a questionnaire to over three hundred missionaries. He thought that the objection "sometimes whimsically made," that missionaries are not reliable reporters, was "improbable and not justified by experience." But any lingering doubts about this could be set to rest since the missionary data and opinions, he had found, were confirmed by "candid and authoritative lay sources."[29]

The resulting strain of ex parte judgment, of description neither enriched nor cross-examined by testimony from those whose civilizations were being described, runs like a faultline through Dennis's conscientious analysis. The former missionary insisted that he wished neither to magnify the evils of the non-Christian world nor to minimize those of Christendom, but he undercut such intentions with strictures against other civilizations that he considered mild and "unmagnified" because he simply took them for granted. The balance Dennis aspired to could scarcely be achieved by a writer who (in a single paragraph) characterized the greatest oriental scholarship as dry, futile, puerile, profitless, irrelevant, vain, vacuous, unwholesome, mentally crooked, and carelessly inexact. With respect to oriental moral philosophies, Dennis could detect little besides confusion, uncertainty, fatalism, and easygoing compliance with evil. The moral structure of Eastern civilization, he wrote,

[29]Barrows, *World's Parliament,* p. 1571; Dennis, *Missions,* 1: vii–viii. Dharmapala, the Indian leader who asked the embarrassing question about Christian knowledge of Buddhism, also surprised the Westerners by informing them that the Buddhists had held a similar parliament twenty centuries earlier. The promoters of the 1893 meeting had been under the impression, as Barrows reported with refreshing candor, "that nothing like a Parliament of Religion had ever assembled before." Ibid., 1: 8.

"if not in a state of collapse, is universally feeble, except as morality is identified with asceticism and external conformity to ceremonial ritual."[30]

By the time Dennis had groped his way to the realm of religious experience and individual character, nearly all the demeaning adjectives had been used; but he discovered new rhetorical resources:

> The personal qualities that are characteristic of an Oriental are complacency, pride, self-confidence, and conscious assurance of the superiority of himself and his environment. He has wrought diligently in his own strength and for his own glory, and, in his estimation, he has succeeded. He delights in his historic past, and is hardly conscious that his present is any the less worthy of admiration. He needs a thorough toning up in intellectual sincerity and moral manhood, and some lessons in humility.[31]

It would be unjust to suppose this is merely Dennis speaking. "The voice is Jacob's voice; the hands are Esau's." Dennis, even if not well remembered by immediately following generations, was roundly praised by his own. The response to his book confirms both the enthusiasm for civilizing emphases in missions and the general myopia about what seem, by evidentiary guidelines common in Dennis's time or any other, serious flaws in his modes of observation and reasoning. The author's casual use of evidence would scarcely have been countenanced in the law courts or scholarship of the Western countries, especially amid the prevailing enthusiasm for empiricism and scientific method. Yet it is difficult to find negative critiques of his work within either the liberal or the more conservative religious bodies.

Dennis's chapters had been presented originally at Princeton and other Presbyterian seminaries, and apparently had been warmly received. Reviewers for such journals as those of the Lutherans and of the Reformed Church offered nothing but praise. The *Christian Missionary*, a Disciples periodical, headlined Dennis's effort as "A Really Great Book," and found his description of the social evils of non-Christian countries not merely unassailable but "intensely touching." This last journal credited Dennis with having "spared no pains to inform himself in regard to these things." A sometime collaborator, Harlan Beach of Yale, did acknowledge defects in Dennis's work, for example its tendency to give Christianity disproportionate credit for social change. The author's "immense mass of facts" tended to exaggerate Christianity's impact and to obscure one's view of "other forces that have cooperated in effecting the changes described."

[30]Dennis, *Missions* 1: 73–74, 378–81.
[31]Ibid., p. 380.

But the dubiety of an entire reliance on Western reports of non-Western societies seemed not to have occurred to Beach: "It is a case of special [i.e. missionary] pleading, without doubt, but we fail to see unfairness of treatment for that reason."[32]

The unspoken assumption, in what passed for intercultural inquiry, continued to be that Western civilization is entitled to phrase the questions as well as provide most of the answers. The unspoken, and mostly unconscious, watchword was still "define and conquer."

From the viewpoint of any fundamental critique of imperialism, therefore, the liberal reformulations of mission theory represented a mixture of gains and losses. Liberal theology had undercut the exclusivity of Christian claims, and both that and the Social Gospel style had helped promote powerful conceptions of Christian service and example as valid modes of evangelization. In the long run, given the tendency for more open religious attitudes to carry over into nonreligious concerns, such contributions were perhaps more weighty than the aid and comfort that the liberal enthusiasms gave to cultural imperialism.

In an immediate sense, however, the predilections of liberal Protestantism, especially in its Social Gospel forms, operated as much to promote cultural aggressiveness as to diminish it. Most liberals, even if they got out of the business of personal evangelism, continued to express ultimate aims in the terminology not only of world evangelization but of Christian finality and "right of conquest." Postmillennial optimism in fact tended to produce more militant images of world conquest than did premillennialism, since the latter when most consistent proclaimed only a limited hope of reaching those few who are to be saved before Christ's return.

It was a replay of the ancient dilemma. To the degree that liberalism offered salvation through social, medical, and educational agencies, a great many institutions in the sending culture were bound to be presented as promoting this salvation, and thus as obligatory elements in what was being urged upon the rest of the world. Though more vocal than conservative evangelicals in faulting political and economic imperialism, liberals thus were likely to be operating on the same wavelength as the imperialists. As many premillennialists and other conservatives continued to "seek another city," both rhetorically and in their choice of missionary activities, socially oriented liberals increasingly viewed themselves not only as chaplains, but as confessors and prophets, within the very secular city of Western expansionism.

[32]*Christian Missionary* 4 (February 1898): 14; *Yale Review* 15 (February 1907): 459–60.

RELIGIOUS CONSERVATISM AND CULTURAL FAITH

Despite these contrasts in theory and general tendency, conservative Protestants often found themselves undertaking the same chaplaincy as that to which their liberal colleagues felt called. One of the more revealing phenomena of the "heyday of missions" is the interweaving of the liberal and Social Gospel formulations with premillennial strains that seemed deeply antagonistic to nearly everything people like George Gordon and James Dennis were saying. The premillennialism that reappeared prominently in American Protestant circles in the 1870s remained a minority faith, even among conservative evangelicals. But it gained well-educated and well-placed adherents within the Presbyterian and other mainline denominations; and by 1900 the Moody Bible Institute and some fifty other training schools were sending out evangelists and other workers committed to some form of premillennial belief.

With premillennialism gaining some hold within older boards, and also spawning vigorous new organizations, this influence was particularly noticeable in foreign missions; premillennial advocates who complained of inadequate progress at home could find comfort in triumphs abroad. Estimates in the 1920s of an 85 percent adherence to premillennialism in the missionary movement were serious exaggerations, or else reflected unnaturally broad criteria for adherence. But by that time one could perhaps speak of a rough equality, within the American mission enterprise, between a postmillennialism that hoped to build the Kingdom before Christ's return, and a premillennial conviction that nothing of the sort could occur before the Second Coming.[33]

The premillennial outlook became steadily more antagonistic to liberal and Social Gospel emphases. Yet with the help of conciliatory attitudes among missionary statesmen, and with just a little obfuscation (on both sides) of theological issues, premillennialists for some fifty years seemed able to march in step with liberals and moderates in the exultant campaign for speedy world evangelization.

On at least three points, to be sure, the divergence between premillennial enthusiasts and their more liberal colleagues could not be easily papered over. The first of these is the easiest to state. It was the premillennial idea itself. Specifically, they disagreed about the timetable for Christ's return (or the importance of discerning one), and about the nature of the coming kingdom.

The second related to the Great Commission: "Go ye into all the world and preach the Gospel." Was Christ's command the prime motive

[33]Weber, *Second Coming*, pp. 26–36, 81.

for missions, or was it not? Liberals, relatively unimpressed by proof-texts and literal injunctions, subordinated the Great Commission or neglected it altogether. Even a moderate like Robert E. Speer, who showed implicit, and sometimes explicit, sympathy for premillennial doctrine, could suggest with some asperity that the Great Commission is persuasive only to minds "unable to appreciate the unexpressed but vital principle" behind it. The real point, said Speer, is Christ's indispensability to the entire world. In the opening paragraphs of a major defense of missions he insisted that Christian obligation would be the same if Christ had never pronounced a Great Commission. But most of Speer's premillennial colleagues were making an exactly opposite case. For them, Christ's "marching orders" were not merely primary; they were sufficient. A. T. Pierson, editor of the *Missionary Review of the World,* had begun *his* most significant work on missions with the statement that Christ's command "makes all other motives comparatively unnecessary."[34]

The third point of disagreement concerned the proper attitude toward other religions. If the liberal emphasis on compassionate motives seemed dangerous—Pierson advised that "God is not addressing the sympathy and compassion of his people chiefly, but their consciences"—this other sort of liberal sympathy was seen as far more so. The liberals' conviction "that a universal and saving element runs through all religious systems, that there is a 'Light of Asia' as well as a 'Light of the world,' " according to the colorfully indignant Pierson had produced an "apathy of misconception," a "paralysis of action," and "a death-like torpor and stupor." Notions that Christianity is "not the only faith that contains . . . redeeming influences," or that there might be a second chance for heathen who die without hearing the Word—such concessions, said Pierson, are "the Devil's master-piece of strategy to keep the hosts of God within the walls of luxurious indolence, when they should be moving outward against the citadels of superstition and idolatry."[35]

Such divergences between liberals and premillennialists are wide and significant. Yet one need not probe very far into the presuppositions on each side to find at least one of the bases for collaboration: a common inability to take seriously any norms or testimonies not originating in Western Christendom, an unwillingness to grant exotic cultures the kind of hearing automatically expected for Christian and Western values. In such matters James Dennis and Arthur T. Pierson were twins, not opposites.

[34]Speer, *Principles and Practice,* pp. 9–11; Pierson, *Crisis,* p. 11.
[35]Pierson, *Crisis,* pp. 292–94.

"Christ's command makes other motives unnecessary." Arthur T. Pierson in 1878. From Delavan L. Pierson, *Arthur T. Pierson* (New York: Fleming H. Revell, 1912), facing p. 130. By permission.

This preexisting harmony in cultural assumptions helped to blur differences between evangelistic and social-service emphases that clearly were taken seriously by the Westerners themselves. Henry Frost, director for North America of the China Inland Mission, seconded Pierson as he complained that under liberal (or simply mindless) auspices, scriptural motivation in missions had been giving way "to the selfish or to the simply humanitarian." The organization Frost helped lead was notable for promoting what might now be called "life-style" adaptations to Chinese ways of life, and for trying to present Christianity shorn of Western embodiments. But Frost's aphorism for all this is revealing: "While it is always true that Christianity civilizes, it is never true that civilization Christianizes." His use of that loaded term, "civilizes," signaled that differences with the liberals concerned priorities and instrumentalities; they were not, generally speaking, disputes about Westernization as one aim and assured result of the mission enterprise. Their respective criticisms of American or Western society, meanwhile, diverged more in form than in intensity: the doubts of social activists about Western capitalism were matched by conservative concern about personal morality and the liquor traffic.[36]

Agreement with the liberals about the rightful triumph of Western civilization is apparent, however curiously, in the very midst of premillennialism's ultimate despair about worldly improvement. Among the conservative leaders, none was more explicitly premillennial than A. B. Simpson, founder of the Christian and Missionary Alliance. Yet Simpson, chiming in with Henry Frost's dictum that "Christianity civilizes," showed no hesitancy about claiming national and social elevation, education, material progress, and the improved status of women among the "fruits of the Gospel." His representations of the people and religions of "missionary lands," meanwhile, were at least as demeaning as Dennis's, and were more blatant (even when unconscious) in their application of Western standards.

"How shall we describe a Japanese?" Simpson asked in an inaptly titled volume of 1893, *Larger Outlooks on Missionary Lands.* "A little dark, thick-set man, always reminding you of a boy." The women, similarly, seemed like girls of thirteen. A Japanese who had become Westernized looked "a little strange and out of place in his foreign dress—something like a Frenchman or a Pole, but much darker and shorter." Laborers and ricksha men were massive, with limbs like great pillars; yet despite this disability they could "run like horses." Simpson

[36]Frost, "Missionary Motives," pp. 85–86.

found all Japanese faces very much alike, so that "one would think it must be very difficult to pick out one's friends in Japan."[37]

Simpson's report on his brief Japanese visit depicted a "frightfully immoral people" whose women dressed immodestly (kimonos "quite too open at the bosom") and whose "habits and customs in public baths are said to be grossly improper." This kind of half-conscious Western ethnocentrism, as a bias affecting nearly everyone—liberals and pre-millennialists, believers and skeptics—lessened the actual distinction between those who went out to civilize and those who felt they were scorning such an approach. Thus Pierson could report enthusiastically, and almost in the same breath, on the biblical inroads and conversions in Japanese schools, and on "the rapid elimination of the Asiatic features from the government."[38]

One must be careful not to push the argument too far. It might seem that few postmillennial liberals could have matched Pierson's raptures concerning the civilization that allegedly does not Christianize:

> We have seen God making a highway for His chariot through
> the iron gates of heathen hostility and Christian apathy. . . .
> While God permitted Protestant England to plant an empire
> toward the sunrise, the Pilgrims were driven to these shores to
> sow the seeds of a Christian republic beside the setting sun.
> Thus Britain was unconsciously reaching out eastward and
> westward to lay the foundations for a world's evangelization.
> Then the providence of God, by the issue of conflicts in Amer-
> ica and India, settled the question that in both hemispheres the
> cross, and not the crescent nor crucifix, was to be dominant.

Yet, as that passage shows, the enthusiasts maintained a certain distance, at least in theory, between Christ and culture. The forces of civilization and empire do not evangelize the world; they open the way for those that do. At a later stage, the missionary converts people to Christ but trusts others to carry through on the civilizing process. While Pierson was gratified that the Japanese, "impressed with the superiority of a Christian civilization," had invited an American missionary to super-intend their school system, he was even more pleased with the missionary's austere reply: "Gentlemen, I have not time to take the superintendence of your schools; I have given myself to the preaching of the gospel."[39]

---

[37]Simpson, *Challenge of Missions*, pp. 35–39; *Larger Outlooks*, pp. 541–43.
[38]Simpson, *Larger Outlooks*, pp. 551, 542. Pierson, *Crisis*, pp. 232–33.
[39]Pierson, *Crisis*, pp. 193–94, 259.

When such distinctions and efforts of separation have been acknowledged, it remains true that American premillennial rhetoric, in this as
in some past eras, foretold a state of things that sounded suspiciously
like an earthly Kingdom of God. For fully two-thirds of Pierson's *Crisis
of Missions,* a reader is likely to be asking, "What crisis? Where?" Pierson's
answer pointed to what he saw as a leveling off of effort abroad, a
dangerous apathy at home, and above all an utterly destructive influence
from liberal theology. But it was A. B. Simpson who offered the calmest
and most internally consistent rationale for this combination of seemingly contradictory attitudes.

This world and its highest civilization, Simpson explained, are indeed
glorious. That, in a way, is the whole point: the more glorious they
are, and the more real their glory, the more we are reminded that the
highest things of this world are as nothing. None of them is of ultimate
worth. Until Christ's return all is penultimate. "Man's highest philan-
thropy," Simpson wrote, "aims to develop and improve the conditions
of this old earth of ours so that some day it shall fulfill the dreams" of
a golden age. Yet if we think the world at its best will fulfill God's
promises, we are holding too mean a conception of the Deity; his
wisdom and love "have something better for our race than civilization,
reformation, social reform and scientific progress; something better
even than a spiritual millennium and the world-wide triumph of the
Gospel and the grace of God."[40]

If the work of conversion, "the world-wide triumph of the Gospel,"
was not progressing as brilliantly as the advance of civilization, this
again, in Simpson's scheme, was not a cause for despair. Christ after
his return will "compel the subjection of all mankind and bring earth's
millions without exception to bow to his scepter." But in the present
age nothing of the sort is to be expected or worked for. God is not
seeking universal conversion, even large-scale conversion; he is sum-
moning only those few who are to be the rulers of the coming age.
The people to be reached and converted are "the 'little flock,' the chosen
bride, the hidden ones who are to unite from every land and tribe and
tongue to sing the millennial chorus that is to welcome the coming
King." Their number is small, and on that understanding the idea of
"evangelization of the world in this generation" is perfectly practicable.

All must hear the Gospel. If few respond, that is as it should be. So
the fact that "numerically we are not making any headway in converting
the whole world" did not faze Simpson. "We cast our nets into the
great sea, but we do not gather all the fish that are in the sea, and when

[40]Simpson, *Challenge,* p. 43.

we have gathered all who are willing to accept the Gospel message, this commission is ended."[41]

As Simpson details the actual message to be conveyed, its activist elements become apparent, and one sees more clearly how such evangelicals could find common ground with liberals. Though he depicted African chiefs hearing with awe "that the Great Chief is coming soon to call them to account," Simpson did not think missionaries should merely preach a Kingdom that comes like a thief in the night. To insist that the infidel must prepare himself is not enough, for Christ's return is itself dependent in marked degree on human action. A. E. Thompson concurred: "I would not cross the street to talk to a crowd of [fellow] premillennialists about the coming of the Lord, unless they were looking for and hastening his coming by sending forth the gospel." "Our missionary work," Simpson wrote succinctly, "is to bring Christ Himself back again."[42]

Since many premillennialists, despite Simpson's disclaimers, engaged in the numbers game, the totting-up of conversions and church memberships, their activism, like that of other mission leaders, often seemed to go well beyond helping God pluck a few brands from the burning. Pierson, in several pages of bracing mathematical projections, wrote of the vast sum that could be made available for missions if each Protestant in the world (Catholics were seen as objects of evangelization) contributed a penny a day. He calculated the number of "contacts" every professing Protestant must make to reach "every living soul" within one generation, and also the number of contacts that would be necessary—it came to a hundred per evangelist—in the event that only one-tenth of the world's Protestants could be enlisted in the effort. As if to dispel any real doubt about the presence of a civilizing vision in this premillennial use of the watchword, he averred that "we are to set up Christian churches, schools, institutions, homes, in the midst of pagan communities, as part of this witness to the power of the gospel."[43]

MAINTAINING CONSENSUS: THE WATCHWORD AND ITS SPOKESMEN

The career of the watchword epitomizes, in itself, a liberal-premillennial collaboration in which cultural enthusiasms and promotional needs outweighed theological differences. The alliance depended in part upon a willingness on both sides to accept—in fact to utilize—the ambiguities in the watchword's key term: "evangelization."

[41]Ibid., pp. 50–54.
[42]Ibid., p. 55. A. E. Thompson is quoted in Weber, *Second Coming*, p. 81.
[43]Pierson, *Crisis*, pp. 324–26.

The usually circumspect Robert E. Speer lent his voice to the confusion when he assured a Student Volunteer Assembly in 1898 that "we do not predict that the world is to be evangelized in this generation," but then went on to report that the number of Chinese Christians had increased 200,000 percent within the lifetime of a certain missionary bishop. In the presence of such results, he told the recruits, one did "begin to feel that perhaps the evangelization of the world in this generation may not, after all, be such a dream."[44]

Other spokesmen were less cautious. When defending the watchword against charges of naiveté or hyperactivism they presented it as a modest hope for worldwide "contact" with potential Christians; but when results were being proclaimed or projected, almost no one settled for the statistics of contact. Quite evidently, among promoters, recruiters, and their home audiences, few were thinking of missions as a dogged proclamatory effort that would be relatively indifferent to conversionary results.

The watchword, like many another campaign slogan, produced cohesion and results partly because of such ambiguities. The strict denotations of "evangelization" and "this generation" were modest, even prosaic. If the first term meant merely reaching everyone with the proclaimed Word, the second, as Mott and others explained tirelessly, simply acknowledged that each generation must fulfill an obligation to the living; and both, as Speer said, expressed hopes, not predictions. Yet the headier connotations were also quite palpable, and most Anglo-American missionary leaders concluded that the electrifying effects of the watchword's use could not be forgone simply because people persisted in making those connotations central. "In the case of a large and increasing number of Christians," Mott asserted in 1902, the watchword had "enlarged vision, strengthened purpose, augmented faith, inspired hopefulness, intensified zeal, driven to God in prayer, and developed the spirit of heroism and self-sacrifice." Despite heavy criticism from many quarters, the leaders found, in the words of Mott's biographer, that any change was precluded by "the difficulties of coining a substitute and gaining its acceptance"—precluded simply by "the appeal of the old motto."[45]

John R. Mott, the leading statesman of the movement in these years, made his mark—as did Speer, Robert Wilder, and Pierson—by an ability not only to tolerate disparate ideals but also to weld or reconcile them.

[44]Speer, "The Watchword," p. 210. See also the speech immediately following: C. C. Hall's "The Beatific Vision of an Evangelized World."

[45]Hopkins, *Mott*, pp. 232–33.

His elaborations of mission ideology and strategy, for example in the book that took the watchword for its title, can therefore be considered broadly representative. By muting or setting aside the more divisive questions of millennial interpretation, Mott could maintain a common front with moderate premillennialists like Pierson, even though he could scarcely harmonize with more determined ones like A. B. Simpson. The watchword, Mott wrote, "does not necessitate a belief in the premillennial view" or "stand in the service of any other particular theory of eschatology." Similarly, by assigning first importance to preaching while beating the drums for all the other missionary pursuits, he could represent nearly everyone except those who, like the Presbyterian John Nevius, still demanded essentially Andersonian limits on missionary activities.[46]

Mott asserted that "the proclamation of the Gospel by the living voice" would always dominate missionary methods. Yet his careful avowals of the subordinate status of other methods seemed barely distinguishable from ringing declarations of their validity and effectiveness:

> The value of medical, educational, literary, and all other forms
> of missionary activity, is measured by the extent to which they
> prepare the way for the Gospel message, promote its accep-
> tance, manifest its spirit and benefits, multiply points of contact
> with human souls and increase the number and efficiency of
> those who preach Christ.

One might say that, up to that point, Rufus Anderson could have agreed. But it was significant that when Mott assigned a precise role for educational work in the scheme of missions, he cited the authority not of Anderson but of Alexander Duff, the Scottish educationist who for Anderson had symbolized where missions had gone wrong. And Mott's own position was clear enough: "In some parts of the world more people have been led to accept Christ through educational missionary effort than through any other agency." Medical work, likewise, could be ranked as "one of the powerful, effective, and directly evangelistic agencies which the Church possesses."[47]

The function that Mott had called most important, "the proclamation of the Gospel by the living voice," often seemed diminished in Mott's writing not just by the prominence he allowed to other missionary activities but by the sheer comprehensiveness of his vision of Christian world conquest. The proclamatory stage did seem almost confined to a generation—indeed to a moment, however vital. Yet carrying the Word

[46]Mott, *Evangelization*, p. 9; Nevius, *Missionary Churches.*
[47]Mott, *Evangelization*, pp. 11–15.

to the present generation, he said, could not be regarded as an end in itself. Contact and proclamation must be followed "by the baptism of converts, by their organization into churches" and then by the building of character and the training of Christians for service. And these achievements are still only "means to the mighty and inspiring object of enthroning Christ in individual life, in family life, in social life, in national life, in international relations, in every relationship of mankind."[48]

To say that mission spokesmen, in promoting such grandiose visions, made use of slogans and rhetorical ambiguity is not to say they always oversimplified the issues. Robert E. Speer's writings, in particular, are laced with direct and sophisticated responses to those who criticized the missionary movement or objected to such features as the watchword. These responses, while not always convincing to those not already convinced, usually succeeded in meeting the cultured despisers of missions on their own ground. Speer recognized that ground, for example, by acknowledging that the entire missionary idea made sense only if one assumed the finality and universal validity of Christianity. What crusading Christians were trying to do, he wrote, was the necessary consequence of their view of Christianity as a unique supernatural life. "If Christianity is not this, but merely a moral system, finer than the moral systems of other religions, and richer . . . [then] indifference to its extension is intelligible—and also indifference to its acceptance."[49]

Speer's frequent allusion to the old civilization/evangelization dichotomy showed a readiness to confront its perennial dilemmas, and also to show respect for those who were seriously troubled by them. He conceded the entrapment of the Christian missionary effort within Western culture, arguing that this was unavoidable but also admitting that it was extremely dangerous. Rejecting common evasions to the effect that Christianity is really non-Western because it began among Galilean fishermen, he stated the resulting difficulty with about as much candor as one could ask for: "We cannot go into the non-Christian world as other than we are or with anything else than that which we have. Even when we have done our best to disentangle the universal truth from the Western form . . . we know that we have not done it." Christian ideas, however "obviously and concededly universal" they may be, are nonetheless enormously difficult to domesticate in other lands.[50]

Given that degree of realism, how could someone like Speer persist in the missionary effort at all, let alone serve as a promoter or spokesman? For many of his contemporaries the answer was that missions

---

[48]Ibid., pp. 14–16.
[49]Speer, *Principles and Practice*, p. 32.
[50]Speer, *Christianity*, pp. 67–70.

constitute an absolute obligation that must be heeded whether the problem of cultural imposition can be solved or not. But Speer himself could not adopt such a damn-the-torpedoes attitude; that was one reason for his repeated assertion that "the last command of Christ is not the deep and final ground of the Church's missionary duty."[51] And it is reasonable to suppose that the motives Speer did think should be paramount—the love of Christ, the world's need for Christianity, the "right" of people everywhere to a knowledge of Christ—would have been far less compelling had he really doubted that Christianity would be able eventually to shed its Western embodiment.

Precisely because Speer was hopeful about such a transformation, he was not forced to choose between a continuing cultural imperialism and an end to the missionary enterprise—between "damn the torpedoes" and "abandon ship." Here he was indeed Anderson's heir: for Speer, the successful Christianizing of the world depended very much upon the success of indigenization. He expressed frustration that non-Western Christians preferred to imitate the West instead of working out "fresh theological statements on the basis of . . . their own new experience of God in Christ." That sort of reluctance, he said, leaves the Westerners with the impossible task of transcending their own cultural and theological forms. Thus the missionary movement must strive more than ever "to be rid of this burden, to build up native churches which will themselves carry this burden, which will deal with their own apologetic problems, work out their own institutions, support their own activities, and evangelize their own lands."[52]

The comparison between Anderson and Speer can be carried one step further. Like his predecessor, Speer was more outspoken than most of his colleagues in insisting that missions must not be in the business of imposing alien modes and institutions. In the course of this plea he in effect rebuked the more avid Social Gospellers. "Our supreme aim," Speer wrote, "is neither to establish republics . . . nor to lead Chinese and Hindu people to wear our dress, nor to remodel their social institutions where these are already wholesome and clean." The idea currently in vogue, that missions must attempt to reorganize the whole social fabric, was a "mischievous doctrine" that the example of Christ and the Apostles does not sanction. In full accord with the Anderson-Venn conception, Speer avowed that he would rather "plant one seed of the life of Christ under the crust of heathen life, than cover that

[51]Ibid., p. 17; *Principles and Practice,* p. 9.
[52]Speer, *Christianity,* p. 73.

whole crust over with the veneer of our social habits, or the vestiture of Western civilization."[53]

The old loopholes, of course, were still available in Speer's formulas. Western cultural imposition was an abomination; but if a native folkway were found less than "wholesome and clean" one could be, well, a little more aggressive. And underlying this was the unclarity about who, exactly, is to make discriminations between wholesome and unwholesome in a given social order. Speer's answer to that—indigenization— admirable though it was, might be ineffectual unless one accepted its most radical implication: the willingness to apply a principle of self-determination across the entire field of a society's values.

The old operational difficulty was there as well: getting the bulky mission organization to go along with the programs of even its most charismatic and revered leaders. In the 1920s, Speer's own Board of Foreign Missions published a book of *Mother Goose Missionary Rhymes* for youngsters in Presbyterian Sunday schools. Most of the rhymes were innocuous ("Little Boy Blue, come blow your horn/ The children in Syria are sad and forlorn") and only faintly invidious ("The money went to China/Where there's ignorance and sin/Now Mary has another box/To put more pennies in"). But a few suggested that the secretary's warnings against cultural imposition, twenty-five years earlier, still were not thoroughly understood in his own organization:

> Ten little heathen standing in a line;
> One went to mission school, then there were but nine.
>
> . . . .
>
> Three little heathen didn't know what to do;
> One learned our language, then there were two.
>
> Two little heathen couldn't have any fun;
> One gave up idols, then there was but one.
>
> One little heathen standing all alone;
> He learned to love our flag, then there were none.[54]

No just critic will allow the missionary movement, even in its heyday of expansionism, to be stereotyped by doggerel verses. But neither is such evidence trivial. Here were educational materials, published down

[53]Speer, *Principles and Practice*, pp. 40, 37.

[54]Richards, *Missionary Rhymes*. I am indebted for this reference to the Reverend George Todd, a Presbyterian, who with a rueful smile pulled it from a shelf in his office at the World Council of Churches in Geneva.

the hall from Speer's offices, that could have been used to illustrate his point that "even when we have done our best to disentangle . . . we have not done it."

Missions as a moral equivalent for imperialism deserved, like later forms of foreign aid, to be seen as preferable to the real thing. But like such other ventures they could at some junctures become that real thing. The magnificent, if frustrated, confidence that this need not happen, that a "fine spiritual imperialism" could be constructed and kept free of contamination, did more than either numbers or charismatic leadership to define the unique enthusiasm of the era.

CHAPTER 5

Activism under Fire

The mission command bids us "go" into all the world, not "fly."

Gustav Warneck, 1910

The World Missionary Conference at Edinburgh in 1910 seemed a landmark event, at the time, to participants and to most observers. But later generations, looking back after a period of relative decline in missions, used a different metaphor: "watershed."

The actual high-point, statistically, for mainline American missions came later, just before the Great Depression. But Edinburgh, like many events and expressions of its era throughout the Western world, would come to seem in retrospect a singular moment of success and untroubled enthusiasm. Within a very few years the coming of the Great War shattered hopes and complacencies on which the missionary movement had been founded, bringing to the surface tensions that had been building for decades, more or less unacknowledged, within the Euro-American Protestant community. After the war, the predominantly activist missionary style that had triumphed under British and American leadership experienced two kinds of assault: one focused in Continental, especially German, critiques of religious activism (by then frequently called simply "Americanism"); a second, picking up some of the same themes, associated with the fundamentalist movement in North America.

These two assault forces—call them pietist and fundamentalist—were cobelligerents, almost never allies. To young Continental churchmen of the twenties protesting against liberal and Social Gospel emphases, American fundamentalism seemed merely a different form of the religious individualism and superficiality they deplored in the American social enthusiasms. Fundamentalism was, to them, American activism in another guise—a part of the problem, not of the solution. Yet these pietists and fundamentalists, along with some others, could agree broadly that foreign missions had taken a wrong direction. They also agreed that the mistake had been to allow education and social service to get the upper hand over true evangelization.

"Activism": The View from Europe

Missionary activism, as an emphasis on civilizing and social service commonly thought to be extreme among the Americans, had always resided to some extent in the eyes and minds of its beholders. So it is fair to raise questions both about the distinctiveness of this style and about its pervasiveness in American missions.

In their practice, as gauged for example by their deployment of different types of mission personnel, Americans and Europeans appear to have differed very little. It is true that in China and India, as of 1910, the Continental European delegations exceeded those of the North Americans in the proportion of ordained persons, and employed slightly smaller proportions of physicians and other laymen. And in other salient items, such as the number of educational institutions, European missions in those vast countries showed marginally less preoccupation with "civilizing" functions. Yet in some fields, such as West Africa, the proportions were reversed, with Europeans more committed to medical and educational work than Americans were.[1]

When one turns from the practical to the ideological, to the modes of missionary apologetic and promotion, the case for a distinctive American style is suggested by the relative unpopularity on the Continent of the Anglo-American "watchword." But at that point the question of pervasiveness arises. One can reasonably question the extent to which the confident activistic rhetoric of mainline promoters represented American Protestantism as a whole, or even American missions.

If these tireless advocates often seemed to have arrogated to themselves a right to speak for the entire American enterprise, the reasons for that appearance are not difficult to discern. In spite of an evident concern that the smaller agencies and sectarian groups be represented in its counsels, the movement was bound to reflect the mainline establishment. Wealth, the weight of numbers, traditions of leadership, the need for consensus, and the concentration of mainline forces in relatively few large units all worked against the sort of genuine inclusiveness and pluralism that might have produced a more variegated impression of American religion and "American" traits.

Among the 120 North American boards and agencies in 1910, 22 were responsible for 65 percent of the missionaries and controlled nearly 80 percent of the total expenditures. These boards, moreover, repre-

---

[1]A contrast of the same sort between Continental and British missions might support the "Anglo-American activist" allegation somewhat better. In India, China, and West Africa, British delegations show a smaller proportion of ordained persons than either the Continentals or the North Americans. ("American" statistics customarily included Canadians.) Dennis et al., *World Atlas;* Richter, "Statistics," pp. 8–9.

sented a massing of personnel and resources that made any one of them more visible and powerful than, say, a dozen sectarian agencies that might collectively dispatch the same number of missionaries to the field. In 1910 the Church of the Nazarenes had twenty-five missionaries; other holiness and pentecostal churches together thirty-seven; the Universalists thirteen; the Mennonites twenty-three. But the four largest boards—the ABCFM and the Northern branches of the Presbyterians, Methodists, and Baptists—each sponsored more than five hundred missionaries. The other major bodies of Presbyterians, Methodists, Baptists, Episcopalians, and Disciples of Christ each supported from 100 to 225 missionaries, as did the Dutch and German Reformed churches taken together, and the ten major Lutheran bodies taken together.[2]

Even more to the point, it was these mainline boards and denominations that made themselves heard in national and international forums; that dominated standard historical accounts of the movement; and that generated theories or theologies of missions. At the Edinburgh Conference, sometimes imagined (then and since) to have represented all Protestants of the Western world, only thirty-five American mission agencies sent delegations. In fact, the bulk of the delegates, and nearly all the American speakers, came from the nine largest organizations. Women, preponderant in virtually all church-membership and missionary statistics, were distinctly underrepresented among the delegates (115 out of 411) and virtually unrecognized on the program.[3]

In the development and publicizing of the ideologies of missions, a mainline (and male) concentration was especially evident. The era saw a literary explosion somewhat commensurate with the organizational one: while only six American books had been written on the theory of missions during the first eighty years of the movement, more than forty appeared between 1890 and 1918. Nearly all were the work of males associated with mainline churches and agencies.[4]

This disproportion in numbers and voices operated, however, to mask other realities that later observers need to keep in mind. The denominations most heavily represented and spoken-for at Edinburgh represented only about 65 percent of American Protestant church membership.[5] Though most holiness, pentecostal, and what would later be called fundamentalist bodies were not yet ready to send out foreign

[2]These and subsequent 1910 statistics, unless otherwise designated, are derived from Dennis et al., *World Atlas*, pp. 86–102.

[3]World Missionary Conference, *History and Records*, pp. 35–107.

[4]Forman, "Mission Theory," pp. 80–81.

[5]*Statistical Abstract of the United States, 1910* (Washington, D.C.: Government Printing Office, 1911), p. 110.

missionaries in large numbers, they did constitute a significant segment of American Christianity. Leaders like Speer or John R. Mott, though unusually (for their time) aware of these sectarian bodies, were not always able, nor necessarily obligated, to speak for them.

One should recognize, in addition, that a few nonmainline organizations were already involved heavily in foreign missions. The Christian and Missionary Alliance in 1910 ranked fifth in the size of its missionary contingent (233). The Seventh-Day Adventists, who were sponsoring 188 foreign missionaries, ranked eighth. The black churches, taken together, with 108 missionaries were not far behind such white churches as the Disciples of Christ. And the Seventh-Day Adventists, though not the others, stood within the top ten denominations in the amount expended on foreign missions.

The dominance of major boards, moreover, was more impressive in some mission areas than in others. Mott and Speer could probably speak for the majority of missionaries in the three largest mission fields—China, India, and Japan—because the mainline bodies themselves held substantial majorities in those areas: 74 percent in China, 70 percent in India and Japan. They could certainly represent the work in countries like Korea, where all but 8 of the 240 missionaries were from the major boards; or Brazil, where the sects were not yet active (14 missionaries out of 204). But they may or may not have spoken for sub-Sahara Africa, the fourth largest mission field, in some parts of which the white middle-class churches were by no means the chief sending agencies. Mainline boards contributed almost 80 percent of the missionaries in Southwest Africa (from the Cameroons southward), but only 45 percent in South Africa and 30 percent in West Africa.

Since the leaders of even the more substantial nonmainline groups were little given to theorizing, especially with respect to issues of cultural interaction, it may be some time before we can fairly estimate how much these groups varied from mainline patterns. What we do know suggests a rich mixture, a spectrum of working assumptions and missionary practice not unlike the spectrum presented by the mainstream movement. The Christian and Missionary Alliance was noted for its insistence on the primacy of evangelization and for attempting, like the predominantly British China Inland Mission, to avoid all forms of secular cultural imposition. And the various Lutheran contingents, however related to the mission establishment, were likely to give a less activist impression than their compatriots in other denominations. Adventists, on the other hand, by virtue of strong medical and educational emphases, were more in tune with concurrent leanings in the mainline movement; and spokesmen for missions of the black churches could sometimes outdo whites in their avidity for taking Shakespeare as well as the Bible to the Africans.[6] In other words, it is possible but by no means certain that more inclusive treatments of mission operations will alter the usual conclusions about a pervasive activistic rhetoric and style.

What cannot be doubted is that Europeans perceived American religion and culture as aggressively activistic, and that such perceptions affected the course of international Christian movements in the twentieth century.[7] It seems evident, also, that American-European tensions, though they have been passed over very lightly in most histories of the missionary and ecumenical movements, had a bearing on the misunderstandings that led to the First World War, and then to the tragically incomplete reconciliation after November 1918.

The identification of American religion as "activistic" was by no means a twentieth-century phenomenon. But the belief that it made a difference—that the American religious style could exert a good or a harmful influence on anyone else—was largely new. Before about 1900, American religion and religious thought had been taken even less seriously, among European churchmen and literati, than had American culture generally. Those Europeans who found American religion even mildly interesting tended to agree about the contrasts with European forms, whether they admired the American characteristics or deplored them.

In 1854 Philip Schaff, a Swiss theologian and historian who had emigrated to the United States, analyzed for a German audience the pros and cons of the activistic style that had been remarked upon since at least the time of J. Hector St. John Crèvecoeur, the "American Farmer" who had published his largely favorable observations in the revolutionary period. The religious life of the Americans, Schaff explained, "is uncommonly practical, energetic, and enterprising." In the various synods and conventions of the churches he noted an unusual amount of oratorical power, and of talent for organization and government. The number of churches, seminaries, and other institutions was by European standards "amazing." Schaff suggested bluntly that Germany and the entire continent of Europe, suffering from a relatively moribund

[6]See Crummell, *Future of Africa*; Blyden, *Liberia's Offering*.

[7]In writing of "European" reactions I am succumbing to the need for a shorthand term. Clearly there were variants, not only among British and Continental observers, but between the most common German reactions and those of Scandinavians, between the Established and the sectarian, the Lutheran and the Calvinistic, and so on. Such variants are spelled out below; in Hutchison, "Innocence Abroad"; and in the early pages of Visser 't Hooft, *Social Gospel* (wherein one finds diverse European churchmen each claiming to be less-activist-than-thou).

Anglo-Saxons and the world's future: a Student Volunteer convention, Des Moines, 1920. From the *Intercollegian* 37 (February 1920): 5, 12. Courtesy of the YMCA of the United States of America.

church life, could learn from America if only they would cease regarding it as barbaric and beneath notice.

Schaff acknowledged, however, that these activistic merits entailed "corresponding faults and infirmities." In what is probably the finest summary, from any period, of the more negative "European" view, he wrote that American Christianity

> is more Petrine than Johannean; more like busy Martha than like the pensive Mary, sitting at the feet of Jesus. It expands more in breadth than in depth. It is often carried on like a sec- ular business, and in a mechanical or utilitarian spirit. It lacks the beautiful enamel of deep fervor and heartiness, the true mysticism, an appreciation of history and the church; it wants the substratum of a profound and spiritual theology; and under the mask of orthodoxy it not infrequently conceals, without in- tending or knowing it, the tendency to abstract intellectualism and superficial rationalism. This is especially evident in the doc- trine of the church and of the Sacraments, and in the meager- ness of the worship . . . [wherein] nothing is left but preaching, free prayer, and singing.[8]

Deeply ingrained perceptions of this kind underlay Continental Eu- ropean responses to the powerful Anglo-American initiatives in foreign missions at the end of the nineteenth century. As Americans collaborated

[8]Schaff, *America*, pp. 94–95.

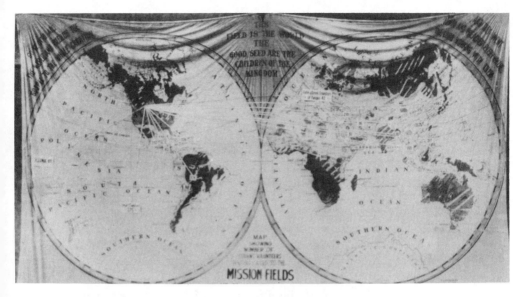

Detail of the map-screen behind the podium, showing the number of student volunteers fanning out (seemingly from Des Moines) to the various mission areas.

with British evangelicals in such enterprises as the Student Volunteer Movement and the China Inland Mission, and especially as the American influence became predominant, the old admiration was reawakened and old objections flourished. Both the astonishment at the Americans' zeal and efficiency, and the doubts about their haste and religious superficiality, grew exponentially. Laced through one European comment after another was the troubled sense that the missionary movement was being taken out of the hands of those who had understood it longest and most deeply, and was becoming oblivious to its true origins in a spiritual and patient Continental pietism.

As I have hinted, one should not fall into the error of supposing that European responses to this changing situation were all, or even mainly, negative. In Scandinavia (one area where the "Americanizing" of religion had been an issue for some decades) the response to John R. Mott, and to the Student Volunteer Movement and its watchword, was overwhelmingly favorable. In Germany, even though Mott and his colleagues encountered extensive resistance in their attempts to foster a student movement on Anglo-American lines, some of the most influential promoters of foreign missions expressed unqualified praise and support.[9]

[9]The point about favorable Scandinavian attitudes was underlined for me in repeated conversations with Professors Bengt Sundkler and Carl Hallencreutz (Uppsala), and the late Professor Torben Christensen (Copenhagen). SVM efforts in Europe are discussed in Clifton Phillips, "Changing Attitudes," pp. 133–35.

Dr. Julius Richter, a scholar and editor who later became Professor of Missions at Berlin, dedicated his *History of Protestant Missions in the Near East* (1910) to the boards of "the great Congregational and Presbyterian Churches of America." English and American views on missionary questions, he acknowledged, differed greatly from the German; so much so that Richter in his English edition recast entire sections— much as an oculist "adapts the spectacles exactly to the eye"—so that English-speaking people would know what he was talking about! But Richter clearly and pointedly praised the very characteristics that most troubled his German and European coworkers. American quantity-mindedness, he wrote, might well solve the central question of finding sufficient laborers for the great harvest. The Laymen's Missionary Movement (founded in the United States in 1906) seemed to promise that "that other perplexing problem, the money question, would be dealt with satisfactorily." And in praising the go-getting American leaders, so often regarded in Europe with condescension or behind-the-hand skepticism, Richter sounded like a convert out to convert others: "In constant intercourse with the leaders . . . I saw of what high types these men really are."[10]

For others who might be less rapturous about American influence, the differences between Germanic and Anglo-American approaches to missions were just what Richter's oculist analogy suggested: differing gifts or strengths, matters not for praise or blame so much as for mutual comprehension and for harnessing. Nils Ehrenström, a Swedish churchman and historian who became a professor at Boston University, later referred to the American-European dichotomy in terms quite congruent with those Schaff had used in 1854. Ehrenström wrote of a "dialectical though sometimes exhausting tension" that had been especially evident in the first quarter of the twentieth century. Over against the American concern with immediate practical consequences, and with the application of factual data to immediate reforms, he set a European mind

> deeply interested in principles, and looking to research for the elucidation of the ways in which Christian principles can be applied to complex modern problems; the American sitting somewhat loose to the existing Churches, the European deeply aware from the start of the problem of the Churches with their varying confessions and widely differing approach to social problems; the American more empirical, the European more

[10]Richter, *Near East,* pp. 5–6.

theoretical, or as the Europeans perhaps would have said, more thorough, in its approach.[11]

European vs. American. Thoroughness vs. urgency (or frenzy). Richter in 1910 had sought directly to counter that prevailing sense of dichotomy by characterizing American nineteenth-century efforts in the Near East as "comprehensive . . . thorough . . . well-founded" and often going forward "quietly, with little recognition from outside."[12] But as much as two generations before that, these alleged virtues had been consistently in question as delegates to the Continental missions conferences, which met about every fourth year after 1866, had considered their relationships to the British and the upstart Americans.

Delegates in 1889, for example, heard the complaints of colleagues who had attended the large London conference of the year before, and who had felt themselves shunned by English-speaking activists. The latter, it was said, were preoccupied with numbers and publicity and quick results; they had no conception of the thoroughness and irenicism of the Continental approach to missions. At the 1897 meeting in Bremen, Gustav Warneck of Halle, the most venerable and eminent mission scholar of the era, delivered a lengthy and severe attack on the watchword; and the delegates, in what Richie Hogg calls an "atmosphere . . . of resigned futility," discussed whether or not there would be any point in sending Continental representatives to the great Ecumenical Missionary Conference being planned for New York in 1900. Neither Warneck nor anyone else, apparently, yearned to attend the New York meeting. But Dr. August Schreiber of the Norddeutsche Missionsgesellschaft remarked plaintively that one might at least make a few new friends by going to New York, and Warneck conceded a duty to send some "sober German words" to counteract those of the Anglo-American enthusiasts.[13]

In the end, Dr. Schreiber agreed to attend the New York meeting, while Warneck sent his sober words to be read at the conference. Warneck's paper complained not only about the rashness of the watchword, but about a propensity, "chiefly noticeable in many English and American mission fields," to export Western language and culture along with Christianity. Ringing the changes on some missionary watchwords that considerably predated Royal Wilder or the Student Volunteers, Warneck pointed out that Christ "bids us 'go' into all the world, not 'fly' "; that Jesus likened the Kingdom of Heaven to a farmer's field, not to a

[11]Ehrenström, "Movements for International Friendship and Life and Work, 1925–1948," in Rouse and Neill, *Ecumenical Movement,* pp. 554–55.

[12]Richter, *Near East,* p. 5.

[13]Hogg, *Ecumenical Foundations,* pp. 65–66.

He sent some "sober German words." Gustav Warneck of Halle. From M. Kähler and J. Warneck, *Gustav Warneck, 1834–1910: Blätter der Erinnerung* (Berlin: Martin Warneck, 1911), facing p. 80.

hothouse; and that our Lord did not command anything sounding like "Go ye and teach English to all nations."

Some of Warneck's reprimands were, apparently, too much for the conference managers, and were simply edited out of the version that was read. The excised passages complained, for example, about "pious rhetoric endeavoring to startle by exaggeration," "a self-righteous adherence to preconceived theories," and catchwords or "romantic will o' the wisps ... more apt to confuse than to enlighten." Enough severe criticism remained, however, after this ill-advised bowdlerizing,[14] to confirm that Warneck, despite pointed American attempts to woo and claim him, and despite his own attempts to be cordial, remained deeply troubled by the "modern Anglo-American view of missions." Mott and Wilder, after a two-hour visit with the great man in April 1899, rejoiced that they had formed a solid friendship and had also persuaded Warneck to modify his opposition. Perhaps they had, but Warneck subsequently recorded his strong and comprehensive dissent not only at the Bremen and New York meetings but also in the American edition of his *History of Protestant Missions,* which deplored even more systematically the "whimsical" notions and exaggerated claims of many American organizations.[15]

Someone was not listening. On the American side leaders like Mott, aloft with their own vision, and too busy with organizational matters to study Continental languages or cultural and religious styles, appeared to regard Warneck as a somewhat isolated problem in public relations, not as the voice of a broad constituency or serious ideological alternative. At one level such men as Mott and Wilder were listening intently to Warneck and other critics; at another, like most contemporaries in or outside the churches, they were inattentive to stirrings of intercultural and interimperial tension that, in hindsight, can scarcely be missed.

At the World Missionary Conference of 1910 (the year of Warneck's death) Anglo-Saxon dominance was even more obvious than in previous forums. Of the 1,200 delegates, over 1,000 were British or North American. Only 170 came from the Continent, and a mere 17 represented the "younger churches" of the non-Western world. If this last figure induces sober reflection about what this generation meant by a term like "world conference," the European numbers tend to confirm the charge that those with most influence thought in quantitative or even materialistic terms. The size of delegations had been determined by "financial giving," by the size of missionary-society budgets. Even numerical criteria of a different kind would have yielded larger Continental delegations. And one based on less tangible assets, such as

[14]Cf. the version actually read (*Ecumenical Missionary Conference,* 1: 289–91) with the longer form published in *Missionary Review of the World* 13 (June 1900): 413–17. Even the latter had been "condensed" from what Warneck had written. Since the editors also hinted that Warneck was a back number, and reported that he had "expected to attend [the Conference], but was prevented by illness," it seems evident that either Warneck or the Americans—and probably both—were pained acutely by this influential dissent from the predominating ideology and optimism.

[15]Hopkins, *Mott,* pp. 232, 252; *Missionary Review* 13: 253–61; Warneck, *History,* pp. 106–16.

historic contributions to missions and mission theory, could have considerably affected the complexion and feel of the conference, especially if Germans and others had been more amply recognized on the speakers list and the various committees.[16]

Continental leaders earlier, responding to the organizers' expressed desire to give them greater recognition, had proposed that the 1910 conference be held in Germany (the two previous "world" meetings had taken place in London and New York). The invitation had been declined, as Hogg reports, "after due consideration and weighing the difficulties of the German language."[17] But if the Anglo-American leadership are to be charged (as I think they must be) with having missed clear and importunate signals, one should note that Europeans to a certain extent missed them as well. The bitterest postwar critic of the Anglo-American influence, Heinrich Frick of the University of Giessen, held that the true and most ominous meaning of the Edinburgh conference had not become clear until another conference nine years later— the political one held at Versailles.

On the surface, as Frick acknowledged in his 1922 attack on "Americanism" in missions, the two conferences had seemed to be opposites: the spirit of vindictive nationalism at Versailles had contrasted sharply with the ecumenical harmony of Edinburgh. But paragraph 438 of the Versailles document, which in effect mandated Allied confiscation of German mission property, gave the lie to such perceptions. The spirit of Edinburgh, Frick now thought, had been one with that of Versailles. "In their innermost meaning, these apparently antagonistic phenomena belong together, because in retrospect one sees they are products of the same spirit: namely, of the Americanism in modern evangelical missions."[18] Warneck in his day had been especially concerned about the haste and superficiality implied in the latter part of the watchword— "in this generation." His postwar successors were more offended by the other part, which they now saw as having meant, all along, the evangelization of the world by and for Anglo-American culture.

Frick, who spent most of his later career at Marburg, within a few years had moderated his negative ideas about American religion and culture, and about the Social Gospel.[19] But at age thirty, and in the

[16]World Missionary Conference, *History and Records;* Rouse and Neill, *Ecumenical Movement,* p. 357; Hogg, *Ecumenical Foundations,* pp. 135, 116.

[17]Hogg, *Ecumenical Foundations,* p. 103.

[18]Frick, *Mission,* p. 392.

[19]The changes, apparently prompted by an American tour as well as by the new alignments forming on social and ecumenical issues, are visible in his "Amerikanische Reiseeindrücke" published in *Christliche Welt* in 1925 and 1926.

Edinburgh had been the prelude to Versailles. Heinrich Frick, critic of *Amerikanismus*. From Ingeborg Schnack, ed., *Marburger Gelehrte in der Ersten Hälfte des 20. Jahrhunderts* (Marburg: Historische Komission für Hessen), facing p. 80. Courtesy of Historische Kommission für Hessen.

immediate backlash of war and national humiliation, he gave graphic expression to attitudes that, justified or not, were emblematic of much that had gone wrong both in missions and in international affairs. In Frick's view the Americans, with an ever-decreasing need for help from their British friends, had effected a grave distortion in the basic idea of missions—first by persuasion and economic power, eventually by force of arms. The preaching of Christ had been displaced by the promotion of an entire pattern of civilization, and Christian evangelism had become cultural propaganda. Nothing was so subtly revealing, from Frick's point of view, as the fact that Americans were spreading themselves through Europe to "convert" people who were already Christian, or who at least were the proper responsibility of their own Christian compatriots. Not so subtle was the British mission pamphlet, before the war, whose cover illustration had set side by side the Cross, the British flag, and the American flag; and whose title had proclaimed "The Spiritual Expansion of the Empire."[20]

That German and some other Continental missions, despite Lutheran and pietist traditions, had allied themselves with national aggrandize-ment[21] did not escape Frick, even at this heated time. Where that had happened, however, it struck him as a case of seduction. The seducer was "religious Americanism."

FUNDAMENTALIST OBJECTIONS

Within American Protestantism, the only large-scale critiques of the mission establishment that bore a resemblance to the Warneck-Frick contentions were those of fundamentalists and their sympathizers. Frick himself had always been more exercised about revivalistic activism than about the Social Gospel variety, and he showed less and less affinity for American fundamentalists as his social commitment (and also his liberal approaches to ecumenicity and world religions) increased in the 1920s. But his Barthian contemporaries, for whom the dreaded American ac-tivism signified theological liberalism and the reduction of Christianity to a purely social evangel, found themselves in league with the fun-damentalists whether they liked it or not (in general they liked it not at all). For both sets of critics, now very much in the position of reformers, the foe to be defeated was a missionary orthodoxy led and

---

[20]Frick, *Mission*, pp. 352–53, 374–76, and 352–416 passim. I have considered this Germanic reaction and its aftermath more fully in "Innocence Abroad," and in "American Missionary Ideologies."

[21]For analyses of the complex relations between German colonial and Germanic mis-sionary developments, see the papers by Glüer, Waldenfels, Besier, Rennstich, Eggert, Dah, and especially Gensichen, in Christensen and Hutchison, *Missionary Ideologies*.

symbolized by the YMCA secretaries; a mission impulse drained, allegedly, of true biblical belief and of all concern for the work of personal conversion.

The credit or blame for firing the first shot in the postwar fundamentalist controversy can be variously assigned. On the conservative side the somewhat reluctant claimant to that distinction was a British Old Testament scholar named W. H. Griffith Thomas, who had taught since 1910 in Toronto, and whose report on China missions initiated the long and bitter struggle within the Presbyterian church that in many ways was central to the larger Protestant conflict.

Thomas's paper, first presented at a meeting of the very conservative Philadelphia presbytery and expanded, in 1921, into a forty-page article for the *Princeton Theological Review,* dwelt on the alarmingly high incidence of modernism in China, and on the vigorous response that conservatives in the field were making to it. Although his own earlier lectures, delivered to China missionaries at a gathering in Kuling, had been held responsible for the formation of the conservative Bible Union of China, Thomas insisted that the antimodernist movement had been under way in China well before that. The specific complaint voiced by this movement was that, throughout China missions and the Chinese church, Bible-believing Christianity was being subordinated to social service.

In support of this charge Thomas cited a condition that liberals themselves acknowledged but on the whole considered a matter for congratulation: in the great thronging centers of Chinese society, evangelism was being left to native Christians. In the Canton area, he reported, all of the two hundred foreign missionaries were engaged either in "institutional" work in the city or in evangelism outside it. Urban evangelistic work was being left to Chinese pastors, supposedly highly trained men who were, unfortunately, "shaky in their theological convictions, and who [held] loose views about the authority and inspiration of the Bible."[22]

The problem, Thomas thought, lay with the denominational mission boards and, of course, the Young Men's and Young Women's Christian Associations. Not only were these agencies failing to demand doctrinal soundness in their workers; they were giving short shrift to the evangelistic part of their enterprise. Mission boards were not, for example, setting as high standards for evangelists as for doctors and teachers. At the same time, Chinese students in Christian schools were being given more meager religious instruction than they would receive even at some

[22]Thomas (here quoting the Reverend Harry Anderson), "Modernism in China," pp. 640–41.

secular schools in the United States. And finally, Chinese who went to the West for higher education—including those who would later be hired as evangelists in cities like Canton—were coming back infected with critical views of the Bible.[23]

Thomas managed to find some consolation in the very inadequacy of these overeducated Chinese pastors. Their failures, he said, served at least to demonstrate once again that "German theology is no use in a revival." But their unsoundness was part and product of an intolerable pattern according to which supposedly Christian institutions in China were sponsoring a combination of non-Christian learning and nonbiblical Christianity. Thomas quoted J. Leighton Stuart, president of the New University at Peking, as conceding that Christianity, while unique and to be preferred over all others, "is not the only religion." Such assessments, Thomas complained, were becoming common fare.[24]

This critic's remedies included at least one that was reminiscent of Andersonian programs in the nineteenth century: curtail the emphasis on education, medicine, and social service. In all these areas, he said, we are in any case discredited by the imperfections in Western societies. Concentrate instead on the preaching of Christ, an activity that can remain unsullied by cultural imperfections. At the least, return to an insistence that all secular pursuits subserve the purposes of evangelism. Finally and especially, send out only Bible-believing Christians for either evangelistic or other mission work. Thomas quoted with approval the culminating proposal of a Bible Union manifesto of 1920: the boards should accept for missionary service only those who would uphold an inerrant Bible and the other articles of the fundamentalist credo.[25]

Most of Thomas's extensive critique was focused rather narrowly on this last issue; that is, on the unsoundness of the candidates the Presbyterian and other mission boards were sending into the field. It was also culpably selective in the choice of cautionary examples, and about as sensational as the production of an Old Testament scholar could well be. Such weaknesses were significant in enabling mission executives like Speer, now as throughout the 1920s, to ward off the fundamentalist challenge. But the tocsin was also being sounded by conservative leaders who took a broader approach and who could command more of a hearing among moderate evangelicals.

The most notable of these was Augustus Strong, the retired president of the Northern Baptist Rochester Seminary. For some years Strong had been a mediating figure between liberals and their critics, welcom-

[23]Ibid., pp. 642, 644.
[24]Ibid., pp. 669, 653.
[25]Ibid., pp. 641–42, 635.

ing much of the higher criticism, hobnobbing with the aggressively liberal Rockefellers, hiring both conservatives and others like Rauschenbusch whom many considered radical.[26] But in his eighties Strong was ready to give aid and comfort to the new fundamentalist movement. In a book called *A Tour of the Missions,* three years before Thomas's explosive attack, he too had assailed the liberals' alleged misuse of scientific biblical criticism, their preoccupation with matters other than personal evangelism, and their failure to insist upon Christianity's status as the one true and final religion.

The venerable Baptist leader had not lost all appreciation for ecumenism, for the Social Gospel, or for vigorous educational work in missions. But he balked when such newer emphases became virtually a new Gospel. What shall we say, he asked, of those who preach these healthy innovations "when they really mean that the preaching of the old doctrines of sin and salvation must give place to 'another gospel' of cooperative Christian work?" Removing the gloves, Strong averred that "to lay greater emphasis upon the fruits of Christianity than upon its roots, is to insult Christ, and ultimately to make Christianity only one of many earth-born religions." Liberal teaching in the seminaries at home, he complained, was producing graduates fit only to be switched off onto "some side-track of social service"—fit to go into all the world, not preaching the Gospel, but serving as YMCA secretaries and passing their religious doubts on to others.[27]

In issuing those complaints Strong was making several assumptions that liberals, by this time, simply did not share. One was that the Christian convictions of a YMCA secretary were—ex officio, as it were— likely to be less firm or deeply held than those of a preaching missionary. Another, closely related to the first, was that education and social service under Christian auspices were ordinarily less effective than evangelistic activity was in commending Christianity to alien societies. "What would Peter have said," he asked incredulously, if advised to avoid preaching and told "to establish schools, and to trust to the gradual enlightenment of the Jewish nation by means of literature?" Liberals, in response, might well have asked how successful Christianity had been in converting the Jewish nation by means of preaching. And countless missionaries, liberal or otherwise, had moved far beyond Strong's language concerning the "senseless idols" and "imaginary deities" of non-Western religions. Just as passé, and as damaging to Strong's credibility, was his assertion that "a pure life . . . a life lived for others, is something which surpasses the power of Confucius or Buddha to produce or to maintain."[28]

[26]Wacker, *Strong,* p. 4 and passim.
[27]Strong, *Tour of the Missions,* pp. 189–90.
[28]Ibid., pp. 193, 201–2, 209.

"What would Peter have said if told to establish schools!" Augustus Strong, critic of social service missions. From *Rochester Theological Seminary Bulletin* 73, supplement (May 1922), facing p. 38. Courtesy of Colgate Rochester Divinity School/Bexley Hall/Crozer Theological Seminary.

Even if one considered such assumptions retrograde, however, and took a more affirming stance toward world religions and social Christianity, Strong's argument remained a coherent and challenging one. He was saying that though applied Christianity is fine, it will not work if one has no distinctive message to apply. An emphasis upon "physical and social agencies, to the detriment of simple gospel preaching" is, he said, like beginning at the roof, and building down to the foundations.[29] (Had Strong known that some of India's greatest temples, because carved out of caves, had been built exactly that way and endured for thousands of years, he might have used a different metaphor.) If making converts was the real goal, as the mission boards still unanimously insisted, then one had to question procedures that seemed indifferent to that goal and mission theories that implied doubts about the final truth of Christianity.

John Horsch, a Mennonite historian and prolific critic of Protestant modernism, carried this argument a step further, in effect recommending a clean and candid break between liberal and conservative missionary objectives. His brief essay of 1920 on *The Modernist View of Missions* was significant for pressing, in that vein, the solution that liberal and moderate spokesmen were resisting. These mission leaders, he said, should admit that they were not primarily interested in evangelism, and that their effort was therefore not the traditional missionary enterprise. They should be frank about this with their financial supporters, who were being seriously misled. Liberals should then go their own way with whatever honest support they could find. Horsch obviously thought such support would be meager; but even if it were not, he would advise distancing the liberals and their influence from genuine evangelistic operations. Until that happened, liberalism, with the great and growing institutional power constructed on its essentially fraudulent appeals, would continue its "undoing of the work of the faithful missionaries of the cross."[30]

Despite this and other hints that modern missions were actually anti-Christian, Horsch was content to focus his attack more moderately on their being antimission, or at least antievangelical. What he wanted was a return to an alleged status quo ante, to a situation in which liberals had been frankly hostile or indifferent to conversionary aims. He quoted Unitarians and others who had acknowledged and indeed boasted that their outreach to the world's people was a matter of interreligious understanding. The problem now was that liberals were advocating the same sort of thing and calling it missions.[31]

[29]Ibid., p. 210.
[30]Horsch, *Modernist View*, p. 15.
[31]Ibid., pp. 3–6.

A Unitarian journalist had expressed pleasure that "our sister churches" were advertising their missionary work in the terminology of world friendship and world service. Horsch, agreeing that this was an interpretation rampant in the mainline churches and boards, charged that liberal strategy involved making capital, again somewhat fraudulently, out of the efforts of others. Professor E. C. Moore of Harvard, a liberal Congregationalist, had observed that "it is seemingly futile to have liberalism and then seek to inject religion into it"; and Horsch of course pounced on this. He said that the liberal strategy at home and abroad was to reverse the order: let evangelicals do the work of converting people to real religion, then subvert the faith of these people and hope for some residuum of religious interest and attachment to the church.[32]

Horsch's own strategy, as this suggests, was to launch various balloons of genuinely liberal manufacture, then puncture them—with arrows dipped in wit rather than in venom. He quoted one China missionary as explaining enthusiastically that Christians were "attacking sin by trying to abolish poverty, ignorance and disease." They were enjoying a hearty response, this worker had reported, in a society still dominated by Confucian modes of thought: "The social message of Christianity is strikingly in accord with the best of Chinese tradition." This is the point exactly, Horsch responded: "All unbiased students will admit that religious liberalism is more nearly akin to Confucianism than to New Testament Christianity."

In their eclecticism, too, liberals and the devotees of non-Christian religions struck Horsch as much alike. The most prominent heathen religions, he explained, present a variety of gods so that adherents can choose those "whose pretensions appeal to them"; one is in fact permitted to profess various religious faiths at the same time. As a rule, these religions gladly accept the Christian God as one among many. "What they object to is the exclusiveness of Christianity." Beyond this, he said, liberal and heathen religion are allied in their common emphasis on the immanence of God. Liberalism's most prominent doctrine, in other words, is "of heathen origin," although Horsch thought radical modernism outdoes the heathen in reducing religion to a psychological formula.[33]

Horsch also, like Thomas, complained that liberals with their social emphases and civilizing ways had committed themselves to exporting some of the more retrograde elements of Western culture, instead of concentrating on the West's one perfect gift to the world, the message of Christian salvation. "The attempt to socialize the non-Christian coun-

[32]Ibid., pp. 10, 12–13.
[33]Ibid., p. 11.

tries," he asserted "has nothing to recommend it to thinking people so long as the endeavors for the socialization of the home lands have failed. Here the proverb is applicable, 'Physician heal thyself.' "[34]

At such points one sees some convergence between the arguments of fundamentalists and those of the people whose influence they most deplored. Liberals in this period were at least as inclined to dwell on the deficiencies in Western culture as conservatives were. But the inferences each party drew for missions were of course different. Critics like Horsch, though they might see presumption in attempts to reform the world socially on the Western model, remained supremely assertive about the exclusive truth and ultimate triumph of Christianity. Liberals, on the other hand, and the mainline boards themselves, seemed to be pondering—cautiously—a collaborative approach to non-Christian religions as well as to non-Western cultures. The activist establishment, clearly enough, was modifying its social enthusiasm too little, and its religious assertiveness too much, to satisfy either its Continental or its American fundamentalist critics.

[34]Ibid., pp. 15–16.

CHAPTER 6

Tradition under Fire

I am weary unto death with this incessant preaching. Let us cease our talk for a time and cut off our talkers, and try to express our religion in terms of living service.

Pearl Buck, 1932

The mission enterprise in the immediate postwar period reflected the contradictions running through American society at large. For missions, in other words, it was an expansive, bustling era even though older certainties had become clouded and some alliances were coming unstuck. American mission enthusiasts maintained a sense of optimism and forward motion despite their awareness that the world was not (and probably never had been) as they had perceived it in 1910, and despite the fact that the "peacemaking" of 1919 had produced cynicism and disappointment. Since American leaders, unlike Professor Frick, responded favorably to the evidences of Anglo-American spiritual ascendancy, they saw in the very failures of peacemakers and politicians a new opening for religious leadership in world affairs. Sobered by the unexpected conflict but still inspired by the Wilsonian response to it, the missionary movement faced the postwar decades with its older civilizing motives transmuted and toughened for the work of reconstruction.

In such respects the movement's sense of this-worldly purpose merely reaffirmed that of the brave prewar era. The mission establishment could feel that a torn and confused political order needed its ministrations now at least as much as a ruthless imperialism had needed them before. Until about 1930, moreover, this sense of purpose, usefulness, and toughened resolve seemed to be ratified by the numbers—by financial support especially, but also by steady growth in most of the other statistics that publicists called upon, in their tireless self-surveys, to certify the pulse and bloodcount of world evangelization.

Still, not all the indices showed growth, nor were the curves of confidence and enthusiasm in all respects moving upward. Recruitment on the college campuses flagged; and while that enervation was not an adequate measure for the health of foreign missions, it did reflect, somewhere quite near the heart of the movement, a decline in confidence and a rearrangement of emotional and practical priorities. The Student Volunteer Movement attracted declining numbers to its conventions, to the signing of pledge cards, and to actual missionary service.[1]

Those young people who did sign on, moreover, had a mind-set different from that of the previous generation. Phrases like "evangelization of the world," which had become downright embarrassing for some of them, for others had acquired a definitely social content; and the student generation, intent on writing such changes into the manifestoes and rhetoric of the movement, found itself nudging aside some figures in the still-revered elder leadership. John R. Mott, whose Anglo-American coloration had earlier marred his effectiveness with student groups on the Continent, no longer could quite be the man of the hour for young American Christians. Unable radically to adapt his ideas, nor to dispel a certain aura of overblown and failed enthusiasms, Mott instead shifted much of his attention and his remarkable talents to the ecumenical movement. Robert E. Speer, more conservative theologically than Mott but better attuned to the problems troubling a younger generation, became for many (along with socialist spellbinder Sherwood Eddy) a more effective guide and role model.

Certainly Speer was the representative "man in the middle" for this era as he strove mightily to contain, but also to conciliate, challenges from left and right. To his left were those who aspired to make Christianity the partner instead of the conqueror of the other religions and spiritual forces of the world; on his right stood traditional mission interests that in the end would view Speer and a "trimming" mainline establishment as the truly dangerous enemies. Like Mott, Speer was closely associated, officially and even personally, with liberals who were coming to see service and "presence" as synonyms for Christian missionary witness; but he also, until his open break with the fundamentalists in the early 1930s, consorted with conservatives who prided themselves on knowing the difference between an altar call and an invitation to the YMCA picnic.[2]

[1]Clifton J. Phillips, "Changing Attitudes in the Student Volunteer Movement," in Christensen and Hutchison, *Missionary Ideologies,* pp. 137–41. See also Ernst, *Moment of Truth.*

[2]John F. Piper, Jr., who is writing a biography of Speer, dissents somewhat from my depiction of Speer's effect on those who (like my own parents) were recruited for missions during the 1920s. Admitting to "a modest bias," he suggests that Speer had always been "the leading statesman," and a more potent force than Mott among collegians. John F. Piper to author, July 8, 1986. Helen Waite Coleman, *The Camp Diamond Story* (privately printed, 1941) documents the range of Speer's personal associations.

If Speer is a key figure in any depiction of the establishment and its dilemmas during this period, John D. Rockefeller, Jr., stands astride the liberal initiatives of these same years—not as a colossus of advanced missionary thinking, but as the friend and financial supporter of those (such as Harry Emerson Fosdick and Ernest Hocking) who did the advanced thinking. And Rockefeller by no means left all the thinking and speaking to others. The liberal advances between the First World War and the Depression are in fact neatly bracketed, at one end by an impatiently liberal Rockefeller pronouncement of 1918 on the future of Christianity, and at the other by the controversial Laymen's Report on Missions, instigated and funded by Rockefeller, that appeared in 1932. The 1918 article, though it occupied merely a few pages in the *Saturday Evening Post,* gained a reputation among conservatives much like the reputation of the Edinburgh Conference among detractors of American activism. It was seen in retrospect as a harbinger, and also a cause, of more massive and terrible depredations.

Rockefeller's piece, called "The Christian Church: What of Its Future?" argued that the church was destined to survive only if it could recapture the loyalty of vast numbers of Christians who were finding its doctrines stifling and its moral stands hypocritical. If it was to be effective either at home or in the mission fields and the wider world, the church must become more inclusive, with doctrines and programs more directly attuned to human needs. That would mean, conversely, becoming less concerned about those doctrines or forms that exclude, divide, and distract.

In phrases much like those that Harry Emerson Fosdick would use four years later in his famous "Shall the Fundamentalists Win?" sermon, Rockefeller condemned what he thought was a Nero-like obliviousness to social conditions and international dilemmas. "In the face of the great problems of sin and evil with which the world is confronted today," he asked, would Christ himself want the observance or nonobservance of particular doctrines to provoke "the separation into rival factions of good men?" He would not, Rockefeller insisted. Christ, even though he established such ordinances as Baptism and the Lord's Supper, aimed to displace the rampant formalism of his day with a spiritual and socially sensitive religion. His modern followers must do the same. Rockefeller acknowledged that "ordinance, creed, ritual, form, Biblical interpretation, theology" all serve to enrich worship; they can bring the believer into fuller understanding of God, and should be used "as each individual or separate church may find them helpful toward that end." But none of these formalisms must be allowed to pose barriers between the soul and its God; between one believer and another; or between the Christian and the neighbor in need.

"A life, not a creed." John D. Rockefeller, Jr., at the time of his proposal for Christian redefinition. Courtesy of the Rockefeller Archive Center.

Rockefeller advanced no new ideas. He was echoing the liberal religion of a century earlier. Particular phrases might suggest the Fosdick of 1922, but pleas for spirit over ordinance evoked the Emerson of 1832, explaining why he was resigning from a stultifying pastorate. Nor was Rockefeller, in this article at least, targeting foreign missions. But for conservatives, including those who would later rail against the

Laymen's Report, his venting of opinion showed exactly what was wrong with a missionary movement they saw as dominated by spineless liberals and fence-sitting board executives. Conservatives were especially alarmed by Rockefeller's vision of a "reborn church" that he said might be called "the Church of the Living God":

> Its terms of admission would be love for God, as He is re-vealed in Christ and His living spirit, and the vital translation of this love into a Christlike life. Its atmosphere would be one of warmth, freedom and joy. . . . It would pronounce ordi-nances, ritual, creed, all nonessential for admission into the kingdom of God or His church. A life, not a creed, would be its test, what a man does, not what he professes.[3]

Fifteen years later, the Princeton Fundamentalist J. Gresham Machen opened his attack on the "Laymen's Inquiry" and its final report by complaining that the study had been financed by a Modernist layman who in 1918 had written an article "advocating admission to the Church without any profession of belief whatever."[4] But it was not Rockefeller—as either he or Machen would readily have agreed—who articulated a mission theory to go with the Standard Oil money and the modernist ideology. The one who, above all others, performed that substantive function was Daniel Johnson Fleming of Union Seminary in New York.

VISION AND REVISION

Fleming, who earlier had served for twelve years as a missionary in India, in his lifetime produced thirty books on missionary subjects. Several of these in the 1920s anticipated, but presented with greater force and individuality, the major conclusions of the Laymen's Report, to which he would also contribute directly. The most impressive of his early writings, carrying the rather hackneyed title *Whither Bound In Missions?* was sponsored, just as the fundamentalists would have pre-dicted, by the publishing arm of the YMCAs and YWCAs. It contended for nothing less than a Copernican revolution in the way Christians of the West conceived and addressed the world.

A number of Fleming's arguments, like Rockefeller's, merely applied new urgency and frankness to an older critique. Quoting an Indian statesman's remark that "your Jesus is hopelessly handicapped by His connection with the West,"[5] Fleming urged more attention to distinc-

---

[3]Rockefeller, "The Christian Church," pp. 16, 37.
[4]Machen, *Modernism and the Board,* p. 5.
[5]Fleming, *Whither,* p. 59.

tions between Christianity and the cultures with which it had become linked, and between Christ and Christianity. This second discrimination, he said, would mean admitting not only that Christ would disown the Inquisition and the Crusades but also that he would deplore the shameful and selfish divisions within his church. Fleming thought those divisions persisted overseas, and led (for example) to foolishly duplicative educational ventures. "Institutions, missions, and denominations seem to find it hard to manifest . . . the quality of self-sacrifice even unto death that has marked the individual missionary." In the same vein, Fleming reiterated older pleas for devolution and indigenization, assailing most efforts to date as halfhearted and proposing a new and tougher test for the fitness of missionary recruits. No misson board, he argued, should certify any candidate for foreign service who could not accept a status of equality or subordination in the overseas post. The new missionary must accept willingly a job description that makes him or her "temporary, secondary and advisory." Those three adjectives, he acknowledged, "are [nowadays] not supposed to appeal to the ambitions of strong men," but they accord with Christ's teaching that the greatest among his followers must be the servant of all.[6]

Fleming's call for these and other "adjustments in quality" brought him into conflict with the conservatives at several points. While he did not renounce all conversionary motives or objectives, his stress on quality did mean a lessening of interest in numbers, both of missionaries and of converts. His preference for an evangelism of service and personal example, moreover, was patent. To Horsch's accusation that liberals were prone to consider the fruits of the Christian life more important than its roots, Fleming gladly pled guilty:

> The most effective popular apologetic on the mission field has passed from origins to consequences, from roots to fruits. . . . Not only the ethnic faiths, but Christianity itself, must stand or fall by their power to enlarge and enrich life. . . . In particular, the people of India, China, and Japan are not going to accept the Bible because of some statement as to its inspired origin. . . . The power of Christianity is to be proved by asking, not whether it can be authoritatively established, but what it accomplishes in the lives of men.[7]

If the clash with fundamentalism were the sole or major story, one could stop here in examining the liberal thinking Fleming represented. But his work is noteworthy for articulating a bolder and broader con-

[6]Ibid., pp. 143, 171–72, 187.
[7]Ibid., pp. 67–68.

ception—an almost literal recasting of the map of the world—that in many respects was destined at length to be accepted as fully by evangelicals as by liberals. Running through all of Fleming's work was an insistence on breaking through the dichotomies of West and non-West, of Christian cultures and heathen cultures, of home base and foreign field. Anticipating the thinking and even the watchwords of ecumenical conferences at mid-century, Fleming questioned the entire vocabulary of foreign missions and of "mission fields." No area is "foreign," and none, more than any other, is a "field." Since we can no longer speak of Christian societies converting non-Christian ones (all societies being less than Christian) we must insist that "the whole world is the mission field; and if a person serves at all he serves in the mission field."[8]

Fleming thought his contemporaries were still wedded to an old and increasingly distasteful rhetoric about the conquest and occupation of new continents. Yet instead of discarding that vocabulary entirely, he made his point by way of an imaginative redefinition of the term "continent." In a newly interdependent world, the continents requiring conquest are not landmasses but rather "the great transverse areas of human activity" such as industrialization, nationalism, materialism, racial injustice, ignorance, war, and poverty. *These* are the new continents which, if we are to think of conquest, ought to be in our minds.[9]

The Laymen's Report would later arouse fear and controversy, along with applause from the religious left, by proposing that Christians devote themselves to the battle between spirituality and materialism, a battle in which they would need to collaborate with other world faiths almost to the exclusion of the traditional competitive stance. Fleming, in 1925 at least, did not go quite that far; but he came close. His emphasis on a permeative rather than a narrowly conversionary form of Christian influence suggested collaboration. So did his view that Christians should rejoice in the spiritual renewal of other faiths, instead of deploring such renewal as the work of the Devil and as, allegedly, a disincentive to Christian conversions.[10]

Calling further on his talent for provocative restatement of scriptural bywords, Fleming also asked in this book whether Christians had been profound enough in their admonitions about giving and receiving, or serious enough in applying the Golden Rule and the concept of human brotherhood.

We have, he said, rightly stressed the blessedness of giving. But we must now rethink the necessity and blessedness of receiving, of being

[8]Ibid., p. 127.
[9]Ibid., pp. 135, 122–44.
[10]Ibid., p. 90; Fleming, *Building with India,* pp. 113–14.

"Others have the same right to their opinion." Daniel Johnson Fleming in the 1920s. Courtesy of E. McClung Fleming.

genuinely teachable. Fleming's art professor at the University of Chicago, Walter Sargent, had argued that of the five major desiderata for great art, China surpassed the West in four. The Union professor believed something of the sort could be affirmed with respect to religion, morals, and other areas of culture: "We have much more to learn from them than *mah jong*." And the willingness to receive, after all, involves a deeper form of giving, the giving of respect and of love. Fleming captured both the strength and the deficiency in the Western outreach of the preceding century when he quoted an Indian Christian's complaint that "you make us feel that you want to do good to us, but you don't make us feel that you need us."[11]

In urging also that Christians rethink the implications of the Golden Rule and of "brotherhood," Fleming was not saying that no such rethinking had begun. Liberals had recognized that the Golden Rule forces one to reconsider proselytizing practices and belittling attitudes that Westerners would not permit, let alone welcome, in their own communities. An implicit message that "your religion is false; it must and will be replaced" would be resented at home, especially if purveyed by aliens; and a great many missionaries, evangelical as well as liberal, by this time were getting along without such attitudes as they themselves served within foreign communities. Many could have agreed with Fleming that "the universal brotherhood of children of God [means] that others have the same right to their opinion as we have to ours."[12] Still others had long since (often because of national laws or community pressures) banned or minimized evangelizing activities in their schools or agencies.

Yet much remained, in missionary practice and in the rhetoric of spiritual "world conquest," that implicitly claimed exemption from Christianity's own ideals of mutuality and brotherhood. Behind such claims to exemption stood an interpretation of Christ's words that was both contradictory and curiously restricted. Because Christianity is true, traditional missions had seemed to say, one may be forced to treat the Golden Rule as not true, or not obligatory. The commandment had been heeded in relatively discrete ethical exchanges, but not applied to Christianity itself. It had been seen as permissible to do unto others what we would not want done to us—for example, to undermine essential religious convictions—so long as what we do is something that others *should* want.

Since that sort of reasoning was more deep and persistent among the domestic supporters of missions than among practicing missionaries, Fleming attempted to vivify (and very literally to "bring home") his contentions concerning the Golden Rule by publishing a remarkable *Christian Century* article called "If Buddhists Came to Our Town." Here he gave detailed and nuanced consideration to the sort of behavior Americans would demand from those who hold an exotic faith and who wish to win people to it. He allowed (perhaps employing too rosy a view of tolerance in American communities) that if Buddhists were

[11]Fleming, *Whither,* p. 27.
[12]Ibid., pp. 196–97.

running the best schools in town, the critics would want them "to feel a real concern that their pupils should become Buddhists." But he pointed out that Americans would resent "any dealing with our children in such a way that they would not later think freely for themselves," or that would bind them permanently to a point of view "alien to all their inheritance."[13]

Fleming put all this in the terms of still another of Jesus' sayings. He offered the uncomfortable proposition that the mission enterprise, once it makes certain that its practices meet Christ's standards, has gone only the first mile. To go the second mile, as we are asked to do, would mean consulting the needs of others as they—not merely as we—define them.[14] To traditionalists with a century of confident expansionist rhetoric behind them, such talk suggested something a good deal worse than just idiosyncratic use of Christ's teachings. It smacked of relativism, pusillanimity, or even a wholesale betrayal of Christianity.

Fleming plainly worried about all those dangers, but he insisted that a collaborative approach to other religions is not a sign of weakness, and does not imply indifference about one's own belief. Teachability and conviction, he said, are not incompatible. And a determination to meet others on their own terms, instead of imposing the terms upon them, is neither unscriptural nor relativistic. On the contrary, it springs from the absolute requirements of Christian love and the Golden Rule.[15]

Fleming's writings of the 1920s were laced with gentle protests not only against the old-time vocabulary of conquest and condescension but against a subtler ethnocentrism that operated when one continued to speak of China or Japan as missionary lands, "as though being our parish abroad was their *raison d'être*." Mission spokesmen were also, he thought, frequently guilty of employing a double language, one for their friends abroad and one for use in stirring excitement and contributions at home. Among a number of testimonies to this practice, Fleming cited that of an Indian Christian who, during four years' study in the United States, had heard one returned missionary after another "distort and conceal the facts" and "deliberately slander the fair name of Mother India." The student may have been oversensitive, Fleming allowed; but perhaps missionaries should themselves risk erring on the side of sensitivity. They should at least make it a rule "always to speak in a way such that you would be pleased to find one of your Korean or Japanese friends in the audience at the close of your address."[16]

[13]Fleming, "Buddhists," pp. 293–94.
[14]Fleming, *Whither*, pp. 24–27.
[15]Ibid., chap. 6.
[16]Ibid., pp. 86–88, 124, 29, 216, 218.

Fleming, though probably the leading American prophet of the sort of "world mission" thinking that would later transform a large part of the mission enterprise, seems to have reached only a limited readership.[17] But foreign missions retained enough hold on the public imagination that hundreds of articles—pro, con, and in-between—appeared during this period in secular magazines such as *Literary Digest, Atlantic Monthly,* and *Ladies Home Journal.*

This literature, along with other evidences of what the educated public was reading and thinking, suggests more polarization, at that level, between critics and defenders than had been evident in earlier decades. This was not because those at either pole were more extreme or strident than before. Somerset Maugham's "Rain," which as a Broadway play generated much of the magazine controversy of 1923, was not a great deal more caustic toward missionaries then Melville's novels of the 1840s had been. T. S. Eliot's version, in "Sweeney Agonistes," of the standard cannibal-missionary joke ("I'll convert *you*! Into a stew. A nice little, white little, missionary stew") was somewhat gentler than Mark Twain's animadversions at the time of the Boxer Rebellion. But it did seem, with iconoclasm and cultural despair on the rise among intellectuals and making some inroads elsewhere in American society, that the Melvilles and Twains were more numerous than before; and that their criticisms called forth louder cries of alarm and defense from mission supporters.[18]

More common than either vituperation or unqualified approval, during the troubled twenties, were calls for mission reform—many of them voiced by workers in the field—that appeared in both secular and religious periodicals. In 1926 and 1927, R. C. Hutchison, a newly minted Ph.D. who was teaching philosophy at the Presbyterian college in Tehran, published two *Atlantic Monthly* articles whose themes paralleled Fleming's but did so in more outright language. Writing on "Islam and Christianity," Hutchison suggested that the rejection of Christianity in the Moslem world had been the most certain, continuous, and disheartening defeat in the entire history of Christianity; and he asked why that should be. His answer was that Moslems see Christianity as having failed consistently to exemplify its own distinctive ethic either in outward relationships or within its own communities. Christians

[17]Most of his books were put out by the YMCA's Association Press, and these seem not to have been widely reviewed. Fleming also published, however, with more commercial houses such as George Doran and Fleming Revell. In addition, his influence on such key figures as Hocking, and on generations of Union Seminary students, should not be ignored. Fleming's thought and career deserve careful study.

[18]Lane, *Missions in Magazines,* chaps. 2 and 6; Forman, "Mission Theory," pp. 95–97.

from the Crusades to the present, he said, far from displaying "a unique or amazing love," have tended (like Moslems themselves, he acknowledged, in some times and places) to achieve their aims by murder, pillage, and war; and their internal divisions have provided almost as poor an example. Moslems are understandably not anxious "to give up their sectarianism for our sectarianism, their strife for our strife, their frenzied theological debates" for ours.[19]

A year later, writing on "Christianity and Proselytism," Hutchison again raised the rhetorical voltage on Fleming's arguments, and also carried some of them a step further. He called upon missionary leaders (with Robert E. Speer, his friend and mentor, unquestionably in mind) to stop trying to please the home folks by insisting that all missionary work is evangelistic in purpose. Such leaders "speak the thought of their great parishes" when they contend that the quest for conversions is the only real aim of missions; but they also, by such assertions, drive away the vast number who could be attracted by a clear presentation of Christianity's "twofold message." One part of that message is evangelistic; the other part, based on the Beatitudes, elicits a dedication to Christian service that has nothing essentially to do with proselytism. Hutchison thought "the most superficial glance at the work of mission institutions" would confirm that these institutions on the whole are offering the fruits of Christian witness and love with no thought whatever of making conversions.[20]

Hutchison, a Presbyterian minister who considered himself an evangelist as well as a teacher, nonetheless was offering evangelism a separate-but-equal status that would in no sense satisfy traditionalists. In a stunning reversal of the language and mathematics of several preceding generations, he proclaimed that Christianity proposes to make its contributions to human welfare "even though from this day to the end of time not a single person surrenders his indifference or deserts his own faith to become a Christian. . . . Though never another Moslem turn to Christ, nor devil worshipper leave his fetishes, nor Hindu stir from his ancient philosophies, still Christianity will offer these services to all." In direct contradiction of fundamentalists who argued that non-evangelizing missions were betraying the wishes of most contributors, Hutchison offered the equally dubious assurance that "it is invariably

---

[19]Hutchison, "Islam and Christianity," pp. 707–9. James King Quay, who in 1928 became secretary of the Cairo YMCA, later recalled that the "religious discussion groups and religious meetings" he directed in Cairo "were not of a proselytizing or theological nature, such as would alienate the Moslems, although we managed to get the Christian emphasis in." Quay, "Four Score and Four Years" (unpublished memoir, 1971), p. 93.

[20]Hutchison, "Christianity and Proselytism," pp. 620–21.

recognized that this gift or service to needy men requires no pay in the form of conversion to Christianity."[21]

Had Hutchison been right in that categorical judgment, the shouting would have been over, and missions could have proceeded without further controversy to a degree of recognition for "service missions" that traditionalists were in fact resisting mightily, and that board executives were unwilling to confer, at least in their public statements. The later ruckus over the Laymen's Report would show that conservatives and the mission establishment were even less prepared to accept a position of mere equality for Christianity or a collaborationist approach to other religions.

WILLIAM E. HOCKING: RE-THINKING MISSIONS

The so-called Laymen's Report of 1932, which attempted systematically to analyze the condition of Protestant missions and to prescribe for their future, at most points was less searching, and less disruptive to traditional ideas, than the work of Fleming and other advanced thinkers had been in the preceding decade. But the conditions of the report's sponsorship and publication thrust its conclusions far more into the arenas of public discussion, both within the missionary movement and beyond it.

The "Laymen's Inquiry," as the overall project was called, began in January 1930 with a meeting of Baptist laymen that had been called by John D. Rockefeller, Jr., and that was addressed by the Methodist layman John R. Mott. Subsequently, on the strength of Rockefeller's financial backing and a tentative blessing from seven of the major denominational boards, the Institute for Social and Religious Research was commissioned to conduct interviews and collect data in India, Burma, Japan, and China. A fifteen-member Commission of Appraisal, representative of the major denominations but independent of their boards, then visited the mission areas and, along with Institute researchers and other professional staff, composed the seven-volume final report. A one-volume version, called *Re-Thinking Missions,* was released by Harper and Brothers in 1932.

The Laymen's Report attracted unusual attention, and aroused controversy, partly because the advanced views of the commission's chairman, Professor William Ernest Hocking of Harvard, enjoyed special prominence in this summary volume. What emerged there most clearly, out of the years of investigation and mounds of information, was an eloquent call, highly characteristic of Hocking, for "world understand-

[21]Ibid., p. 621.

ing on the spiritual level." Spiritual collaboration was to be the objective of missions; they ought not to operate in hostility to other world religions, nor seek to displace them.

This was not necessarily the view of all those laypersons (women having been substantially represented) who had collaborated in the Inquiry. And certainly it was not just what denominational executives had had in mind when they granted friendly advance support to the project. Hence the ensuing scramble, especially among the missions boards, to associate and dissociate, to endorse some of the findings and reject or condemn others.

Missions, in the Hocking formulation, were not to become mere generalized agencies for promoting worldwide spiritual uplift. As a specifically Christian enterprise, missions were "to seek with people of other lands a true knowledge and love of God, expressing in life and word what we have learned through Jesus Christ, and endeavoring to give effect to his spirit in the life of the world." But certainly Hocking wanted a fundamental shift of emphasis or perhaps the acknowledgement of a shift that had already happened. A determination to "give effect" to the knowledge and love of God clearly, in his rendition, allowed for autonomous humanitarian service. Hocking, like Hutchison, noted and approved the current "visible tendency to regard [educational and other associated interests] as having a value of their own, and as being legitimate functions of Christian missions apart from any explicit evangelization." In an observation that conservatives would consider accurate to the point of banality, he added that it was "as if 'salvation' had begun to take on a new meaning."[22]

Hocking was an eminent philosopher, a Congregationalist layman, and the author of *The Meaning of God in Human Experience* (1912), a minor classic in the liberal Protestant tradition. He had come to the missions project as one whose prime concern, personal as well as professional, was to discover a "world faith" capable of overcoming the heartless forces of modern secularism. When Rockefeller and his colleagues approached Hocking in 1930, the latter responded by wondering whether or not he was qualified. He also had numerous questions, he said, about the missionary enterprise as traditionally conducted, and felt some doubts about its continuance.

Rockefeller replied that these were exactly the questions and doubts that the sponsors wished an independent research organization and fair-minded appraisers to investigate. Hocking, writing to his department chairman to request a leave, remarked that the unusual assignment made

[22]Hocking, *Re-Thinking*, pp. 25, 59, 61.

"World understanding on the spiritual level": William Ernest Hocking. From *Fortune* 25 (February 1942): 90. Photographed for *Fortune* by Barrett Gallagher and reproduced here by permission.

sense because his role would be that of a philosopher more than of a Christian layman.[23] To anyone who knew Hocking's work, and Rockefeller's views, it might have been clear from all this that the Inquiry would be posing questions that, within the movement at least, had not been asked before; or that had never been asked in such an intense and public way.

That many of the participants, or Hocking himself, were predisposed to find that the mission enterprise should close down seems unlikely. The verdict, at any rate, was that it should not. The commission held that neither Christianity nor any other great religion should be asked to cease all attempts to convey its version of the truth. To ask whether Christian missions should continue, Hocking wrote, is as fruitless as asking whether good will should continue.[24]

Yet the great changes that had overtaken the movement in the twentieth-century world—an altered theological outlook, reform within the various religions, the emergence of a world culture, and the rise of nationalism in the East—had removed some of the grounds for mission activity, had transformed other motives, and had created new mission imperatives. Above all, many of these changes had forced attention to a new and overwhelming challenge, that of combating a corrosive secularization. The danger, throughout the world, lay in "the loss of traditional restraints as the spread of world-culture undermines the sanctions of ancient custom and religion."[25]

Hocking, like Fleming and virtually every other liberal who sought to redefine missions, struggled with the obvious objection (obvious at least from a traditional point of view) that genuine collaboration among religions would undermine Christianity's claims to distinctiveness, to say nothing of its claims to uniqueness and superiority. But like these other liberals Hocking denied such allegations. Christians, he wrote, need not relinquish the beliefs that distinguish them. In particular, they would still hold that Christian love is the element especially needed for the spiritual rejuvenation of the world. In that sense, and in the sense of Christianity's consequent fitness for leadership, belief in the superior or even supreme value of Christianity would remain. What must not remain, Hocking thought, is a parochialism that in effect denies the God-given right of others to hold a similar loyalty to their own religious systems. In that respect, he said, to boast about a unique or superior

[23]Rouner, *Human Experience,* pp. 263–65.
[24]Hocking, *Re-Thinking,* p. 4.
[25]Ibid., p. 23.

grasp of religious truth is not only unnecessary; it constitutes "a humiliating mistake."[26]

The new missionary, as the commission argued throughout the report, should be an ambassador more than either a soldier or a high-pressure salesman. The ambassador for Christ would be accredited, or even selected, by those he or she was to serve. The religious ambassador, like secular ones, would be expected to believe in his cause and to hope that others would be drawn to it, but not to press others to change their own allegiance. In one case as in the other, restraint on the part of the emissary would in no sense imply a lack of conviction.[27]

Hocking (himself sounding like something of a diplomat) contrasted past and future missionary ideologies not as wrong notions versus right ones but as temporary expedients now ready to give way to permanent modes of action. A missionary agenda predicated on the superiority of Western and Christian institutions, and announcing the right of Christian soldiers to conquer and displace other systems, may have been inevitable, he thought, at a certain stage of history. What was emerging, however, was a "permanent" stance that would recognize the right of all peoples to autonomy and respect, and would acknowledge the spiritual vitality and reforming zeal in other world religions. Christianity and Western culture must question, with respect to achievement if not to aspiration, their own convictions about a superior spirituality. At the least they must be content to cherish such convictions without parading them, or maintaining them as working assumptions, in their relationships with the East.[28]

The idea of ambassadorship, at least for Hocking and his colleagues, implied a missionary force that could be much smaller than the current one, and that must be far better. The finding in the Laymen's Report that stirred most controversy—along with the report's equivocal stance toward evangelism and its collaborationist approach to world religions—concerned the quality of missionary personnel. "Resentment" might be a better term for the reaction than "controversy"; the good people who ran or participated in missions were doubtless more hurt by this particular criticism than they could admit. The appraisers concluded that the missionary force as presently constituted was not up to the delicate work of ambassadorship.

Far too many missionaries, they had found, were not operating well even under traditional, less demanding guidelines. Their chairman paid

[26]Ibid., pp. 49, and 46–52 passim.

[27]For Hocking's most explicit references to the ambassadorial model, see *Re-Thinking*, pp. 26, 115.

[28]Ibid., pp. 24–30.

tribute to the many missionaries "of conspicuous power, true saintliness, and a sublime spirit of devotion, men and women in whose presence one feels himself at once exalted and unworthy." But his report on the majority was damning: "the greater number seem to us of limited outlook and capacity." He thought that their vision of the inner meaning of what they were doing had become obscured. They had been beaten down by the intricacies and frictions of "a task too great for their powers and their hearts." The attempt to combine Christian service with the drive to make converts had too often led to the commissioning of second-rate doctors, educators, agronomists, and social workers; or else had distorted and deflected the energies of first-rate ones.[29]

Hocking told of an able young physician whose efforts over the years to run his hospital and also preach to the patients had left him no time for professional development or even for meditation, and whose clinic had thus become notorious for sending out five hundred patients each morning with a good Bible text and, too often, the wrong medicine. Correct diagnoses were not attempted; serious diseases were overlooked. Everyone got a smile and a cheerful message; but the dwindling clientele of this doctor had at length dragged the reputation of Christianity down with it. The nationals, having "discovered the inadequacy of the medical service they received . . . wonder if the good doctor's Gospel message was not as erroneous as his treatment." The traditional evangelistic endeavor, already hampered by doctrinal narrowness and sectarian division, had been further vitiated by an unwise and often improper linkage between humanitarian service and personal evangelism.[30]

For the Christian ambassadorship of the future, competence in one's speciality, whether ministerial or medical, would be essential; but even that would not be enough. The new missionary must also be far more expert in understanding and relating to the social problems of the host country. The commission here referred especially to macroeconomic and macrosocial issues. They were calling for a missionary force so lean and well-trained, and so well attuned to modern social research, that its members could, if invited to do so, provide mediation in major social or economic controversies. What they had found among present personnel were missionaries proposing Sunday rest days in non-Christian countries, advocating Prohibition laws about which American Christians were themselves divided, and pressing for Western-style social welfare without the knowledge required to adapt it to Eastern conditions. But the appraisers also reported—and this was by far the un-

[29]Ibid., pp. 15–18.
[30]Ibid., pp. 202–3. See also pp. 67–70, 162, 177, 193, 199.

kindest cut—that most missionaries were inadequate for the micro- as well as the macro-problems; they were ill equipped even to provide the traditional "cup of cold water."

The commission had found almost no social workers, for example, who were "trained to deal scientifically and intelligently with human beings trying to adjust themselves to [a] new factory environment." The report conveyed a sense that the missionary hero, justly celebrated for sacrificial efforts in the slums or villages, was nonetheless a kind of loose cannon, bumbling and banging around in virtual ignorance of his surroundings.[31]

Though this public scolding of missionaries and their sponsors was difficult for the movement to accept, the associated notion of a reduction in force may well have been more deeply threatening. The commission was seeking to squelch the quantitative emphasis that even judicious leaders like Speer had indulged. A. T. Pierson had estimated the number of pennies and the number of right-hearted evangelists required to bring the millennium. The Student Volunteer Movement had tempered such bald calculations by insisting on the kind of college and seminary training that would ensure quality; but numbers and quantitative goals had remained very much in view. The Hocking Commission was now urging that in the new conditions contraction would be as important as expansion. This was not only a reversal of the quantitative dynamic that had made missions in truth a "movement"; in applying its own definitions of quality the commission was proposing standards diametrically opposite to those most urgently sought by fundamentalists. The latter wanted to recall missionaries who were not preaching the Virgin Birth. Hocking with almost equal decisiveness advised that where missionaries in the field were ill-qualified for the work of social reconstruction "they should be withdrawn and only persons of the highest type and quality should be sent out for the future."[32]

Criticizing the Critics: The Battle over the Laymen's Report

Publication of the Laymen's Report prompted an extensive, generally high-minded debate within and beyond the missionary movement. This debate confirmed that, with radical critiques and ideas now being put forward by people who claimed to champion Christian missions, a distinct landmark had been passed. One could now preach (as well as practice) a social emphasis, or even collaboration among world religions, without being seen as a maverick.

[31]Ibid., pp. 244–47.
[32]Ibid., p. 108.

Archibald Baker of the University of Chicago, who wrote the best analysis of the early responses, thought the battleground of mission discussions had moved to an advanced territory somewhat beyond the issues that were dividing fundamentalists from liberals and moderates. Baker, a liberal with strong humanist leanings, conceded that the majority of church members still held to something resembling the Bible-centered stance of the fundamentalists. But he believed that within the mission leadership the crucial debate was now between a moderate, Christo-centric position, focused on the Christ who fulfills but does not destroy, and the advanced liberalism of the report.

Baker alluded to a fourth, more radical position, one that was entirely homocentric and naturalistic. Though this was still outside the boundaries of missionary discussions, he thought it would eventually, if current trends continued, present "the main issue for the Church." In making such a prediction he was, like most observers at the time, underestimating both the continuing viability of fundamentalism and the potential of the fledgling neo-orthodox movement to challenge both naturalism and liberalism. But Baker was right that a collaborationist view of missions had rather suddenly become an accepted subject of discussion within the church organizations, and he was right in thinking this a signal event in the modern history of Christian missions.[33]

For the time being, however, a centrist position clearly dominated. This was the position taken, independently but with near-unaminity, by the denominations that had given qualified support to the study. The mission boards of these churches varied in their reactions, with the ABCFM offering the most favorable response to the Laymen's Report; the Methodists and the Episcopalians showing a bit more uneasiness; and the Northern Baptists, Presbyterians (North), United Presbyterians, and Dutch Reformed each raising a larger number of objections. Yet they all were agreed in finding the programmatic elements of the report more admirable than its theology. And all of them made the same point about the theology. This point, as stated in mildest form by the Congregationalists, was that the report showed too little "conviction of the uniqueness of the revelation of God in Christ."[34]

A further common experience for the various boards and bureaucracies was, of course, that all were caught in the middle. Having recorded their objections to Hocking, they were immediately assailed on the other flank because of the mildness of those objections, and usually because they had lent their prestige to the survey in the first place.

[33]Baker, "Reaction," pp. 392–98.
[34]Ibid., p. 385.

J. Gresham Machen. Courtesy of
Westminster Theological Seminary.

Robert E. Speer. Courtesy of Margaret Bailey Speer.

Pearl Buck. Courtesy of the Library
of Congress.

The family feud among the northern Presbyterians was the most
dramatic, and the most revealing of major positions and their relative
strengths. The setting and dramatis personae were exceptional. In the
immediate background was, first of all, the Laymen's Report, but secondly a bitter conflict at Princeton Seminary that had recently ended
in a stunning triumph of moderates over fundamentalists. In the cast
of characters the leader actor was Speer, filling a familiar role as man-
in-the-middle, but now forced to play that role with more combative-
ness than usual. To his left was the Presbyterian missionary and novelist
Pearl Buck, who had come out foursquare for the Laymen's Report.
To his right was J. Gresham Machen, the former Princeton Seminary
professor now holding forth at the newly founded Westminister Seminary (Philadelphia) and assailing Speer for, among other things, not
dismissing Pearl Buck.

Buck as spokesperson for a theory of missions could not rank with
the other two; in that way the picture lacks symmetry. But events had
thrust her into a strategic position. The daughter of China missionaries,
the wife of a missionary educator employed by the Presbyterian Board,
generally considered a missionary herself (though she insisted that,
technically, she was not),[35] Mrs. Buck had come home on furlough
about a year after publication of *The Good Earth* in 1931. As a suddenly
celebrated author (she would win the Pulitzer Prize for 1932), she was
called upon for a *Christian Century* article on the Laymen's Report,

[35]Board of Foreign Missions, *Annual Report, 1932* (Philadelphia, 1932), p. 288;
Harris, *Buck,* p. 308.

and was scheduled by the Presbyterian Board for many speeches around the United States. She declined most of the speaking engagements, on the ground that she was not really employed by the Presbyterians and did not wish anyone to think the Board was supporting her financially. But one talk that she did give, to an unexpectedly large assemblage of Presbyterian women and Board officials at the Astor Hotel in New York, caused a minor sensation. Both this speech and the *Christian Century* article appeared to confirm what conservatives in their most anguished moments believed about the direction the missionary enterprise was taking.

Buck's review honored Hocking's book with what was probably the most lavish praise it received from any quarter.[36] As an author who had shown herself capable of acerbic criticism, and who had belittled some of the commission's researchers, when she encountered them in China, as "men . . . of rather small caliber," she nonethelesss had decided the final report was "the only book I have ever read which seems to me literally true in its every observation and right in its every conclusion."

Buck could accept the charge leveled against missionaries in the field—that *they* tended to be of small caliber—because she thought that to a large degree this was not their fault; the more culpable mediocrity was that of the people who sent the missionaries and the system that controlled their activities. As she was to say again to her surprised hearers at the Astor Hotel, church people were keeping their best talent at home to serve as their own lawyers and businessmen and ministers.

[36]Buck, "Laymen's Report," pp. 1434–37.

The mission boards then compounded the problem by, in effect, en-
forcing mediocrity: the dedicated souls they sent out were narrowed
rather than broadened by the nature of their assigned duties. More
specifically, the pressure from home for "results" meant that, instead of
rising to the real needs of the people they lived with, the missionaries
became bogged down in an irrelevant pursuit of converts. They were
afforded neither time nor encouragement for the desperately difficult
task of learning what Chinese or Indian society was all about. Give a
young person two years to learn about four thousand years of history?
Buck thought this ludicrous. In not even addressing that enormous
problem, a misguided system with its fanciful expectations was in effect
submitting the missionary to "a spiritual slavery degrading beyond
words."

Despite all this, Buck professed to feel more encouraged about the
future of Christianity and of missions that she had ever felt before,
during forty years of living in China. The report itself was the ground
for her optimism. "If Christians take this book seriously at all, I foresee
possibly the greatest missionary impetus we have known in centuries."
Like Hocking, she looked forward to an era in which missionaries would
be far fewer and better, and would be trained to meet very specific
personal and social needs.

Such needs, she was convinced, would seldom include being preached
at by Western Christians. "I am weary unto death with this incessant
preaching. . . . Let us cease our talk for a time and cut off our talkers,
and try to express our religion in terms of living service." To be sure,
she said, "the seed is the Word." But since when did the Word mean
simply talk? And what people had ever understood the meaning of the
Word until it was made flesh and dwelt among them? The new missionary would truly dwell among the people, doing not his work but
theirs. "He would . . . be a part of a native work, throwing his life into
it as it was and working through it as one of its members. Preaching
would be his last task."

Buck's Astor Hotel speech, several days after the article's appearance,
reiterated most of these ideas but also took a broader and deeper look
at the dilemma of individual missionaries. The latter, she said, share
many of the doubts about traditional doctrines that are widespread
among churchpeople at home, and are forced to ask, "Is there a case
for foreign missions?" If one no longer holds in quite the old way to
the divinity and indispensability of Christ; if one also does not detect
many churchgoers at home actually living by Christ's teachings; if one
cannot feel sure that the more admirable qualities of our civilization

depend upon Christianity; "then why should I ask anyone to give anything to a cause like that? Above all, why should I give myself?"[37]

Clearly these were questions Buck was asking herself. Her "resignation," divorce, and permanent return to the United States two years later might suggest that her own response to them would have been negative. Yet it was not. She believed the missionary movement must continue, though in a chastened and strengthened form. Even if it should be learned some day that Christ had existed only as "the essence of men's dreams of simplest and most beautiful goodness," she would be unwilling to relinquish those dreams or to cease sharing them with others. To assert the superiority of Christianity over other religions is not necessary; it is only necessary to recognize that we cannot live without Christ, and then to act on that recognition. She asserted that she herself could not live without Christ. Missionary work in some form was therefore obligatory: "What selfishness if I keep him for myself alone, or for my race!"

Pearl Buck later recalled that when she had finished the Astor speech "deadly silence fell upon the room" and she felt as if she were alone in the middle of the Sahara. Yet an ovation followed (in which the people at the head table did not join) and she rushed to her hotel "knowing I had done something devastating." Certainly she had made news. Among those ringing her phone immediately was an editor of *Harper's* magazine. *Harper's* in all probability displaced another article to insert hers in the next month's issue. Her publisher, John Day, responded to a continued demand by reproducing the speech as a pamphlet.

Robert E. Speer's analysis of *Re-Thinking Missions* also appeared in January of 1933. This was a polite rebuttal, acknowledging the need and usefulness of even the severest criticism; and praising the motives, hard work, and good sense of those who had carried out the appraisal. One-fifth of Speer's article (later a small book) responded appreciatively to twelve Hocking recommendations that the Presbyterian Board had specifically welcomed; and Speer acknowledged many other points of agreement that he had no space to discuss.[38] He praised the report's emphasis on self-support in the native churches, its call for ever-higher standards of quality, and its demand that Christianity be applied and not just proclaimed. But Speer also complained of serious flaws. The

[37]Buck, "Is There a Case?" Cf. Hutchison, "Can I Give My Life to Foreign Missions?" pp. 109–20; and Silver, "Pearl Buck."

[38]Robert E. Speer, *"Re-Thinking Missions" Examined,* pp. 47–49.

investigators, he said, had operated with too little exposure to missions or mission history; their judgments were hasty and unfair. In addition, a number of their schemes were simply impractical, while their insistence on promoting one missionary style and banning others showed a streak of intolerance. Finally—overarching and distorting everything else—their theology was faulty. In the end, the report for all its merits would have to be charged with seriously dividing the churches at home and abroad, and with having damaged the enterprise it intended to serve.[39]

In expanding on these points Speer frequently seemed quintessentially the politician—beholden to too many constituencies, too quickly falling back upon practical considerations in serious matters of principle. When he insisted that mission history was not a story of attempted "conquest," he seemed to be allaying the doubts of his liberal constituency. When he asserted, on the other hand, that Christianity must "make no compromises" with other religions but "anticipate the absolute triumph of Christ as acknowledged Lord and Saviour," he could be seen as resorting to traditional language that would reassure conservative supporters. His appeals to practicality, meanwhile—doubts about the churches' willingness to share control of mission funds, questions about trusting foreign peoples to define their own needs, warnings that donors would not underwrite the report's theology—could suggest to some critics that missions were in even more trouble, and were more deeply mired in Western paternalism, than Hocking and his colleagues had imagined.[40]

The question of Christian finality—whether Christianity is one version of divine truth or is ultimately the only version—was the do-or-die issue in this debate. It not only stood out in explicit discussion; it lurked behind most other, more limited, questions, enhancing their importance and also the emotion with which they were argued. So one is not surprised to find Speer, on that point, expressing himself with special force. Professor Hocking's definition of uniqueness as the capacity to make a singular and indispensable contribution to the world's salvation was simply not enough. Christ, Speer wrote, "is still *the* way, not *a* way, and there is no goal beyond Him or apart from Him, nor any search for truth that is to be found outside of Him, nor any final truth to be sought by a universal religious quest, except it be sought in Him."[41]

This was strong stuff. Though a fair enough representation of the kind of exclusivity that Christians, or indeed true believers in any faith,

[39]Ibid., pp. 49–60, 16–18, 36–38, 42, 23–35, 59–63.
[40]Ibid., pp. 17, 34, 26, 42, 36–38.
[41]Ibid., p. 31.

were likely to assert within their own conventicles, it did not represent what Christian spokesmen, Speer himself included, were likely to say to Gandhi or to a Buddhist leader. And it was stronger language, probably, than the former Princeton tackle would have used had he not feared a blind-side block from Professor Machen.

But in contesting the report's definition of "Christian uniqueness," Speer plainly had caught Hocking and his colleagues, who also were men and women "in the middle," trying to satisfy too many constituencies. On other points as well, he either held his own as chief spokesman for the mission establishment or successfully took the offense to expose the report's inner contradictions. One argument, however, the one over quality of personnel, almost inevitably ended in a draw. Both sides were trying to generalize about ten thousand scattered Americans. More important, the commission was invoking standards of excellence that, whatever their merits, were not the same as those being applied by mission boards. Some missionaries were bad by any standard, as Speer readily acknowledged. More were just not up to the demanding roles, as specialists and as ambassadors, that the Hocking commission had in mind for them.

Hocking of course had fully intended to champion standards of excellence and expertise so high that very few could measure up to them. But this entailed two further contradictions that Speer was quick to point out. One was that the report deplored "exclusivism and partisanship" but then showed a desire, remarkably like that of the fundamentalists, to limit support to one type of missionary and have the others sent home. The report had argued rather plainly that foreign missions should not continue if they must operate in the old way. In a similar exclusivist vein, it had professed to find "true evangelism" indispensable yet had repeatedly shown distaste for the traditional evangelism of verbal persuasion. Speer suggested that the commissioners would really like to be rid of all the preaching missionaries.[42]

The secretary's final blast against the report had to do with its divisive impact on the churches at home, in Europe, and in the mission fields of the non-Western world. Here a reader can sense the exasperation of an executive and conciliator who had devoted forty years to the complex mission enterprise and who found it hard to put up with meddling by less experienced hands. In that sense the point was routine and unexceptional. But Speer's alarmed reaction also provided a bulletin on European-American tensions of long standing.

[42]Ibid., pp. 23–25, 44–47.

European complaints against American activism had risen to a crescendo in the 1920s, particularly in debates surrounding the international Stockholm conference of 1925, which had considered Christianity's social role. At the Jerusalem meetings of the International Missionary Council three years later, the Europeans, as Speer reported, had continued to express "their fear of what seemed to them to be the domination of American missions by a humanistic activism and an intellectual and religious syncretism." After some conciliation and meeting of minds at Jerusalem, the Europeans had been aroused all over again between 1930 and 1932 by an activistic "survey report" on foreign work issued by the YMCA and YWCA. In the summer of 1932, at meetings in Herrnhut, Saxony, the Americans had barely averted a withdrawal of the Europeans from the International Missionary Council. The timing of the Hocking Report in juxtaposition to these events had been as infuriating as it was accidental.[43]

By the same token, Speer's ability to maintain his usual composure was remarkable. Undoubtedly, though, he was buoyed and emboldened at just this time by renewed support from fellow moderates in the Presbyterian Church and in Princeton Seminary. Forced as Speer himself had been to take sides on fundamentalism, these moderates had carried through the reorganization of the seminary that had caused Machen and the fundamentalists in 1929 to withdraw to their new seminary in Philadelphia. Princeton's reorganization, and the victory of the moderates, had been endorsed at every stage by the Presbyterian General Assembly. Speer had been honored, immediately thereafter, by the seminary's invitation to give the Stone Lectures. (He offered these, interestingly enough, on *The Finality of Jesus Christ.*)

Machen, though he had his new seminary and his own devoted constituency, appeared at this juncture to be fighting a rearguard action. His protest following the issuance of the Laymen's Report was framed as a criticism of Speer, rather than as an assault against a document Machen considered too outlandish to merit much attention. ("A public attack," he called it, "against the very heart of the Christian religion.") Yet such a criticism was extraordinarily difficult to mount. Toward Speer the younger man expressed an admiration that combined awe and despair. He complained that "hosts of Christian people throughout this country are convinced that whatever Dr. Speer favors must be absolutely sound." Poignantly, and perhaps with some thought of Moses' apologies to the Lord along similar lines, he stressed that he was no match for Speer. "He is one of the most eloquent men in all the world; and God

[43]Ibid., pp. 60–63.

has given me no eloquence at all. I have no skill in debate; I have no contagious fire of eloquence." Speer's personal force, which had helped sustain a diverse movement in bad times as well as good, had seldom been more warmly attested.[44]

Machen's praise for Speer, though transparently genuine, served the diplomatic purpose of balancing an otherwise heavy-handed and virulent indictment. Machen accused the Board of Foreign Missions of acting, in its tacit accommodations to liberalism, in such a way as to mislead the supporters of missions and betray the faith. It had employed unsound people and countenanced dangerous doctrine. Almost systematically, it seemed, the Board had managed to participate in the wrong conferences, recommend wicked books, sponsor liberal and radical missionaries, approve Christian converts who were not really Christian, and retain key officers who had signed antifundamentalist manifestoes. Speer and others had participated in the missionary conferences at Lausanne and Jerusalem. In doing so, Machen thought, they had associated themselves with relativistic views, with notions that the difference between Christianity and other religions is one between superior and inferior, or perfect and imperfect, "instead of being, as it truly is, the difference between the true and the false." In 1932, moreover, Speer had chaired a Committee on Cooperation in Latin America, which in turn had recommended publication in Spanish of books by Fosdick and other unsound authors. The Board was employing one secretary who had approved the "Auburn Affirmation," a plea for doctrinal tolerance signed by 1,274 Presbyterian ministers in the mid-twenties. Another official (John A. Mackay, later president of Princeton Seminary) had expressed admiration for the heterodox Moral Re-Armament movement, and had praised a dangerous Swiss theologian named Karl Barth.[45]

On top of all this, in Machen's view the Board had shown itself quite unrepentant. Accused of giving official backing to two Christian workers of unsuitably broad sympathies, Sherwood Eddy and Toyohiko Kagawa, Board members had responded defiantly that they wished the charge were true: "Many worse things could be done than aid Eddy in his virile student evangelism, and Kagawa in his sacrificial devotion to the doctrine that 'God is Love,' which the 'disciple whom Jesus loved' thought was orthodox." Finally, and worst of all, the Board had failed to dismiss the "outstanding advocate of modern unbelief," Pearl Buck; or to condemn sufficiently the book she had lauded, *Re-Thinking Mis-*

---

[44]Machen, *Modernism and the Board,* pp. 6, 57, 60.
[45]Ibid., pp. 48, 3, 18–26, 52–53. Loetscher, *Broadening Church,* p. 117.

sions. They had failed to disavow leading missionaries like A. K. Reis-chauer of Japan who were guilty of admiration for the Hocking Report.[46]

To liberals and also many evangelicals this "enemies list" sounded like an honor roll of contemporary Christian leadership. It still does, and the historian who even summarizes Machen's earnest argument could be accused of wasting everyone's time. What the attack reveals, however, is the extremity to which fundamentalism, at least for the time being, had been driven. Machen was, or had been, the giant among scholarly fundamentalists. That he had been reduced to endless chron-icles of guilt-by-association and heresy-by-omission suggested the need on the conservative side for new structures of thought.

These were already forming, stimulated especially by the Barthian and Niebuhrian orthodoxies that fundamentalists also considered un-sound. From Machen's point of view, however, the entire outlook was bleak. Expressing the prophet's despairing sense that "I alone am left," he acknowledged that it would do little good to dismiss the secretaries who were approving liberal missionaries; the cancer had spread too widely for that. One could not even correct matters by dismissing the Board that had appointed the secretaries. One would need to deal with the General Assembly that controlled the Board, and beyond that the churches that sent delegates to the General Assembly.[47] One would have to dismiss the Presbyterian Church.

This, in effect, was what Machen did as he retreated from one redoubt to another. Having renounced Princeton, he next repudiated the Board and established the Independent Board for Presbyterian Foreign Mis-sions, which many of his associates at Westminister Seminary could not support. In 1935, Machen's presbytery suspended him from the min-istry "until such time as he shall give satisfactory evidence of repentance." The General Assembly in the same year assured Speer of the Church's "full confidence . . . and heartfelt love." In 1936 Machen founded his own denomination, the Presbyterian Church of America.[48]

The decisiveness of this centrist victory did not mean, of course, that conservative boards and missionaries were becoming extinct. Yet the opinion reflected by Archibald Baker, that the main differences now lay between the Speer and the Hocking positions, was not simply a wishful attempt by academics and elitists to dispose of the religious right. The statistics did seem to support such a view. Even if one counted holiness, pentecostal, and adventist missionaries along with fundamentalists, the

---

[46]Machen, *Modernism and the Board,* pp. 49, 12–18, 6–12, 55–57.

[47]Ibid., p. 38.

[48]Loetscher, *Broadening Church,* pp. 150–55. In 1939, the Presbyterian Church of America became the Orthodox Presbyterian Church.

proportion of workers supported by conservative boards in the mid-thirties was only about 10 percent in Japan, 7 in Korea, 16 in India, and 26 In China.[49] Machen's Independent Board, though it had created a stir, claimed only a dozen missionaries, worldwide, in 1935. While many fundamentalists and conservatives worked for mainline boards (numbers would be hard to estimate) there were also moderates, if not liberals, among those sponsored by some conservative agencies.

Thus, though the supposedly self-destructing fundamentalists had not disappeared, and conservative mission ideals remained very much alive, the mainline boards retained a ten-to-one dominance throughout the Depression decade. With respect to this major segment of the movement, and the churches at home that supported it, the incursions of liberal thinking had been substantial. For them, at least, the era of "foreign missions" was ending; conceptions of "world mission" had taken hold; and even the notion of a world faith had gained some hearing.

[49]Parker, *Statistical Survey,* pp. 84–121.

CHAPTER 7

Familiar Debates in an Unfamiliar World

The world was writing the agenda . . . the right of the world to do this was largely taken for granted and Uppsala tried to read the writing, understand it and respond to it.

Norman Goodall, 1968

While the word "mission" is repeatedly used, its meaning is *nowhere* that of communicating the good news of Jesus Christ to unbelieving men in order that they might believe and live.

Donald McGavran, 1968

A historian in the early 1980s, concluding a study of missions and American foreign relations, set down a bit of conventional wisdom that was both accurate and wildly incorrect. He wrote that "the Protestant missionary movement began to wane in the 1920s and, despite periodic atavism and latter-day nostalgia, the decline continues to this day."[1] This was a reasonable interpretation of what had happened to the mission enterprise "as we had known it"—to missions as a formal expression and extension of American mainline Protestantism. If one looked beyond that ambit, however, the statement was far from true. The 14,000 career missionaries of the late 1920s did indeed shrink by several thousand during the early years of the Depression. But then the numbers soared: from 11,000 in 1935 to 35,000 in 1980.

The point, of course, is that 32,000 of the foot soldiers in this new missionary army represented agencies not related to the churches that had earlier dominated the mission enterprise. Since the emergent groups were usually, though not invariably, more conservative than the oldline or "ecumenical" ones, it was fair to speak of an almost exact reversal in the proportions of "ecumenicals" and "evangelicals" in missionary ranks. By 1982, an official of the Overseas Ministries Study Center could take it to be "well known that the North American conservative

[1]Reed, *Missionary Mind*, p. 197.

agencies . . . [account] for ten out of eleven North American Protestant career missionaries working overseas."[2]

To assume, given these striking figures for "missionary personnel," that the older liberal-to-moderate (say, Fleming-to-Speer) forms of practical missionary effort had become negligible would again be too superficial. By the 1980s there were some five hundred organizations—religious and secular, governmental and private—whose work overseas was primarily educational or humanitarian. These agencies—though most of them, like the Peace Corps, kept no statistics on the numbers of Methodists and Presbyterians they sent abroad—unquestionably were employing thousands of "ecumenical Protestants," along with many people of other religions or no religion, in work that was virtually indistinguishable from what the mission boards and YMCAs had been sponsoring in the 1930s.[3]

Equally worthy of notice were the differences in mission theory and operation among those 32,000 generally called "evangelical." To be sure, the larger and faster-growing portion of this contingent stood for religious and cultural ideologies that would have been too conservative for Mott and Speer; and some, because of their premillennial and other commitments, quite clearly would have embarrassed J. Gresham Machen. But a large, vocal, and highly organized segment of the evangelicals, with nearly 14,000 overseas personnel, by the 1980s had become liberal or radical (though still wary about those terms) at least in their "cultural" assumptions. More differences remained between these mainstream evangelicals and the ecumenicals, despite concessions on both sides, when it came to such explicitly religious issues as the balance between evangelism and social action. But by that time it was important, as it had been in the years around 1930, to recognize a three-way division. In historical terms, one could with due caution speak of the heirs of Fleming and Hocking, the heirs of Mott and Speer, and the heirs of Machen and militant fundamentalism.

THE ECUMENICAL-EVANGELICAL STANDOFF

In the period just after World War II, however, the situation was somewhat simpler. The strains and animosities of those decades made for a binary division: ecumenicals versus evangelicals. This was a time when the liberal and radical juices were running so strongly in churches of ecumenical outlook that more conservative mission interests felt driven

[2]Coote, "Uneven Growth," p. 118.

[3]Technical Assistance Information Clearing House, *U.S. Nonprofit Organizations in Development Assistance Abroad* (New York: TAICH, 1983).

into a bitter and seemingly unified opposition; or at least into a degree of collaboration that conservative evangelicals had seldom achieved in the past. In a conscious effort to counterbalance the "DOM" agencies (those affiliated with the Division of Ministries, National Council of Churches), and to provide shelter for groups dissatisfied with the liberal DOM, the evangelicals managed to draw the wagons around two organizations: the Interdenominational Foreign Mission Association (IFMA), founded by nondenominational "faith missions" in 1917; and the Evangelical Foreign Missions Association (EFMA), created in 1945 by dissenters from mainline ecumenism.

Between ecumenicals and evangelicals in this post-1945 period, mutual recriminations were common enough to remind one of the late unlamented twenties. Eugene Smith, New York executive secretary for the World Council of Churches, served as an observer at the 1966 evangelical mission conference at Wheaton College in Illinois. He came away appalled at the virulence and, as he thought, the severe distortions in the conservative outlook. "The distrust of the ecumenical movement within this group," Smith reported, "has to be experienced to be believed."[4] And liberal responses to this distrust were scarcely temperate. Smith himself remarked that evangelicals' readiness to "redeem" sinners without so much as challenging their racial bigotry had produced "nausea, wide-spread and justified." When the evangelicals, in their Wheaton Declaration, voiced unprecedented self-criticism on that and other points, a writer for the *Christian Century* complained that the conservatives had not flagellated themselves sufficiently. Having confessed to an undue isolation from the world, Maynard Shelly wrote, the evangelicals "might also have confessed their isolation from the church, from missions, and from themselves."[5]

The acuteness of feeling on both sides testified to the suddenness with which, for liberals in particular, the world and national landscapes had appeared to change. Though the breakup of colonialism, for example, had been gradual, the soaring political strength of regional and ideological groupings in the non-Western world had scarcely been anticipated. It was not surprising that the ecumenicals, awakened to such challenges, could be impatient with those who they thought were still asleep.

In other ways, though, the bitter feelings and impatience stemmed not from new ideas or external conditions but from the fact that a long-

[4]Quoted in Lotz, "Evangelization," p. 301.

[5]Eugene L. Smith, "Renewal in Mission," in McGavran, ed., *Debate,* p. 261; Maynard Shelly, "Evangelical Congress on Worldwide Mission: 'The World' Discovered," *Christian Century* 83 (May 25, 1966): 695.

ignored conservative opposition had found a voice and could no longer be ignored. Most of the liberal notions now excoriated by evangelicals had been advanced soon after 1920 within the ecumenical establishment in Europe and America, and then had visibly gained strength as the ecumenical movement itself, almost oblivious to the existence of serious conservative dissent, either outside the movement or on its fringes, had boomed along in the series of great international meetings from 1925 (the Stockholm assembly) to the 1960s. Ecumenical enthusiasm and self-confidence, which easily became a new triumphalism, not only gave offense to those who felt shunted aside; it also helped ensure that most of those nurtured in the ecumenical version of recent history would find dissent hard to deal with.

As is usual in such intramural debates, both sides laid claim to the same tradition. Yet there was also a tacit agreement—again, not un- naturally—to divide the historical territory. Evangelicals in general claimed the Edinburgh Conference, along with nearly everything and everyone—William Carey to John R. Mott—that had led up to it. Ecu- menicals saw themselves as the rightful heirs of Edinburgh (everyone claimed that) and of all that had been unfolding, at least in the limelight of international meetings and pronouncements, since that great mo- ment. In the newly emerging contention over tradition, Edinburgh stood as the apostolic age, in relation to which later events were seen either as fulfillment or as apostasy.

For liberals around mid-century, the importance of Edinburgh, apart from its sheer magnitude as an ecumenical event, had lain in its initiation of a shift from "foreign missions" thinking to "world mission" thinking. That the prophets of this change had come from the pitifully small band of non-Western delegates now seemed an embarrassment, yet this also had been a meaningful sign of the way world initiatives would shift. V. S. Azariah's assertion, at Edinburgh, that the relation of mis- sionary to Indian national was still one "between master and servant" had not jolted the great majority of delegates in 1910, but now it had become a bit of usable history. Similarly, one could discern in retrospect that Edinburgh had applied new urgency (and perhaps new sincerity) to those ideas of indigenization and Western devolution that had been promoted but little realized during the first century of the missionary movement. The Edinburgh subcommission that now seemed most im- portant had opened its report on "The Church in the Mission Field" by suggesting that the very phrasing of its title was erroneous: "The whole world is the mission field, and there is no Church that is not a Church in the mission field. Some Christian communities are younger and some are older, but that is all the difference." This committee, touching on an idea later made prominent by the Hocking Commission, had felt that even the older-younger distinction, with its connotations of a pupillary status for the latter, should be seen as "transitional and not permanent."[6]

At the Jerusalem Conference of 1928, where the younger churches were far better represented than before (52 out of 231), Mott himself had called for an end to the vocabulary of "sending" and "receiving" churches. At the same meeting, the emphasis upon social reform and interfaith collaboration provoked conservative alarm, in Europe and America, that was to be refueled by the Laymen's Report shortly afterward. The Dutch scholar Hendrik Kraemer, articulating that alarm, had then weighed in with eloquent arguments for the uniqueness of Christian revelation and the radical discontinuity between Christianity and other world religions; but most delegates at the next great conference, at Madras in 1938, rejected or bypassed the Kraemer position.[7] It was scarcely surprising that liberal ecumenism, in the years following the Laymen's Report, firmly assumed itself to be the wave of the future; and that conservative evangelicals, partly because of that liberal self-confidence, increasingly saw the mainline mission leadership as a dangerous and overweening establishment.

This is not to say that ecumenicals, in rejecting hard-line reactions like Kraemer's, were necessarily coming to accept the premises and conclusions of William Ernest Hocking. Before the 1960s, at least, nothing of that sort could justly be asserted. If there was a normative ecumenical stance, it was represented, among the Americans, by such thinkers as Kenneth Scott Latourette and Edmund Soper. This was a stance plainly affected both by the theological realism of American neo-orthodoxy and by the missiological realism of Fleming and Hocking. But with respect to Christian attitudes toward other religions, it was the position, essentially, of George A. Gordon and the liberals of 1900. Latourette in 1936 acknowledged that "the tragic events of the past three decades have made us aware, as our confident nineteenth-century predecessors were not, of the weaknesses in so-called Christian civilization. We are more appreciative than were most of them of the virtues of other cultures." Yet he came out, fundamentally, where Gordon had: preaching a Christ who comes to fulfill and supersede, not to collaborate. Soper, seven years later, reviewed thoroughly both the Hocking and the Kraemer positions and placed himself squarely in the middle: He wrote that the view represented by his *Philosophy of the Christian*

---

[6]Bassham, *Mission Theology,* pp. 17–18; World Missionary Conference, *Report of Commission II,* pp. 4–6.

[7]Bassham, *Mission Theology,* pp. 21–25.

World Mission "must be called that of uniqueness together with continuity."[8]

Liberals who were not content with the "definite maybe" of such a view, and who moved toward positions that brought upheaval and division in the 1960s, were most often to be found in the gatherings and literature of the international student movement. That movement, having in the 1920s decreased its use of the watchword and its preoccupation with personal evangelism, continued to serve as liberal pacesetter for the ecumenical leadership. This was evident in areas of social concern and in the repeatedly emphasized wish to meet other religions in "humble dialogue." It was even more striking in the zeal with which the student movement promoted a shift in conceptions of the church: from the traditional notion of a church that presses its own agenda within the secular order, to that of a Christianity and Christian mission whose objectives are virtually determined by that order and its terrible dilemmas.[9]

Ecumenicals, across this moderate-to-radical spectrum, had reasonable grounds for considering themselves the heirs of post-Edinburgh developments. They also, however, whatever their degree of liberality, inherited the ambiguities with which earlier reformers had struggled. Some ambiguities, like the ones relating to millennialism that inhered in the watchword, could simply be sloughed off; others, such as evangelism itself, could not be. Like their predecessors (in fact, like liberals at any time), ecumenicals at mid-century were attempting to honor and retain the latter sort of concept by means of redefinition. Unwilling, especially under fire, to admit any lack of concern for evangelism—whether in city work at home or in overseas missions—the most ingenious and socially active of the ecumenicals called upon the image of a Christ who lived among and for others. They redefined mission as Christian "presence" throughout the world; and conversion as, above all, the radical remaking of social structures. "Christian presence," as a paper of the World Student Christian Federation explained in 1964, "does not mean that we are simply there; it tries to describe the adventure of being there in the name of Christ, often anonymously, listening before we speak . . . involved in the fierce fight against all that dehumanizes, ready to act against demonic powers, to identify with the outcast, merciless in ridiculing modern idols and new myths."[10]

One might also evangelize in the more traditional sense, attempting to turn people from their religions or nonreligions to acceptance of

[8]Latourette, *Missions Tomorrow*, pp. 134, 136; Soper, *Philosophy of Mission*, p. 225, and pp. 212–31 passim; Forman, "Mission Theory," pp. 106–8.

[9]Bassham, *Mission Theology*, pp. 69, 45–48.

[10]Ibid., p. 72.

Christ as the only way to personal salvation. The 1964 Federation document allowed that "once we are there, we may witness fearlessly to Christ if the occasion is given." But it also called for a kind of diffidence that traditional thinking and martyrology had not in the least accepted; bluntly, "we may also have to be silent." With respect to Christian conviction, as presumably with respect to any other firmly held belief, attempts to persuade others might or might not be in order.

What was not in order, in the new dispensation, was any believer's presumption that he or she has been specially anointed to convey God's answers; or even, indeed, to phrase God's questions. One test of valid mission, therefore, was whether or not, in taking up the concerns of others, one also accepts "their issues and their structures." When that idea, and the idea of "Christian presence," were applied explicitly to dealings with other faiths, as they were in a publishing venture of the early 1960s, it was fair to conclude that sharply modified understandings of Christian finality had gained acceptability within a mission estab-lishment that had unanimously resisted such concessions in 1932. Ecu-menicals were appropriating a distinction that had been common in other religions and in democratic political thought, but not so common in the rhetoric of Christian missions: they were saying that even the deepest convictions about the finality of one's own faith do not nec-essarily call for, or depend upon, a willingness to "speak out" in direct or implicit detraction of other faiths.[11]

The resulting reformulations of mission ideas gained their most pro-vocative expression in the latter part of the 1960s. Those who planned the Uppsala (Sweden) Assembly of the World Council of Churches for 1968 directed attention to "the world," as distinct from "foreign fields," as the arena for missions. Starting from an assumption that the mission of the church is fundamentally the same everywhere—a point long since settled for most ecumenists—they pressed farther by proposing that the world and not the church must set the agenda for missions. Norman Goodall, editor of the assembly documents, thought the delegates "not only recognized that . . . the world was writing the agenda for the meet-ing; the right of the world to do this was largely taken for granted and Uppsala tried to read the writing, understand it and respond to it."

The sources of such an attitude were not theoretical—not some abstract theological decision about where Christians should be looking for divine leadings. The common perception, rather, was that this was one of those times in the history of the church when the world's agenda

[11]Ibid., pp. 72–73, 81, 110. The "Christian Presence Series" appeared between 1959 and 1966 under the imprint of SCM Press, London.

trivialized almost any other. As Goodall wrote, "the most obvious and widely acknowledged feature of the Assembly was its preoccupation—at times, almost, its obsession—with the revolutionary ferment of our time, with questions of social and international responsibility, of war and peace and economic justice, with the pressing, agonizing physical needs of men, with the plight of the underprivileged, the homeless and starving, and with the most radical contemporary rebellions against all 'establishments,' civil and religious."[12]

This did not mean (though critics were sure it did) that the world's agenda had been suggested by the headlines of that year, or even of the decade. Throughout the postwar period, while many ecumenicals had been rallying behind slogans derived from Barthian and neo-orthodox theology—"Let the Church be the Church"; "The Church Against the World"—many others had continued marching to the softer but steadily growing drumbeat of what would come to be called "secular theologies." Anyone puzzled by the apparently sudden emergence of those theologies in the 1960s, in mission thinking and elsewhere, must look beyond the sources usually mentioned, such as the writings of Dietrich Bonhoeffer. Reconsideration of the secular had become an obligatory day-to-day task for theologians, activists, and leaders of the student movement who found themselves questioning the pretensions of the Christian establishment in almost all its forms, from the local parish to the most comprehensive form of earthly establishment: "Christendom." To the innocent question the child reportedly asked as he looked up at the cathedral—"Is God in there?"—the response now was, "Yes, but not so much as we had thought."

A CHURCH FOR OTHERS: THE HOEKENDIJK PRESCRIPTION

The guru for this sort of thinking, from the 1940s until his death in 1975, was Hendrik Kraemer's compatriot and opposite number, Johannes Hoekendijk. Hoekendijk's career bridged theology and activism, Europe and America, student work and missions. Having been secretary of the Student Christian Movement in the Netherlands, and then of the Netherlands Missionary Council, he became, successively, secretary for evangelism of the World Council of Churches, professor of theology at Utrecht, and finally (1965–75) professor of missions at Union Seminary in New York. His writings, notably *Evangelism in France* (1950) and *The Church Inside Out* (1966) sought to perform a further bridging operation, his boldest so far. Hoekendijk wished to construct a bridge between the traditional terminology of "evangelism," on one side, and

---

[12]In Goodall, *Uppsala Report*, p. xvii.

on the other a conception of the church's role that to most contemporaries seemed decidedly untraditional if not heretical.

From Hoekendijk's point of view, however, it was the evangelical tradition that by biblical standards had been guilty of heresy, from the time of the post-Zinzendorf Moravians to the present. (This new attempt, out of European pietism, to locate the apostolic age a bit earlier than 1910 was itself an important contribution to ecumenical thinking, especially among Americans.) "Evangelism" as refracted and distorted through the assumptions of modern culture in the West, had been a response not to God's call for renewal but to some very human apprehensions about the church's loss of its central place in society. The word "evangelize," he complained, had too regularly been "a biblical camouflage of what should rightly be called the reconquest of ecclesiastical influence."

Pietists and evangelicals had presumably recognized, in the eighteenth century and after, that the entity called Christendom had not held together. In view of that reality, Hoekendijk suggested, they ought to have stationed themselves humbly in the world that God had, after all, created and within which he was working as much as ever. Instead they had condemned the world and summoned individuals to reject it in favor of a church that supposedly would regain its strength and reconquer what had been lost. Evangelism did reach out into the world, both at home and overseas, but wherever it went its impulse had been "to isolate individuals and assemble them in an island of the saved, floating on a flood of perdition."[13]

In foreign missions especially, Hoekendijk claimed, this rejection of the world and its structures had been fatally infected with illusions that Christendom was not dead after all, that Christendom lived on in the forms and institutions of Western civilization. One evangelical venture after another, finding it impossible to follow Zinzendorf's advice (to "gather individual souls" and "stay away from all social and cultural work"), had given in to the temptation to "prepare" mission grounds for evangelism by establishing something called Christian civilization, which in reality was Western civilization. The resulting missionary tradition, dominant from early Moravian times to those of David Livingstone and Gustav Warneck, was one that, Hoekendijk insisted, "cannot guide us any longer." Its principal spokesmen "all believe, in one way or another, in the possible realization of the *Corpus Christianum,* and our experiences with this kind of Christendom have been too bitter for us to follow them any farther."[14]

[13]Hoekendijk, "Call to Evangelism," p. 43.
[14]Ibid., p. 44.

Those portions of Hoekendijk's plea that seem especially to have influenced ecumenical thinking in the sixties portrayed a church that had been using the illusory idea of Christendom as a "protective shell." In that sort of thinking, he wrote,

> Christendom becomes a shock breaker. Influences from outside are filtered; condemnations hurled at the church are intercepted; in this well-protected area the church can have its own style of life, speak its own language, determine its own time. The direct intercourse between church and world has ceased. The wolves are kept far from the little fold. A splendid (very Christian-tinged) isolation is possible. Life may change, but the church in this field of Christendom remains a bastion of the past, related to outworn social structures.[15]

"Mission" in such a context had become what Heinrich Frick, and before him the theologian Martin Kähler, had complained of: "propaganda." True mission sows and plants without knowing what God will produce, but propaganda presumes to *trans*plant; that is, it reimplants a fully formed Lutheran or Catholic or Methodist grain. Worse, what it implants is a German Lutheranism, or a Dutch Catholicism, or a bourgeois Methodism. "The propagandist tries to make exact copies of himself. He attempts to make man in his image and after his likeness."[16]

Hoekendijk, enthusiastically planting his own seeds for the more constructive formulations of the 1960s, pled in 1950 for an evangelism that would express itself through flexible structures capable of direct action in society. The precedent from Christian tradition would be the diaconate; the model in the secular order was the laboratory. The Church must go where the need is, and once there it must operate experimentally. The diaconate as a structure for evangelism has traditionally operated with "no other relation to the outside world than that of a humble service." It envisions Christianity lived out at the level of the "little group, living in a concrete situation, and serving each other and their environment by reforming the structure of a segment of society."[17]

Hoekendijk over the next two decades never relented in his castigation of traditional church structures. At a student conference in 1960 on "The Life and Mission of the Church," he called the parish system immobile, self-centered, and introverted, "an invention of the Middle Ages . . . completely inadequate and unfit to give expression to the life of a community which believes that Christ and this modern world are

[15]Ibid., p. 45.
[16]Ibid., p. 48.
[17]Ibid., p. 54.

bound together." While approving the growth of a liturgical seriousness in the churches, he was appalled by a "sacro-mentality" that he thought bespoke an estrangement from the larger world in which life is really going on. "People do not dare to behave like normal human beings," he complained, and there is "a terrifying increase in clerical collars."

Hoekendijk's negative analyses served always as a background for affirming the "simple and rather primitive" missionary methods pioneered by the great founders of pietism and evangelicalism, but then abandoned. He proposed that "after two centuries of reflection, of thought, of experiment" Christians should now return to Wesley's and Zinzendorf's reliance on "creative minorities . . . small, flexible, mobile groups of dedicated members who live in commitment and *disponibilité*—availability."[18]

The reports of the working groups that prepared for the Uppsala meeting, and those that emanated from it, nearly all displayed the same forthright insistence on relocating the church within the structures presented by the secular order. At some points, challenging the most hallowed assumptions of traditional evangelism, these reports raised serious questions about bringing converts into the existing churches. Hoekendijk in 1966 had phrased the same doubt with characteristic acerbity, calling it an "illegitimate scandal" that people should be induced "to adapt themselves to the various patterns of the present chaos of denominations." The European and American working groups, in both of which the Dutch theologian was involved, agreed with him to the extent of denouncing denominational differences as dysfunctional and irrelevant in the modern world; and denouncing proselytism as a one-sided conception of conversion. It was one-sided because the more important kind of "conversion" arises "on the corporate level in the form of social change," and also because the church must go out to the world, not simply wait and invite outsiders in. The European working group asked that the church henceforth be organized into "go-structures." The term, more suggestive of American activism than of the pietist traditions so often invoked, conveyed by its very awkwardness the zeal for rejecting all static, finished conceptions of a merely "waiting church."[19]

CONTESTING RIGHTS TO THE HERITAGE

The advance reports for the Uppsala assembly, published in 1967 as *The Church for Others and the Church for the World,* marked a high point

---

[18]Hoekendijk, "Christ and the World," pp. 81–82, 79.
[19]Hoekendijk, "Notes," pp. 46–47; World Council, *Church for Others,* pp. 35, 75–76, 18–19.

Combating the "terrifying increase in clerical collars." Johannes Hoekendijk
in 1970. Courtesy of Letty Russell.

of antitraditional thinking among ecumenicals, and by the same token
served as an unusual provocation to stronger evangelical opposition.
After protests about these documents from conservatives (many of whom
soon withdrew from World Council affiliation), the dissident "church
growth" line of thinking gained some recognition at the assembly. The
final Uppsala Report referred to the church as the structure within
which "the signs of the new humanity are experienced," and conceded
that Christians find their true life in its life of word, sacrament, and
fellowship. "The growth of the Church . . . both inward and outward,"
was acknowledged to be of urgent importance. But such statements
might have been printed in a separate section labeled "Minority Opinion." The Uppsala Report, as David Hubbard of Fuller Seminary com-

plained, was a "hotchpotch" of the views of people whose disagreements remained fundamental. It was, as he said, a patchwork quilt whose seams were visible.[20]

Some of the vital interests of the conservatives never so much as made it into the quilt. Among these was the traditional missionary emphasis on personal evangelism. Just before the assembly met, Professor Donald McGavran of Fuller Seminary had asked in print, "Will Uppsala Betray the Two Billion?" From his point of view the Uppsala working groups had not only maligned the church; they seemed utterly to have forgotten about the multitudes who "live and die in a famine of the Word of God more terrible by far than the sporadic physical famines which occur in unfortunate lands." In view of this alleged neglect, he found the ecumenicals' use of terms like "evangelism" and "mission" infuriating if not downright dishonest. It seemed to conservatives that once again, as so often in the past, modernists with shaky Christian credentials had stolen the evangelicals' rhetorical clothing and were trying desperately to wear it. McGavran observed that while the word "mission" was repeatedly used, "its meaning is *nowhere* that of communicating the good news of Jesus Christ to unbelieving men in order that they might believe and live." The liberals, he complained, were appropriating words that had had settled meanings for at least 250 years, and without warning or explanation were forcing these words to bear radically different freight. Though McGavran said his readers would have to judge whether or not this constituted a "pious fraud," he did not leave them without guidance in making such judgments. Nor was he to be satisfied by the concessions embodied in the final assembly document. Uppsala *had* betrayed the Two Billion.[21]

If liberals could be accused of stealing some parts of the tradition—carrying them off to their theological tailor-shops to be altered beyond recognition—they might be charged with abandoning other parts entirely. Though plainly intent on claiming biblical authorizations, and those of the Reformation, the radical Reformation, and the Social Gospel, ecumenicals on the whole left the nineteenth-century missionary movement for someone else to appropriate. In their historical recollections the figures of William Carey and Adoniram Judson, while not despised, were also not much emphasized. A. J. Gordon and A. T. Pierson were not in the pantheon at all; and memories even of Mott and Speer had become a bit hazy.

Evangelicals, it turned out, were ready to fight for the contested traditions and also, with some stridency, to take up those the ecumen-

---

[20]Goodall, *Uppsala,* p. 29; Bassham, *Mission Theology,* p. 83.
[21]McGavran, *Debate,* pp. 233, 235, 237.

"Uppsala has betrayed the two billion." Donald McGavran in the 1960s.
Courtesy of Fuller Theological Seminary.

icals had abandoned. "Seeking an identity," as Rodger Bassham puts it,
through an emphasis on explicit contrasts between their positions and
those of the liberal churches, Carl F. H. Henry and other evangelicals
sought in the sixties both to vindicate their definitions of mission and
evangelism and to rehabilitate the language of "proselytism" and the
watchword.

Throughout the early sixties, evangelicals showed determination to rebuild lost connections with the Edinburgh Conference, its rhetoric, and its ebullient spirit. A Chicago meeting in 1960 sought to revive the watchword, which was then featured in the ringing peroration of the "Wheaton Declaration" six years later. While conscious of the negative connotations that had come to be attached to the term "proselytism" (though perhaps less aware, at this time, of the deep aversion to it in Third World countries), the Wheaton delegates sought also to refurbish that conception. The intent was not to fuel sectarian rivalries or to condone ancient forms of coercion; such methods and aims were soundly renounced. Nor were evangelicals bent on reviving elements of Western paternalism. The usual stance, in fact, was somewhat at odds with such purposes; one was called upon, after all, to proselytize for the faith not merely in the Third World but among Catholics in Europe or Latin America, and among the heathen in Darkest America.[22]

That evangelicals went about seeking converts in the supposedly Christian West as much as in the Third World was not a sufficient answer for ecumenicals; for many of the latter, it simply raised other troublesome questions. But it is worth noting how much of the evangelical surge in missions *was* a matter of missionizing the nominally Christian societies of Europe, Latin America, and the Caribbean. In the mid-seventies, American Protestant bodies reported 400 missionaries in Germany, nearly 400 in France, 2,000 in Brazil, 750 in Colombia, 200 in Spain, over 100 in the United Kingdom. Forty-three percent of North American Protestant overseas personnel were serving either in Latin America (36 percent) or in Europe. While some of these were attached to ecumenical agencies such as Church World Service, more were evangelists and workers for conservative groups. The northern Presbyterians in 1975 were sending only about one-sixth of their missionary personnel to these regions; but for the Southern Baptists the proportion was two-fifths. A number of conservative agencies listed more missionaries in Europe than in Asia and Africa combined. Such deployments could suggest the oft-criticized "American" insistence on converting other Christians to American Christianity—or to some new and very special revelation arising therein. More ominously, it could and occasionally did mean strident anti-Catholicism. But it could also lend credence to the evangelicals' claim that they, as much as the liberals, were thinking in "world mission" terms.[23]

In at least one further respect, however, evangelicals were enthusiastically looking backward, not so much to Edinburgh as to the pre-

[22]Bassham, *Mission Theology*, pp. 178, 210–30; Lindsell, *Wheaton*, p. 237.
[23]*Mission Handbook* for 1973 and 1976; Lindsell, *Wheaton*, pp.111–23, 225–26.

Edinburgh era: they sought to reinstate the Great Commission as a leading, or even as an entirely sufficient, justification for missions. Speer and others in the emergent leadership of 1910 had deplored reliance on the Great Commission, which they saw as a particularly overused and simplistic form of biblical literalism; its focus on imperatives internal to Christianity had, moreover, masked too much aggression or insensitivity in the past. But the Wheaton document of 1966, and those of the American-organized evangelistic conference in Berlin the same year, referred frequently to the Great Commission, and occasionally seemed even to offer a warrant for the old heedlessness and *ex parte* argumentation. John R. W. Stott of London opened the first of three addresses on the Great Commission by asserting that "in the last resort, we engage in evangelism today not because we want to or because we choose to or because we like to, but because we have been told to. The Church is under orders. The risen Lord has commanded us to 'go,' to 'preach,' to 'make disciples'; and that is enough for us."[24]

Billy Graham, in a keynote address at the Berlin conference, used much the same language: "If there were no other reason . . . the command of Christ would be enough! It is not optional—we have no choice." Reiterating favorite objections to liberalism and ecumenism, he deplored the "syncretistic" search for points of unity with other world religions, and the "universalist" persuasion that Christ is somehow present in all peoples and societies, so that all will be saved. He called attention, beyond that, to the liberals' dangerous move from a spiritual to a secular conception of the church's task, from the statement that "the Church has a mission" to a notion that "the Church is mission." Evangelism had been thoroughly subsumed, he said, into a primary concern for education, social reform, and, above all, "evangelization of the structures of society."[25]

The appeals for a new conservative solidarity were strident, the appeal to the past quite prominent, the case against the ecumenicals often unfairly drawn. Rodger Bassham, despite considerable sympathy for the new evangelicals, justifiably views this particular period in their development as triumphalist, polemical, and lacking in either maturity or a penitent spirit. Yet even at this early and militant stage the new evangelicalism was not simply a copy or continuation of the old. The watchword and the Great Commission had been reasserted, and with them the potential for renewed tribalism and condescension; but the old attendant rhetoric, involving active depreciation of other faiths and revelations, was notably absent. The primacy of personal over social evangelism had been trumpeted; but it was also clear that many evan-

[24]In Henry and Mooneyham, *Berlin,* 1:37.
[25]Ibid., pp. 24–26.

gelicals were seeking new and more serious modes of accommodation between that firm commitment and liberal-to-radical social programs. The nineteenth century had been reinstated; but this included the nineteenth century of Rufus Anderson and Henry Venn, and the zeal of those leaders for indigenization.[26]

To be sure, all such attempted adjustments could pale against the backdrop of alarmed vehemence concerning ecumenical Christianity. They could also seem mere gestures toward modern social problems, or self-serving attempts to burnish the image of evangelicalism's past performance. Billy Graham, at Berlin, ran through the obligatory references to great social reformers whose work had been initiated by conversion to Christ: Wilberforce, Booth, George Williams of the YMCA, Keir Hardie of the British Labour party. So many speakers at that conference did the same that a black evangelist finally retorted that whatever the situation may have been in nineteenth-century England, evangelicalism in his own lifetime had meant passivity in social matters, a tacit support of the status quo, and evasive pleas to the effect that one cannot change human hearts by legislation. "Frankly I am a bit weary," said William Pannell, "of hearing that Lord Shaftesbury and Wilberforce effected social change in England." Legislation, another black delegate added, "did for me and my people in America what empty and highpowered evangelical preaching never did for 100 years."[27]

It was also true, however, that Carl Henry and others had been directing a similar appeal, along with broad admonitions to self-criticism and repentance, toward fellow evangelicals for at least a decade. Much more was to come in response to those appeals, but some early results were visible in the Wheaton and Berlin pronouncements.

REALIGNMENTS AND SECOND THOUGHTS

The years around 1968 saw not merely disagreement and tension between ecumenicals and evangelicals but actual leave-takings and institutional divergence. The failure of evangelicals to influence the final Uppsala Report as much as they wished, and then a similar disappointment with the Bangkok deliberations of the World Council in 1973,[28] helped ensure that the conservatives would continue to stage their own international meetings, and that recriminations would continue. Ecumenical-evangelical relationships were affected, however, by another

[26]Bassham, pp. 244–45; Lindsell, *Wheaton*, pp. 213–14.
[27]Henry, *Berlin*, 1: 28; Bassham, *Mission Theology*, pp.⁵225–28; Lindsell, *Wheaton*, pp. 193–203.
[28]Bassham, *Mission Theology*, p. 96.

clear and highly significant pattern: a growing differentiation between "affiliated" and "unaffiliated" evangelicals. (The former were the evangelicals united in the IFMA or EFMA. The latter belonged to neither, though some of them, among the pentecostals for example, were "affiliated" in their own sizeable umbrella organizations.)

Between 1960 and 1980, missionary personnel associated with the ecumenical churches and agencies declined (in round numbers) from 10,300 to 3,100. About 60 percent of this decline occurred not because the Presbyterians or Methodists were sponsoring fewer missionaries, but because missionary organizations that found themselves too conservative for the ecumenical camp had, over those two decades, dropped their affiliation with the World and National Councils. Similarly, the gain for "affiliated" evangelicals (from 10,800 to 13,700) came about largely because of the transfer of missionary agencies.

That the net growth in the best-organized, most articulate sector of evangelicalism was so modest—a gain of only 3,000 while ecumenical missions were declining by 7,000—may well occasion surprise. It is accounted for by the fact that the affiliated-evangelical sector, like the ecumenical, was losing agencies. It was losing them to that "unaffiliated" world of missionary societies that had come to constitute the real growth sector for Protestant overseas activity. The numbers in this third category swelled from 7,000 missionaries in 1960 to 17,000 in 1980. The organizations that commissioned this rapidly increasing number of workers were generally extremely small—with important exceptions such as the Southern Baptists and the Wycliffe Bible Translators.[29]

The massive rightward movement in the missionary enterprise might have been seen as merely a footnote to the growth and aggressiveness of American conservative religion, except that each of the three groupings could be correlated with a fairly distinctive attitude toward overseas missions. Such correlations were only approximate, since many who called themselves evangelicals continued to operate within ecumenical bodies, and some organizations avoided "affiliation" for reasons other than extreme conservatism. But in general it was possible, as Edward Dayton wrote, to characterize the ecumenicals as withdrawing from mission activities, the affiliated evangelicals as "accommodating" to new structures involving non-Western initiative and leadership, and the non-affiliated societies as still "operating independently" in relation to the native churches—or at any rate as not operating under their direction. To that extent, the unaffiliated evangelicals were to be noticed as those

---

[29]Coote, "Uneven Growth"; *Mission Handbook* for 1979.

who, above all others, were carrying the torch for traditional missionary methods.[30]

It is not necessary, in making such distinctions, to propose that all nonaffiliated agencies and their workers, however conservative or fundamentalist, were perpetuating an older cultural imperialism. As always, some of the most conservative missionaries outdid all others in "going native" and blending with the local culture. The point is rather that moderate evangelicals, in seeking generally to unify conservative missions, had become increasingly united in their zeal for indigenization. This is what Edward Dayton meant by their "accommodation"; not theological adjustment, or a diffidence about evangelism, but rather the Westerner's (or, in Europe and Latin America, the North American's) willingness to work in subordinate status.

It was fair to say, however, that where rapprochement occurred, after 1968, between ecumenicals and the affiliated evangelicals, the adjustments did involve changes in theology, and did affect the balances between evangelism and social action. Some evangelicals may have imagined that the "cultural" adjustment signified by zealous indigenization would not affect theology or mission priorities. But genuine moves toward indigenization (as distinguished from the show-window recognition of nationals so common in the past) tended to operate as an entering wedge for changes in priorities. As the evangelical contingent, like its liberal counterpart, held its meetings increasingly in non-Western locations, and sometimes drew more Third World delegates than the ecumenicals did, Western evangelicals heard pleas for change more compelling than those they had been hearing and resisting from their Western or their white American colleagues. At Berlin, American blacks had offered the most stinging challenges. At the Lausanne meeting of evangelicals in 1974, the strident voices against a church-growth or convert-counting emphasis were those of Latin Americans. René Padilla, for example, told evangelicals that "there is no place for statistics on 'how many souls die without Christ every minute,' if they do not take into account how many of those who die, die victims of hunger." And Samuel Escobar warned that spirituality without involvement in social, economic, and political concerns is mere religiosity.[31]

---

[30]Dayton, "Current Trends," p. 3. David Stoll, in a meticulous and balanced appraisal of this third force (*Fishers of Men*) writes as follows of a major Wycliffe project: "While . . . organized as an intrigue, it is clearly an evangelical intrigue with its own jealously guarded objectives. The deeper problem is the group's naiveté, its capacity for looking the other way and serving dictatorships, if that will serve the Great Commission" (p. 86).

[31]Bassham, *Mission Theology,* p. 237.

Evangelicals of Europe and North America were also affected, however, by accelerating appeals from within their own ranks, particularly from younger adherents involved in the antiwar and civil rights movements. A 5,000-delegate Congress on Evangelism at Minneapolis in 1969 had focused on social issues and had found itself (to the distress of many participants, to be sure) defining evangelism to include a social witness. The organization named Evangelicals for Social Action, the magazine called *Sojourners,* and a "Chicago Declaration" of 1973 all represented the emergence and growing influence of, in Bassham's words, "a small but disciplined and articulate [radical] group." As part of the same process, evangelicals developed a less alarmed and more discriminating reaction even to fairly extreme ecumenical formulations such as *Church for Others.*

Thus John R. W. Stott was not alone in acknowledging, by the time of the evangelicals' Lausanne meeting in 1974, that views like his own had been altered in the preceding eight years. The ecumenicals' insistence that "the Church is mission" he still considered an overstatement. But he clearly spoke for many others in accepting the shift in focus signified by terms like *missio dei* (i.e., this is not the church's mission, fundamentally, but God's), and by admonitions to turn the church "inside out" in response to the world's agenda. As Stott now saw the matter, Christ commanded believers to follow his living example, and this example was one of service in and to the world. The divine commission, therefore, "must be understood to include social as well as evangelistic responsibility, unless we are to be guilty of distorting the words of Jesus."[32]

The outcome, for such evangelicals, was a conception of the relations between activism and personal evangelism much like the one R. C. Hutchison had proposed in 1927, and at that date had found too advanced for the mainline mission boards. Stott now conceived social action and evangelism to be partners. "As partners the two belong to each other and yet are independent of each other. Each stands on its own feet in its own right alongside the other. Neither is a means to the other, or even a manifestation of the other. For each is an end in itself."[33]

In a number of other respects, too, the organized evangelicals by the mid-seventies were sounding less like strident opponents of the ecumenicals, more like a centrist or mediating party. The more advanced evangelical contingents, not content with an emphasis on indigenization

[32]Ibid., pp. 269–74; Douglas, *Lausanne,* p. 68; Stott, *Christian Mission,* p. 23.
[33]Stott, *Christian Mission,* p. 27.

(or "contextualization," as it was coming to be called), even seconded one of the more extreme ecumenical proposals: that a "moratorium" on Western missionary activity might be called for in some parts of the world.

Evangelical discussions, moreover, while still on guard against such traditional menaces as syncretism and universalism, now embraced the possibility of sympathetic "dialogue" with persons of other faiths: and less was said about a prescriptive and sufficient Great Commission as the warrant for missions. In all these areas, an attitude of penitence—not merely on behalf of conservative evangelicalism, but more generally with respect to Christian action in the world—had modified the triumphalism of a decade earlier.[34]

With these mainstream evangelicals conceding a number of important points to the ecumenicals, and with the latter making good-faith efforts to incorporate more personal evangelism in their programs, talk of a "new consensus" in the late 1970s was more than a benign exercise in wishful thinking. The ecumenicals and the "organized evangelicals" had indeed developed large areas of agreement, and were well justified in expecting to stress them and build upon them.

Those who wrote hopefully about a new consensus felt constrained, nonetheless, to add a question mark,[35] and for at least two reasons. One was that, for every evangelical who had joined Dr. Stott in positions representing a working harmony with ecumenicals, there were perhaps two others, on the right flank of the mission enterprise, who were quite ready to take their place in promoting more traditional missionary attitudes. The old adage seemed to apply: *Plus ça change, plus c'est le même chose.* Foreigners in particular—European or Latin American as well as those outside the West—were likely to think that little had changed. As a matter of everyday observation, they found the spectrum of "American missionary" attitudes and practices indistinguishable from what they or their parents had known earlier in the century.[36]

The new consensus was limited, secondly, by the degree to which the old cleavage between evangelizing and civilizing missions—in its more modern form: evangelism versus collaborative social amelioration—lived on behind even the sincerest protestations about common objectives. One revealing testimony to this continuing disagreement

[34]Bassham, *Mission Theology,* pp. 141–42, 235, 240, 332–33, 244.

[35]Ibid., chap. 8.

[36]The last statement arises from my own discussions with audiences of all kinds, and conversations with religious leaders and media persons, in perhaps fifteen countries from Sweden to the South Pacific. The statement, if anything, understates the extent to which "traditional" forms of proselytizing, cultural as well as religious, are thought to be in operation.

was provided by an eminent British ecumenist and former missionary who wrote out his thought for an American publication in 1982. Lesslie Newbigin, a Presbyterian who had been one of the first bishops of the ecumenical Church of South India, and who later had taught at a missionary training center in England, called it "strange and sad" that the so-called ecumenical and evangelical positions were still frequently seen as mutually exclusive; and he attempted yet another assault on that stubborn dichotomy. But his own stand, while conciliatory in intention, was "ecumenical" in a most progressive sense, and thus offered an accurate taxonomy of the enduring problem.

Like many of the conservatives, Newbigin believed the dichotomy should not exist. But, like them, he urged the reunion of these concepts in terms that many of his opposite numbers could not accept. Behind the insistence that evangelism must be given priority over compassionate action, Newbigin argued, lies "a real misreading of the New Testament." Giving yet one more lick to the misuses of the Great Commission, he wrote that these words of Christ are "nowhere cited in the New Testament as the basis of missions. At no point does any of the apostolic writers seek to lay upon the conscience of his readers the duty to evangelize as an act of obedience to the Lord." The so-called Great Commission is rather a "shout of joy" announcing that death is overthrown and that God the Holy Spirit will gather the nations together by his own mighty power.[37]

Calling upon historical experience as well as biblical warrants (or their absence), Newbigin proposed that "many of the greatest triumphs of the gospel have been the results of informal contacts of which we know nothing." Though our vision in these matters may have been clouded, up to now, by the fact that "most of the histories have been written by the missionaries," he thought it probable that "a whole history of the 'expansion of Christianity' could be written with very few missionary names in it!" Throughout that history, whoever writes it, one sees clearly that attempts to separate "Word" and "act" have been fatal. Whenever evangelists have invited men and women to take refuge in the name of Jesus without at the same time standing witness against the kingdom of evil, the church has then stood not as a sign of God's kingdom but as a countersign: "the more successful it is in increasing its membership, the more it becomes a sign against the sovereignty of God. . . . We have, surely, the authority of the Lord himself for saying that church growth that does not bear fruit is only providing fuel for Hell."

[37]Newbigin, "Cross-Currents," pp. 154–55.

Newbigin acknowledged that the word of evangelism need not always have an overt deed attached to it. Yet he warned those who claimed to be holding the line against broad social definitions of mission that they, like the religious authorities who opposed certain activities of the earliest Christians, might find that they were opposing God himself. "To offer, in effect, 'cheap grace' to individuals by peeling off all the social and political implications of the gospel is to denature the gospel." Where missions are dispatched, their primary aim should not be conversion, which is God's doing, but rather the bringing into existence of "a Christian presence in a milieu where previously there was no such presence or where such presence was ineffective."

In establishing that presence, especially in juxtaposition to other religions, the Christian should be using the language neither of condemnation, nor of invidious comparison, nor of intended conquest. Newbigin's reasons for saying this were not those of a universalist—that no-one will be lost whatever his or her religion—but more nearly those of Roger Williams. "Christians," he wrote, "are called to be witnesses, and they may never speak as though they were the judge." They must be wary, on biblical grounds, of assuming any judgmental qualifications. "The grave and terrible warnings that the New Testament contains about the possibility of eternal loss are directed to those who are confident they are among the saved."

This was an ancient and perennial plea for Christian humility in the face of God's transcendence. In a more topical mode, Newbigin worried about the persisting vocabulary of Christian world conquest and world conversion. He saw the church not only retaining the inappropriate language of the Crusades (a crusading spirit having been "foreign to Jesus"), but falling in with the dubious crusades of the secular authorities. He recalled that when Indian tanks rolled into Bangladesh, his own Church of South India had discovered a previously unproclaimed enthusiasm for sending missionaries to Bangladesh, whether the existing Christian churches in that country wanted them or not. In the continuing calls for world evangelization one could still, in 1982, detect "the strong stench of imperialism."

Newbigin was not necessarily hurling these rebukes against all evangelical mission and Bible societies—even those on the far right—and he was presumably aware that prominent evangelicals such as Stott, his compatriot, already concurred with much that he was saying. Nor was he ready, one assumes, to exculpate all liberals. Yet the gravamen of his charge lay against a changing evangelicalism that still, in his view, had not sufficiently outgrown the nineteenth century.

The immediate "invited response" to Newbigin's article came from among the affiliated or mainstream evangelicals. Both Paul B. Schrotenboer, of the Reformed Evangelical Synod, and C. Peter Wagner, of Fuller Theological Seminary, took issue with Newbigin on the matter that he had made central: whether traditional evangelism is to be accorded a primary or merely a co-equal status. And both critics indicated that, given more space, they would oppose him on the connected questions of Christianity's unique salvific function and the Christian's duty to proclaim it. Schrotenboer found himself coming down "on the opposite side" from Newbigin on that issue, and Wagner went farther by differing with Newbigin on the nature and goals of evangelism itself. Mounting an argument that appeared even to go beyond the position so laboriously staked out by the generation of John R. Mott, Wagner argued that the task of evangelism (and presumably the meaning of its intended outcome: evangelization) is not proclamation but conversion. Proclamation, witness, "making known the good news" are all necessary but not sufficient. "The goal of evangelism is the conversion of sinners, saving souls, making disciples. When people turn from darkness to light, from the power of Satan to the power of God, evangelism has occurred."

Both respondents were plainly uncomfortable, as well, with Newbigin's notion that Christians should witness to their faith without presuming to judge or condemn the faith of others. While Schrotenboer was not so sure that affirming the lost status of those unreached by the Gospel should be called "an act of judging," he nonetheless was "not impressed by Bishop Newbigin's comments that we are not judges." He cited the second chapter of First Corinthians as authority for insisting that "the person who is spiritual judges all things."[38]

Despite such disagreement, the parties to this debate professed to find a good deal of common ground, and one would not want to dismiss their professions as mere cordiality. Yet as Bishop Newbigin, given *his* chance to respond, retraced the theological arguments for a certain restraint in missions (insisting that evangelism is human work while conversion is God's work; warning that the assertion of judgmental rights for "the spiritual" begs an important question), a reader might easily wonder whether a new consensus had formed even at the moderate center.

The notion of a new consensus was plausible if one were using it to contrast the agreements effected by 1985 with the hostility evangelicals and ecumenicals had felt toward each other in 1965. But it was more helpful, perhaps, to speak of a "new mainstream" that embodied as much consensus, and as much dissensus, as that of about 1920.

[38]Schrotenboer and Wagner, "Response," pp. 152–54.

This new mainstream, if one did speak in those terms, was not a replication of the old one, not simply "more of the same thing"; it embodied a marked leftward shift in cultural and religious assumptions. But what of the right wing, the large and proliferating force of "un-affiliated evangelicals"? It was this phenomenon on the right, after all, that provoked the thought that nothing had really changed, in the total mise-en-scène, except the names and positioning of the players.

The idea of a permanent or persisting "third force" was of course profoundly disturbing for the mainstream interests, evangelical as much as ecumenical. Yet for some of them it was also gratifying that long-avoided truths about the persistence of sectarian religion were finally sinking in. A few sociologists and other pundits might in fact have said, "We tried to tell you!" Clearly some of them, at least since the 1950s, had tried in both empirical and theoretical terms to suggest that religious impulses—quite definitely including sectarian ones—do not disappear, or even necessarily decline, in the process of secularization. Such impulses "relocate," whereupon we proclaim their disappearance because we are looking for them in the wrong places; or, as in the case of fundamentalism, because we manage to wish them away. We also, as the sociologist Rodney Stark pointed out, theorize them away, for example in our ignoring, ex hypothesi, that secularization provokes the formation of new sects even as it promotes the disappearance or churchly assimilation of older ones.[39]

None of that, of course, could answer to the fears and extreme annoyance of those who deplored religious aggressiveness, whether the aggressive soul-saver was to be observed handing out his tracts abroad, or on suburban doorsteps at home, or in the airports in between. But that very quality of ubiquity, as I have tried to suggest, was important when one attempted, in the 1980s, to understand the apparent surge of conservative mission activity. With so much that was called "foreign missions" directed to Catholic or other Christian societies, the practices in question could be viewed as deriving less from the foreign missionary movement of the past than from the domestic heritage of revivalism and street-corner evangelism. More to the point, the conclusion one might hastily come to, that extreme conservatives now outnumbered everyone else in the traditional foreign mission areas, in general was not valid.

If for such reasons it remained uncertain just how much one should be impressed by sectarian mission activity, there could be little doubt

---

[39]Rodney Stark, "Church and Sect," in Phillip Hammond, ed., *The Sacred in a Secular Age* (Berkeley: University of California Press, 1985), pp. 139–49.

that the old ideological debates would continue, and often in forms reminiscent of the nineteenth century. And if evangelical-ecumenical dialogue now occupied a ground different from that of a half-century earlier, the wider and more acerbic arguments frequently did not.

Insofar as ecumenicals were obliged to engage in the latter kind of "argument"—to deal with perceived challenges from extreme conservatives—the response of cooler heads among them was not some attempted extirpation of sectarian activity but the determination to strengthen a different kind of Christian witness.[40] In doing so they could be heartened, or at least should have been, by another example of the phenomenon of "relocation." As I have suggested earlier, American liberal Protestants were spread over the world, in religious and other agencies of service and education, in incomparably greater numbers than they had been at the high-point of the foreign mission enterprise.

Admittedly there was a difference, one bearing some heavy emotional freight, between being a Christian missionary and being a teacher or social worker who was also a practicing Christian. Yet the theological and traditional grounds for not pressing such a distinction were substantial. And, speaking more practically, for these churches there appeared to be little choice. They would effect their witness, and even their conversions, through these new-style missionaries, lay and clerical, or else would witness scarcely at all.

Still another form of relocation needed to be considered before the old-line churches made too much of their own seeming withdrawal from the mission enterprise. Wherever "indigenization" had at long last occurred, the work once carried on by Western missionaries was now situated in national churches and agencies. One found relatively few official American Presbyterian workers in Korea because evangelism and other functions were being managed by Korean Presbyterians, few Methodist missionaries in Fiji because postcolonial Methodism had become largely a Fijian operation. The Moravians, they of the great missionary heritage, by the 1980s were sponsoring only two American workers in Tanzania; but before exclaiming about that fact one needed to consider where the Moravian church, internationally, was now "located." The largest clustering of Moravians was no longer in America or Germany. It was in Tanzania.

---

[40]This was evident, for example, in the work and writings of the Uruguayan Methodist leader Emilio Castro, who served the World Council of Churches, first as director of its Commission on World Mission and Evangelism, and after 1984 as its general secretary. See his *Freedom in Mission* (Geneva: WCC Publications, 1985).

That kind of growth and indigenization, whether it represented the triumph of an old ideal or merely the working of extrinsic forces, meant that the statistics for American mission personnel might tell one precious little about ideological balances in world Christianity. Disputes familiar to Americans, such as those between liberals and conservative evangelicals, could be found elsewhere—often in similar forms and occasionally in more strident form. But where such analogous divisions did exist, ecumenical Christianity abroad, as in the United States, occupied a position significantly stronger than might be suggested by the one-to-eleven imbalance in missionary personnel. In 1980, over 40 percent of Japanese Protestants belonged to bodies that found themselves able to affiliate with the World Council of Churches. For India, the figure was over 60 percent.[41]

Despite these necessary qualifications, the reversals in missionary statistics were highly significant. They did not mean that ecumenicals had somehow, despite that designation, withdrawn from the world, nor that those still called missionaries were all happily persisting in nineteenth-century modes. Ecumenicals and "mainstream evangelicals" often differed marginally if at all in their practical commitment to such goals as indigenization, or to the culturally leveling recognition that "the whole world is the mission field." What the dissimilar statistics did proclaim, however, was that the churches once dominant in American religion and the mission enterprise, churches that still could claim to represent roughly half of America's Protestants, had effected a decisive break with the past. They had announced, far more distinctly than most of their evangelical counterparts, an unwillingness any longer to work with the rubrics and terminology of the classical era. In that sense the American "foreign mission movement," if it had not come to an end, surely had come under revised management.

[41]David B. Barrett, *World Christian Encyclopedia* (Nairobi: Oxford University Press, 1982), pp. 419, 370.

Afterword: Mission for a "People among Peoples"

Many of us, looking to the United States, feel that we are looking at ourselves in the process of becoming: ourselves as we might be and do.

Conor Cruise O'Brien, 1980

By the mid-1980s, attitudes toward the earlier mission enterprise had
become more sophisticated. Commentators of all kinds—secular and
religious, ecumenical and evangelical—seemed willing to make distinctions. In scholarly contexts but also in more popular ones, questions
about one's view of missions or missionaries were more likely than
before to be met with, in effect, a request for specificity: "Which missionaries do you have in mind?"

Clearly the time-honored habits of thought—hagiographic habits on
one side, automatically dismissive ones on the other—would die hard.
This was true especially because reasonably open-minded people still
equated "missionary" with "evangelist," and "evangelist" with, say, Billy
Sunday or perhaps Elmer Gantry. In the summer of 1985, the director
of a university oral-history project announced a discovery that he thought
would surprise others and that doubtless had surprised him. He reported that the onetime China missionaries whose recollections were
being recorded had turned out not to be "your stereotypic Bible-
thumping soul-savers." Basically, as he told a journalist, "they were Peace
Corps types before the Peace Corps."[1]

The remark was richly revealing. In real life, as opposed to legend,
a "Bible-thumping soul-saver" image described the missionaries of most
times and places about as well as the image of a street-corner evangelist
would have served, back home, to depict the average Presbyterian minister or Episcopalian social worker. Even the more irenic approaches
to proselytization, as conservatives had complained bitterly from about
1900 on, had become difficult to find within the hugely dominant
mainline missions. If one had polled the missionary offspring still numerous in the 1980s within university and seminary faculties and in
overseas agencies, one would have found few who remembered, among
hundreds of missionary acquaintances, any Bible-thumpers at all.

[1]R. Wayne Anderson of Northeastern University, quoted in the *Boston Globe* (August
12, 1985), p. 41.

If otherwise well-informed people had gained a different impression, as clearly they had, that was not entirely the fault of novelists intent on producing the best story, or of cartoonists and movie-makers seeking out the bizarre. It owed something, as well, to decades of ever-so-slight prevarication by mission publicists and returned missionaries who, telling the home folks what they wanted to hear, had regularly exaggerated both the centrality and the success of evangelism. Admittedly, without the missionary-as-converter—complete with clerical collar, pith helmet, and expectant cannibals—the *Saturday Evening Post* and *New Yorker* would have been deprived of an entire subgenre of magazine art. But it is also safe to say that Sunday night audiences in church basements had rarely gathered to hear, and in general had not been offered, homilies emphasizing the missionaries' customary restraint about active proselytizing, or their vigorous day-to-day collaboration with people of other faiths.

Whatever the sources of the stereotypes, several long-standing objections would remain in place even if the older images could be dispensed with or refined. A critic, having been led to recognize the prevalence of "Peace Corps types" in the mission forces, might well hold that these workers, with their Western technology and reforming zeal, had been more prone to cultural imperialism than their preaching colleagues. As for proselytization, had not the doctors and teachers and translators, according to their own repeated insistence, been proselytizers in the larger sense? Bible-thumpers or not, surely they had been avid participants in a movement dedicated fundamentally to the disparagement and displacement of other people's religions.

Several responses seem warranted by the history of American mission thought and activity. The first is an acknowledgment that if "imperialism" be defined with the breadth and depth most historians now consider appropriate, the American missionary movement takes its place as an active contributor. To be sure, if one were to define the term more traditionally that would be far less true, since missionaries and their sponsors often stood in an equivocal relation, at most, to colonialism and to military or commercial expansionism. But if "imperialism" connotes the attempt to impose one's ideas and culture on another, and the possible instruments of imposition are not limited to guns and power politics—if the tools of the trade include, for example, ordinary persuasiveness backed by vastly superior resources—then the missionary movement unquestionably qualifies as an arm of this broader sort of imperialism.[2]

[2]See Arthur Schlesinger, Jr., "The Missionary Enterprise and Theories of Imperialism," in Fairbank, *Missionary Enterprise,* pp. 336–73.

To contend, after such acknowledgment, that the missionaries and their theorists were remarkably enlightened about the dangers of cultural imposition may seem a backhanded compliment. If one is saying that the missionaries in their educational and serving functions were the best of a bad lot, then it might be kinder to omit the point. But the point ought not to be omitted, because the sensitivity that some mission theorists brought to the dilemmas of cultural interaction was more than just enlightened for its time. Often it was enlightened for any time, our own included.

The more naive or unreflective civilizers, activists who simply offered the education or technology they knew and believed in, deserve substantial credit. But condescension is even less warranted in relation to their troubled colleagues, those who combated the cruder forms of Western expansionism and in addition were alert to dangers in the forms they themselves represented. The fact that all Western missionaries were somehow enmeshed in political imperialism and its assumptions should not be denied, as apologists have sometimes attempted to do. But just as historians can applaud the achievements of abolitionists despite the racist frame of much abolitionist thought, it should be possible to admire, and even learn from, the selective imperialists who were vocal and prominent within the missionary movement.

But what of that second line of criticism: that the missionary social worker or science teacher was enmeshed in another questionable system, one of religious aggression? Were not such persons, for all their willingness to witness quietly for a serving and healing Christ, part of a movement bent on spiritual conquest of the world?

One can hear cries of indignation as soon as such a question is posed. How unreasonable! Are we to rule that a Christian (or Marxist, or anyone else) shall serve an alien people only on condition that he or she suppress any deeply held convictions about the rightful shape of human destiny? The indignation might in part be justified, since objections to missionaries—especially what one might call knee-jerk objections—have sometimes implied exactly that sort of censorship. But we should not begin caricaturing the critics. Even strident ones like Herman Melville and Mark Twain were content that people of Christian conviction should serve, witness, and perhaps preach in exotic settings. Melville thought no Christian could oppose the fundamental idea of missions. Twain, in the course of excoriating a particular missionary and his sponsors for abetting imperialist designs, insisted that he thought well of "almost all" the missionaries he had known or heard of.[3] It

[3]Mark Twain, "To My Missionary Critics," p. 532. Melville's views are treated in Chapter 3, above.

seems to have been possible, somewhere near the outer limits of polite discussion between the mission movement and its critics, to agree about Christianity's right to be heard in the world even though its evangelists and other representatives were quite likely to cherish a hope of eventual spiritual conquest.

The fundamental disagreement, it would seem, usually began at just that point, the point where "right to be heard" and "hope of conquest" came together as something quite different from either—that is, as Christianity's supposed "right," anchored in a revelation acknowledged only by Christian believers, to displace other religions and effect a spiritual conquest of the world. Beyond the stage of apologetics represented by such a claim, the critics and the more resolute defenders consistently found conversation difficult. Critics saw the movement as, on the ground of this encompassing assertion, expanding the simple plea for a hearing into a demand, conscious or not, for rights of advocacy that Christian societies had not often accorded to others. They found mission spokesmen making intracultural distinctions ("we shall destroy your religion, but not harm your other cultural forms") that these spokesmen would not allow anyone to pose in relation to their own civilization.

Much else that critics saw as dubious, on biblical as well as other grounds, tended to flow from an assumed right of conquest. For example, if the record of mission advocacy yielded a rather complimentary portrait of selective imperialists, it produced another picture, less flattering, of selective biblicists and selective providentialists. The God constantly depicted as opening doors for missions seemed often to be ignored when he closed the doors to particular ardently held objectives. In 1967, a professor of missiology at the Catholic University of America presented criticisms that, even at that date, were seldom voiced in such precincts:

> Despite the efforts of Christianity to convert the Jews over the centuries, Judaism remains firm. . . . Must we not conclude then that it continues to exist precisely because Almighty God, for His own reasons, wishes it to continue? And would we not perhaps find ourselves opposing God Himself if we were to try in the future to overthrow Judaism or any other non-Christian religion?[4]

That particular kind of prophetic correction had been, to say the least, unusual within a missionary movement that had become thor-

---

[4]Ronan Hoffman (in a section entitled "Are Conversion Missions Outmoded?"), "Yes! Conversion and the Mission of the Church," in McGavran, *Conciliar-Evangelical Debate,* p. 82.

oughly infused, in the nineteenth century, by a psychology of conquest and displacement. As some biblical norms had been elevated and others subordinated, the rhetoric of an American and Protestant errand to the world had seemed to abandon the generally tender phrasings of the seventeenth century (the church as the woman seeking protection in the wilderness) and instead had exploited, quite incessantly, nearly all the military metaphors of a confident Western expansionism. Errand had become Crusade.

Insofar as rationales for Christian world mission might continue in the late twentieth century to spell "crusade," the issues between critics and apologists would probably continue to be nonnegotiable. The critics, whether ecumenical, evangelical, or secular, were unlikely to relent and approve the more hegemonic interpretations, past or present, of Christian rights in the world. And those mission promoters who were still heavily invested in a nineteenth-century heritage might, on their part, find it almost impossible to renounce a language of Christian world conquest. Some of the more thoughtful of these, as well as others who merely clung to shibboleths, would continue to consider any such renunciation a betrayal, a surrender to relativism, and perhaps an acknowledgment that one was not a Christian believer at all. Because "we have our orders," as Stott and Graham had put it in the 1960s, for many traditionalists it would continue not to matter, finally, that other estimable people and religions have their orders as well.

The resulting standoff in fundamental assumptions mirrored, on the American scene, a tension between competing secular interpretations of the "American mission." As always, one must beware of facile reductions. Differences of opinion about religious outreach were not simply, or even mainly, contentions over America's place in the world; mission ideologists, anywhere along the spectrum from religious pluralism to thoroughgoing Christian triumphalism, could plausibly claim an independent biblical and theological stance. Pluralists, holding that humans and their religions are relativized by the fact of God's sovereignty, did not depend on Thomas Jefferson as their mentor; and triumphalists were even more certain of a biblical warrant. Yet the historical record could scarcely be taken as promising any considerable insulation, for missions or the church, from the winds of political and geopolitical doctrine. And if that was the case, the Christian triumphalism that many still considered a test of faith might be expected to undergo further revision only to the extent that an ingrained American and Western triumphalism was also revised.

For a time in the late 1970s, it had seemed to many judicious observers that rethinking of that kind was proceeding, in the larger American society, at an unprecedented rate. Conor Cruise O'Brien, an Irish academic and statesman who had spent a number of years in the United States, thought he detected a widespread American willingness, in the wake of the Vietnam and Watergate experiences, to proceed without "the comforting notion of a special purity in the national heart."

All peoples, O'Brien acknowledged, have considered themselves "chosen" to perform distinctive roles in the human drama. And most have committed about as many crimes as Americans have against their own and other people. But no other nation, he thought, has submitted the alleged chosenness, despite the crimes, as "a case for canonization." (O'Brien's illustrator pictured a stern American eagle looking in the mirror and seeing there a chaste and beautiful swan.)

But now all that might be changing. Not only had a loss of innocence occurred; Americans seemed to be accepting the loss with equanimity. Being number one, especially in righteousness, had been more taxing than they had realized. Their society, at the same time, had achieved enough in its civil rights revolution that others plagued with racial and religious antagonisms could take heart as well as take warning. "There are many of us who, looking to the United States, feel that we are looking at ourselves in the process of becoming: ourselves as we might be and do, given the opportunity, for good or ill."[5]

Sacvan Bercovitch, a Canadian-born specialist in American cultural history, carried similar observations a step further. Bercovitch agreed that recent "encroachments of history," including the civil rights struggle, had been highly destructive to American myths of chosenness and innocence whose enervation would not be an unmixed blessing. He believed, however, that other formulations, also biblical but more congruent with reality, were available to enrich or replace what had been partially lost. Even the Israelites, after all, had been warned that they were not God's *only* chosen people—the prophet Amos having put God's chilling rhetorical question: "Are you not like the Ethiopians to me?" Perhaps, Bercovitch suggested, the American errand in its more ecstatic form "may yet come to rest, where it always belonged, in the bush gardens of the imagination." Perhaps Americans were at last prepared to accept their real-world status as *goy b'goyim*, a people among peoples.[6]

[5]"Innocent Nation, Wicked World," *Harper's* (April 1980): 32–34.

[6]From a speech to American studies scholars in Europe, published with some alterations as "The Rites of Assent: Rhetoric, Ritual, and the Ideology of American Consensus," in Sam B. Girgus, ed., *The American Self: Myth, Ideology, and Popular Culture* (Albuquerque: University of New Mexico Press, 1981), pp. 5–42. Professor Bercovitch added the reference to Amos in a later conversation with the author.

Liberal internationalists seemed able, at least for a brief shining moment, to anticipate that by 1992, the quincentennial of the world's discovery of America, Americans would be ready to return the compliment. A renewed national assertiveness in the 1980s, even if interpreted as a rear-guard action, made such projections more doubtful; by the mid-80s observers at home and abroad were less prone to speak of either an American or an American Christian acceptance of equal status among the peoples of the earth. Yet these conservative, occasionally xenophobic, turns in opinion and policy were unlikely to affect (except possibly to strengthen) the "encroachments of history" upon traditional claims to innocence and privileged treatment.

If heightened acceptance of a new status could be anticipated anywhere, one might expect to find it in the context of a world Christianity in which the West's dominance, numerically and otherwise, appeared to have ended definitively. So far as that acceptance did indeed occur, the successors to missionaries who had served, among their several functions, as chaplains to the old imperialism would be those now intent on maintaining Christian effectuality within the new religious and cultural pluralism.

Bibliography

The bibliography with a few exceptions lists works that are cited more than once in the footnotes, and that pertain directly to mission thought at the American home base rather than to operations or discourse in the field. Since the entries serve as "first references," they have necessarily been listed alphabetically and not grouped either by topics or by types of material. I have therefore provided indications, according to the following code, of the uses I have made, and that other investigators probably would wish to make, of given items on the list.

S   Foreign mission *statistics*.
G   *General* histories of missions.
I   *Indian* missions, mainly colonial and North American.
H   *Historical* description and analysis of foreign mission topics.
R   *Reports* on foreign mission activities and conferences.
B   *Biography*.
T   Foreign mission *theory*, apologetics, promotion.
C   *Criticism* and *controversies*.
P   Other *primary* materials.

R   American Board of Commissioners for Foreign Missions. *Annual Reports*. Boston: various publishers, 1810–38.

H   Anderson, Charles R. *Melville in the South Seas*. New York: Columbia University Press, 1939.

T   Anderson, Rufus. *Foreign Missions, Their Relations and Claims*. New York: Scribner, 1869.

R   ———. *History of the Sandwich Islands Mission*. London: Hodder and Stoughton, 1872.

R   ———. *Memorial Volume of the First Fifty Years of the ABCFM*. 4th ed. Boston: ABCFM, 1861.

H   Andrew, John A., III. *Rebuilding the Christian Commonwealth: New England Congregationalists and Foreign Missions, 1800–1830*. Lexington: University Press of Kentucky, 1976.

I   Axtell, James, *The Invasion Within: The Contest of Cultures in Colonial North America*. New York: Oxford University Press, 1985.

C   Baker, Archibald G. "Reaction to the Laymen's Report." *Journal of Religion* 13 (October 1933): 379–98.

R   Barrows, John Henry. *The World's Parliament of Religions*. 2 vols. Chicago: Parliament Publishing Co., 1893.

H   Bassham, Rodger C. *Mission Theology: 1948–1975.* South Pasadena: William Carey Library, 1979.

I   Baudert, S. "Zinzendorf's Thought on Missions Related to His Views of the World." *International Review of Missions* 21 (July 1932): 390–401.

S   Beach, Harlan P., and Charles H. Fahs, eds. *World Missionary Atlas.* New York: Institute of Social and Religious Research, 1925.

H   Beaver, R. Pierce, ed. *American Missions in Bicentennial Perspective.* South Pasadena: William Carey Library, 1977.

H   ———. *American Protestant Women in World Mission.* Grand Rapids: Eerdmans, 1980.

T   ———. "Missionary Motivation Through Three Centuries." In Brauer, ed., *Reinterpretation in American Church History.*

T   ———. *To Advance the Gospel: Selections from the Writings of Rufus Anderson.* Grand Rapids: Eerdmans, 1967.

I   Benz, Ernst. "Pietist and Puritan Sources of Early Protestant World Missions (Cotton Mather and A. H. Francke)." *Church History* 20 (June 1951): 28–55.

G   Bliss, Edwin M. *A Concise History of Missions.* New York: Fleming H. Revell, 1897.

        ———. *Encyclopedia of Missions.* 2 vols. New York: Funk and Wagnalls, 1891.

R,T   Blyden, Edward W. *Liberia's Offering.* New York: John A. Gray, 1862.

I   Bowden, Henry W. *American Indians and Christian Missions: Studies in Cultural Conflict.* Chicago: University of Chicago Press, 1981.

H   Bradley, Harold W. *The American Frontier in Hawaii: The Pioneers, 1789–1843.* Stanford: Stanford University Press, 1942.

T   Brauer, Jerald C., ed. *Reinterpretation in American Church History.* Chicago: University of Chicago Press, 1968.

B   Brumberg, Joan Jacobs. *Mission for Life.* New York: The Free Press, 1980.

C,T   Buck, Pearl S. "Is There a Case for Foreign Missions?" *Harper's* (January 1933): 143–155.

C   ———. "The Laymen's Mission Report." *Christian Century* 49 (November 23, 1932): 1434–37.

T   Carver, W. O. "Baptists and the Problem of World Missions." *Review and Expositor* 17 (July 1920): 317–29.

I   Chaney, Charles L. *The Birth of Missions in America.* South Pasadena: William Carey Library, 1976.

T   Christensen, Torben and William R. Hutchison, eds., *Missionary Ideologies in the Imperialist Era: 1880–1920.* Aarhus, Denmark: Aros Publishers, and Cambridge, Mass.: Harvard Theological Review, 1984.

T   Clarke, William Newton. *A Study of Christian Missions.* New York: Charles Scribner's Sons, 1900.

H   Conforti, Jospeh. "Jonathan Edwards's Most Popular Work: 'The Life of David Brainerd' and Nineteenth Century Evangelical Culture," *Church History 54* (June 1985): 188–201.

S   Coote, Robert T. "The Uneven Growth of Conservative Evangelical Missions." *International Bulletin of Missionary Research* 6 (July 1982): 118–23.

R,T   Crummell, Alexander. *The Future of Africa.* New York: Negro Universities Press, 1969 (originally published 1862).

S   Dayton, Edward R. "Current Trends in North American Protestant Ministries Overseas." *Occasional Bulletin of Missionary Research* 1 (April 1977): 2–7.

S   Dennis, James S., ed. *Centennial Survey of Foreign Missions.* New York: Fleming H. Revell, 1902.

T   _____. *Christian Missions and Social Progress.* 3 vols. New York: Fleming H. Revell, 1897–1906.

G   _____. *Foreign Missions After a Century.* New York: Fleming H. Revell, 1893.

S   Dennis, James S., et al., eds. *World Atlas of Christian Missions.* New York: Student Volunteer Movement, 1911.

R   Douglas, J. D., ed. *Let the Earth Hear His Voice: International Congress on World Evangelization, Lausanne.* Minneapolis: World Wide Publications, 1975.

R   *Ecumenical Missionary Conference, New York, 1900.* 2 vols. New York: American Tract Society, 1900.

B   Edwards, Jonathan. *Memoirs of the Rev. David Brainerd . . . Chiefly Taken from His Own Diary.* New Haven: S. Converse, 1822.

H   Ernst, Eldon G. *Moment of Truth for Protestant America: Interchurch Campaigns Following World War One.* Missoula, Mont.: Scholars' Press, 1972.

I   Ellis, John Tracy, ed. *Documents of American Catholic History.* 2 vols. Chicago: Regnery, 1967.

H   Elsbree, Oliver W. *The Rise of the Missionary Spirit in America, 1790–1815.* Williamsport: Williamsport Printing Co., 1928.

T   Emmons, Nathaniel. "God Never Forsakes His People." In volume 5 of *Works.* 6 vols. Boston: Congregational Board of Publication, 1862.

H   Fairbank, John K. "Assignment for the '70's." *American Historical Review* 74 (February 1969): 861–79.

H   _____, ed. *The Missionary Enterprise in China and America.* Cambridge, Mass.: Harvard University Press, 1974.

T   Fleming, Daniel Johnson. *Building with India.* West Medford: Central Committee on United Study of Foreign Missions, 1922.

T   _____. "If Buddhists Came to Our Town." *Christian Century.* 46 (February 28, 1929): 293–94.

T   _____. *Whither Bound in Missions?* New York: Association Press, 1925.

G,T   Forman, Charles W. "A History of Foreign Mission Theory." In Beaver, ed. *American Missions in Bicentennial Perspective.*

H   Foster, Charles I. *An Errand of Mercy: The Evangelical United Front, 1790–1837.* Chapel Hill: University of North Carolina Press, 1960.

I   Fox, George, *The Journal of George Fox.* 2 vols. Cambridge: The University Press, 1911 (originally published 1694).

T,C   Frick, Heinrich. *Die Evangelische Mission.* Bonn: Schroeder, 1922.

T   Frost, Henry. "What Missionary Motives Should Prevail?" In *The Fundamentals.* 12 vols. Vol. 12:85–96. Chicago: Testimony Publishing Co., 1910–15.

B   Garrett, John. *Roger Williams: Witness Beyond Christendom, 1603–1683.* New York: Macmillan, 1970.

I   Goen, C. C. "Jonathan Edwards: A New Departure in Eschatology." *Church History* 28 (March 1959): 25–40.

R   Goodall, Norman, ed. *The Uppsala Report, 1968.* Geneva: World Council of Churches, 1968.

T   Gordon, George Angier. "The Gospel for Humanity." In William R. Hutchison, ed., *American Protestant Thought in the Liberal Era.*

H   Grabill, Joseph L. "The 'Invisible' Missionary: A Study in American Foreign Relations." *Journal of Church and State* 14 (Winter 1972): 93–105.

T   Griffin, Edward Dorr. *The Kingdom of Christ.* Greenfield: John Denno, 1805.

T   _____. *Sermon Preached in Sandwich.* Boston: Nathaniel Willis, 1813.

T   Hall, C. C. "The Beatific Vision of an Evangelized World." In *The Student Missionary Appeal.* New York: Student Volunteer Movement, 1898.

R   Hamlin, Cyrus. *Among the Turks.* New York: R. Carter and Bros., 1878.

B   Harris, Theodore F. *Pearl S. Buck: A Biography.* New York: John Day, 1969.

R   Henry, Carl F. H. and Stanley Mooneyham, eds. *One Race, One Gospel, One Task: World Congress on Evangelism, Berlin, 1966.* 2 vols. Minneapolis: World Wide Publications, 1967.

H   Hersey, John. *The Call.* New York: Alfred A. Knopf, 1985.

H   Hill, Patricia. *The World Their Household.* Ann Arbor: University of Michigan Press, 1984.

R,T,C Hocking, William Ernest, et al. *Re-Thinking Missions: A Laymen's Inquiry After One Hundred Years.* New York: Harper and Bros., 1932.

T   Hoekendijk, Johannes. "The Call to Evangelism." In Donald McGavran, ed., *The Conciliar-Evangelical Debate: The Crucial Documents, 1964–1976.*

T   ———. "Christ and the World in the Modern Age." *The Student World* 54 (1961): 75–82.

T   ———. "Notes on the Meaning of Mission(ary)." In Thomas Wieser, ed., *Planning for Mission*.

H   Hogg, W. Richie. *Ecumenical Foundations*. New York: Harper, 1953.

H   ———. "The Role of American Protestantism in World Mission." In R. Pierce Beaver, ed., *American Missions in Bicentennial Perspective*.

B   Hopkins, C. Howard. *John R. Mott, 1865–1955: A Biography*. Geneva: World Council of Churches, 1979.

P   Hopkins, Samuel. *A Treatise on the Millennium*. Boston: Thomas and Andrews, 1793.

C   Horsch, John. *The Modernist View of Missions*. Scottdale: Fundamental Truth Depot, 1920.

T   Humphrey, Heman. *The Promised Land*. Boston: Samuel T. Armstrong, 1819.

H   Hunter, Jane. *The Gospel of Gentility: American Women Missionaries in Turn-of-the-Century China*. New Haven: Yale University Press, 1984.

T   Hutchison, Ralph Cooper. "Can I Give My Life to Foreign Missions: The Journal of an Outgoing Missionary." *International Review of Missions* 16 (January 1927): 109–20.

T   ———. "Christianity and Proselytism." *Atlantic Monthly* 140 (November 1927): 620–25.

T   ———. "Islam and Christianity." *Atlantic Monthly* 138 (November 1926): 706–10.

T   Hutchison, William R. "American Missionary Ideologies: 'Activism' as Theory, Practice and Stereotype." In F. Forrester Church and Timothy George, eds., *Continuity and Discontinuity in Church History*. Leiden: Brill, 1979.

T   ———, ed. *American Protestant Thought in the Liberal Era*. 2d ed. Washington, D.C.: University Press of America, 1984.

C   ———. "Innocence Abroad: The 'American Religion' in Europe." *Church History* 51 (March 1982): 71–84.

T   ———. *The Modernist Impulse in American Protestantism*. Cambridge, Mass.: Harvard University Press, 1976.

H   Jacobs, Sylvia M., ed. *Black Americans and the Missionary Movement in Africa*. Westport, Conn.: Greenwood Press, 1982.

I   Jennings, Francis. *The Invasion of America: Indians, Colonialism, and the Cant of Conquest*. Chapel Hill: University of North Carolina Press, 1975.

B   Judson, Edward. *The Life of Adoniram Judson*. New York: Randolph, 1883.

I   Kelsey, Rayner. *Friends and the Indians, 1655–1917*. Philadelphia: Associated Executive Committee of Friends on Indian Affairs, 1917.

I   Kennedy, J. H. *Jesuit and Savage in New France*. New Haven: Yale
         University Press, 1950.
P   King, Henry C. *The Moral and Religious Challenge of Our Times*.
         New York: Macmillan, 1911.
C   Lane, Ortha May. *Missions in Magazines*. Tientsin, China: Tientsin
         Press. (Ph.D. dissertation, State University of Iowa, 1935.)
G   Latourette, K. S. *The Great Century, 1800–1914*. Vols. 4–6 of *A
         History of the Expansion of Christianity*. 7 vols. New York, Harper
         and Bros., 1938–46.
T   ———. *Missions Tomorrow*. New York: Harper and Bros., 1936.
R   Lindsell, Harold, ed. *The Church's Worldwide Mission: Proceedings of
         the Congress at Wheaton, Illinois, 1966*. Waco: World Books,
         1966.
C   Loetscher, Lefferts A. *The Broadening Church: A Study of Theological
         Issues in the Presbyterian Church Since 1869*. Philadelphia: Uni-
         versity of Pennsylvania Press, 1957.
H   Lotz, Denton. " 'The Evangelization of the World in This Genera-
         tion': The Resurgence of a Missionary Idea Among the Con-
         servative Evangelicals." Ph.D. dissertation, University of
         Hamburg, 1970.
C   McGavran, Donald, ed. *The Conciliar-Evangelical Debate: The Crucial
         Documents, 1964–1976*. South Pasadena: William Carey Library,
         1977.
I   McLoughlin, William G. *Cherokees and Missionaries, 1789–1839*. New
         Haven: Yale University Press, 1984.
C   Machen, J. Gresham. *Modernism and the Board of Foreign Missions of
         the Presbyterian Church in the U.S.A.* Philadelphia: privately
         printed, 1933.
I   Mather, Cotton. *India Christiana: A Discourse Delivered unto the Com-
         missioners for the Propagation of the Gospel among the American
         Indians. . . .* Boston: B. Green, 1721.
I   ———. *Magnalia Christi Americana*. 2 vols. Hartford: Silas Andrus
         and Sons, 1853–55 (originally published 1702).
C   Melville, Herman. *Omoo*. London: Constable, 1922 (originally pub-
         lished 1847).
C   ———. *Typee*. London: Constable, 1922 (originally published 1846).
H   Michener, James A. *Hawaii*. New York: Random House, 1959.
B   Miller, Char. *Fathers and Sons: The Bingham Family and The American
         Mission*. Philadelphia: Temple University Press, 1982.
I   Miller, Perry. *Errand Into the Wilderness*. Cambridge, Mass.: Harvard
         University Press, 1956.
T   Miller, Samuel. *Sermon Delivered in the Middle Church, New Haven,
         at the Ordination of William Goodell et al*. Boston: Crocker and
         Brewster, 1822.

S   *Mission Handbook: North American Protestant Ministries Overseas.* 10th and 11th eds., Monrovia: Missions Advanced Research and Communication Center, 1973 and 1976.

T   Mott, John R. *The Evangelization of the World in This Generation.* New York: Student Volunteer Movement, 1905.

T   ————. "The Tasks of Tomorrow." In *Addresses and Papers of John R. Mott,* vol. 1. New York, Association Press, 1946.

G   Neill, Stephen. *A History of Christian Missions.* Harmondsworth: Penguin, 1977 (originally published 1964).

T   Nevius, John L. *The Planting and Development of Missionary Churches.* 4th ed. Philadelphia: Presbyterian and Reformed Publishing Co., 1958 (originally published 1885).

T,C   Newbigin, Lesslie. "Cross-Currents in Ecumenical and Evangelical Understandings of Mission." *International Bulletin of Missionary Research* 6 (October 1982): 146–51 and reply to critics, 154–55.

G   Newcomb, Harvey. *A Cyclopedia of Missions.* New York, Scribner: 1854.

S   Parker, Joseph I., ed. *Interpretative Statistical Survey of the World Mission of the Christian Church.* New York: International Missionary Council, 1938.

B,C   Patterson, James Alan. "Robert E. Speer and the Crisis of the American Protestant Missionary Movement, 1920–1937." Ph.D. dissertation, Princeton Theological Seminary, 1980.

I,B   Pettit, Norman. Introduction to Jonathan Edwards, *The Life of David Brainerd.* New Haven: Yale University Press, 1985.

H,T   Phillips, Clifton. "Changing Attitudes in the Student Volunteer Movement of Great Britain and North America." In Christensen and Hutchison, *Missionary Ideologies.*

H   ————. *Protestant America and the Pagan World.* Cambridge, Mass.: East Asian Research Center, Harvard University, 1969.

T   Pierson, Arthur T. *The Crisis of Missions.* New York: Robert Carter and Bros., 1886.

H   Rabe, Valentin. *The Home Base of American China Missions, 1880–1920.* Cambridge, Mass.: Harvard University Press, 1978.

H   Reed, James. *The Missionary Mind and American East Asia Policy, 1911–1915.* Cambridge, Mass.: Harvard University Press, 1983.

P   Richards, Anna Russell. *Mother Goose Missionary Rhymes.* New York: Board of Foreign Missions, c. 1925.

R   Richter, Julius. *A History of Protestant Missions in the Near East.* New York: Revell, 1910.

S   ————. "Statistics of the Protestant Missionary Societies of the World for 1910." Interleaved in *Missionary Review of the World* 24 (January 1911): 8–9.

C   Rockefeller, John D., Jr. "The Christian Church: What of its Future?" *Saturday Evening Post* (February 9, 1918), 16 and 37.

I   Rooy, Sidney H. *The Theology of Missions in the Puritan Tradition.* Delft: W. D. Meinema, 1965.

T   Rouner, Leroy S. *Within Human Experience: The Philosophy of William Ernest Hocking.* Cambridge, Mass.: Harvard University Press, 1969.

G   Rouse, Ruth and Stephen Neill, eds. *A History of the Ecumenical Movement, 1517–1948.* London: Society for the Propagation of Christian Knowledge, 1954.

I   Salisbury, Neal. "Red Puritans: The Praying Indians of Massachusetts Bay and John Eliot." *William and Mary Quarterly* 31 (January 1974): 27–54.

C   Sanders, Elizabeth E. *Remarks on the "Tour Around Hawaii."* Salem: privately printed, 1848.

P   Schaff, Phillip. *America,* ed. Perry Miller. Cambridge, Mass.: Harvard University Press, 1961 (originally published 1854).

B,T   Schneider, Robert A. "The Senior Secretary: Rufus Anderson and the ABCFM, 1810–1880." Ph.D. dissertation, Harvard University, 1980.

T,C   Schrotenboer, Paul G. and C. Peter Wagner. "Response to the Article by Lesslie Newbigin." *International Bulletin of Missionary Research* 6 (October 1982): 152–54.

I   Shuffelton, Frank. "Indian Devils and Pilgrim Fathers: Squanto, Hobomok, and the English Conception of Indian Religion." *New England Quarterly* 49 (March 1976): 108–16.

C   Silver, Charles. "Pearl Buck, Evangelism and Works of Love: Images of the Missionary in Fiction." *Journal of Presbyterian History* 51 (1973): 216–34.

T   Simpson, A. B. *The Challenge of Missions.* New York: Christian Alliance Publishing Co., 1926.

R   ———. *Larger Outlooks on Missionary Lands.* New York: Christian Alliance Publishing Co., 1893.

H   Smith, Bradford. *Yankees in Paradise.* Philadelphia: Lippincott, 1956.

T   Soper, Edmund D. *The Philosophy of the Christian World Mission.* New York: Abingdon-Cokesbury, 1943.

T   Speer, Robert E. *Christianity and the Nations.* New York: Fleming H. Revell, 1910.

S   ———. "A Few Comparisons of Then and Now." *Missionary Review of the World* 51 (January 1928): 5–10.

P   ———. *The Finality of Jesus Christ.* New York: Fleming H. Revell, 1933.

T   ———. *Missionary Principles and Practice.* New York: Fleming H. Revell, 1910.

C,T   ———. *"Re-Thinking Missions" Examined.* New York: Fleming H. Revell, 1933.

B   ———. *Studies of Missionary Leadership*. Philadelphia: Westminster Press, 1914.

T   ———. "The Watchword of the Movement: The Evangelization of the World in This Generation." In *The Student Missionary Appeal*. New York: Student Volunteer Movement, 1898.

I   Stein, Stephen J. Editor's Introduction. In Jonathan Edwards, *Apocalyptic Writings*. New Haven: Yale University Press, 1977.

H,C   Stoll, David. *Fishers of Men or Founders of Empire? The Wycliffe Bible Translators in Latin America*. Cambridge, Mass.: Cultural Survival, 1982.

T   Stott, John R. W. *Christian Mission in the Modern World*. Downers Grove: InterVarsity Press, 1975.

R   Strong, Augustus. *A Tour of the Missions*. Philadelphia: Griffith and Rowland, 1918.

G   Strong, William E. *The Story of the American Board*. Boston: Pilgrim Press, 1910.

C   Thomas, W. H. Griffith. "Modernism in China." *Princeton Theological Review* 19 (October 1921): 630–71.

B   Thompson, Augustus C. *Discourse Commemorative of Rev. Rufus Anderson*. Boston: ABCFM, 1880.

H   Thomson, James C., Jr., et al. *Sentimental Imperialists: The American Experience in East Asia*. New York: Harper and Row, 1981.

C   Twain, Mark. "To the Person Sitting in Darkness," and "To My Missionary Critics." *North American Review* 172 (1901): 160–76, 520–34.

T   Visser 't Hooft, W. A. *The Background of the Social Gospel in America*. Haarlem: Willink, 1928.

B   Wacker, Grant. *Augustus H. Strong and the Dilemma of Historical Consciousness*. Macon: Mercer University Press, 1985.

H   Walls, Andrew. "British Missions." In Torben Christensen and William R. Hutchison, eds., *Missionary Ideologies*.

G   Warneck, Gustav. *Outline of a History of Protestant Missions*. New York: Fleming H. Revell, 1901.

T   Wayland, Francis. *The Apostolic Ministry*. Rochester: Sage and Brother, 1853.

T   Weber, Timothy. *Living in the Shadow of the Second Coming: American Premillennialism, 1875–1982*. Grand Rapids: Academic Books, 1983.

R   Wieser, Thomas, ed. *Planning for Mission*. New York: United States Conference for the World Council of Churches, 1966.

R,T   Wilder, Royal. *Mission Schools in India*. New York: A. D. F. Randolph, 1861.

T   Williams, Daniel Day. *The Andover Liberals: A Study in American Theology*. New York: King's Crown Press, 1941.

I   Williams, George H. *Wilderness and Paradise in Christian Thought*. New York: Harper and Bros., 1962.

I,T   Williams, Roger. *The Complete Writings of Roger Williams.* 7 vols. New York: Russell and Russell, 1963.

H   Williams, Walter L. *Black Americans and the Evangelization of Africa.* Madison: University of Wisconsin Press, 1982.

R,T   Winslow, Miron. *Hints on Missions to India.* New York: M. W. Dodd, 1856.

I,B   Winslow, Ola Elizabeth. *John Eliot, Apostle to the Indians.* Boston: Houghton Mifflin, 1968.

I,B   ————. *Jonathan Edwards, 1703–1758: A Biography.* New York: Macmillan, 1940.

T   Woods, Leonard. *Sermon Delivered at the . . . Ordination of the Rev. Messrs. Samuel Newell et al.* Boston: Samuel T. Armstrong, 1812.

T   ————. *Sermon Occasioned by the Death of the Rev. Samuel Worcester.* Salem: Whipple, 1821.

I   Woolman, John. *The Journal of John Woolman and A Plea for the Poor.* Seacaucus, N.J.: Citadel Press, 1972 (originally published 1774).

T   Worcester, Samuel. *Paul on Mars Hill: Or a Christian Survey of the Pagan World.* Andover, Mass.: Flagg and Gould, 1815.

T   World Council of Churches (Western European and North American Working Groups). *The Church for Others and the Church for the World.* Geneva, 1967.

R   World Missionary Conference, 1910. *History and Records and Addresses.* Edinburgh: Oliphant, Anderson, and Ferrier.

R   ————. *Report of Commission II. The Church in the Mission Field.* Edinburgh: Oliphant, Anderson and Ferrier.

Index

Africa, 46, 54; American missions to and attitudes toward, 118, 126, 129; Catholic missions to, 16; Southern, 128; American missions to sub-Saharan, 128; West, 46, 126, 128

Allouez, Claude, 23

American Board of Commissioners for Foreign Missions, 1n, 43–44, 165; "Address to the Christian Public," 46, 57; early history, 45–47, 55, 56; and establishment of denominational boards, 95–97, 101–2; in the imperialist era, 127; and liberals, 103; mission to Hawaii, 69–77; missions among American Indians, 63–69; and Anderson, 77–90, 95–98

Anderson, Charles, 75

Anderson, Rufus: deputation of 1854–55, 84, 97–98; *Foreign Missions,* 81n; *Memorial Volume,* 79; opposition to policies of, 91, 92, 93, 95–99, 120; as senior secretary of ABCFM, 77–90, 102; and Speer as heir, 122; "The Theory of Missions to the Heathen," 81n, 82; mentioned, 140, 192

Andover Seminary, 47, 50, 78; liberals and future probation, 105, 113

Andrew, John A., 52

Arnold, Edwin, *Light of Asia,* 109

Auburn Affirmation, 173

Azariah, V. S., 179

Baker, Archibald, 165, 190

Bangladesh, missions to, 199

Baptist missions: with the ABCFM, 45; Board of Foreign Missions, 58; in the early republic, 46, 49; in the imperialist era, 127; indigenization in, 26, 78, 84, 95, 98; post-World War I, 165, 190

Barrows, John Henry, 105, 109

Barth, Karl, 138, 173–74, 183

Bassham, Roger, 189, 195

Beach, Harlan, 110–11

Beaver, R. Pierce, 3

Beecher, Lyman, 65

Bercovitch, Sacvan, 208

Berlin Conference (1966), 191, 192, 194

Bible Union of China, 139–40

Bingham, Hiram: leader of mission to Hawaii, 70–73; ordination sermon, 51; mentioned, 68, 93, 102

Black church missions, 3, 128

Bonhoeffer, Dietrich, 183

Booth, William, 192

Boudinot, Elias, 65–68

Bowden, Henry, 28

Brainerd, David, 27–35, 37–38, 64

Brazil, missions to, 128

Brébeuf, Jean de, 17, 21

Brethren missions, 46

British missions, 93–94, 126n, 131–38; "The Spiritual Expansion of the Empire," 138; thought, 8, 40, 78, 107, 120

Buck, Pearl, 146, 166–69, 173; Astor Hotel speech, 167–69; *The Good Earth,* 166

Buddhism: missionary view of, 47, 106, 141, 154–55; and World's Parliament of Religions, 105, 109, 109n; mentioned, 13

Bunyan, John, 13

Burma, missions to, 46–47, 48, 50, 58, 158

Bushnell, Horace, 104

Calderón, Bishop of Cuba, 19

Calvinism, 33, 41, 49–54

Canada, Catholic missions to, 16, 25

Candlin, George T., 107

Carey, William, 179, 188

Carribean, missions to, 190

Castro, Emilio, 201

Ceylon: Dutch missions to, 24; American missions to, 46, 62, 84–85
Chamberlain, Daniel, 71
Chambers, Talbot, 97
Chicago Declaration (1973), 195
China: American missions to, 46, 96, 115, 119, 126, 128, 151, 158, 166–68; Boxer Rebellion, 156; Catholic missions to, 21–22, 25; historiography of missions to, 3; missionaries and Communism, 1; missionary attitudes toward, 106, 115, 123, 153; modernism and missions to, 139–40, 144, 175
China Inland Missions, 115, 128, 131
Christian and Missionary Alliance, 115, 128
Church growth movement, 187, 194
Church of the Nazarene missions, 127
Church World Service, 190
Civil rights movement, 208
Clarke, William Newton, 103–6
Concert of prayer, 38
Confucianism, 106, 141, 144
Congregational missions: in the colonial American period, 26–33, 38–42; in the early republic, 43–51; in the imperialist era, 95–96, 101, 132
Congress on Evangelism, Minneapolis (1969), 195
Cornwall, Connecticut, Indian school, 65–67
Crèvecoeur, J. Hector St. John, 129

Dayton, Edward, 193–94
Dennis, James, 112, 113, 115; *Christian Missions and Social Progress,* 107–10
Dharmapala, 109, 109n
Disciples of Christ missions, 46, 127, 128; *Christian Missionary,* 110
Duff, Alexander, 120
Dutch missions, 24–25

Ecumenical Missionary Conference, New York (1900), 133
Ecumenical missions, 176–88, 191–207
Eddy, Sherwood, 102, 147, 173
Edinburgh Conference. *See* World Missionary Conference, Edinburgh (1910)
Education in missions, 12, 201, 204–5; conservatives and, 115, 116, 118, 139–44, 157–58, 191; controversy over, 80,

82–90, 97–102, 125–26, 134, 139–44; in Hawaii, 70; in the imperialist era, 111, 115, 116, 118, 120; to Indians, 65, 68; liberals and, 111, 201
Edwards, Jonathan: as Brainerd's biographer, 29–30; on the millennium and missions, 38, 40–41, 53–54; as a missionary thinker, 40–41; mentioned, 48, 50–51, 61
Ehrenström, Nils, 132–33
Eliot, John, 15, 24, 27–28, 34, 36–37, 64
Eliot, T. S., 156
Emmons, Nathaniel, 61
Encomienda, 19
Episcopal missions, 46, 127
Episcopalians, 165
Escobar, Samuel, 194
Europe, missions to, 190
European missions: critique of Americanism, 125–38, 171–72, 196; statistics, 100–101, 126; thought, 8, 40, 93, 125–26
Evangelical Foreign Missions Association (EFMA), 178
Evangelical missions (post–1940 evangelicalism), 152, 176–79, 184, 187–207; unaffiliated, 193–94, 200–201, 207
Evangelicals for Social Action, 195
Evangelizing/civilizing tension: in American missions to Indians, 62–69; and Anderson, 77–90; in Catholic missions, 15, 18–21; in ecumenical missions, 184–87, 197–99, 201–2; European observations regarding, 125–38; in evangelical missions, 187–92, 194–96, 201–2; explained, 9–14, 204–5; in fundamentalist mission thought, 139–45; in Hawaiian mission, 69–77; in the imperialist era, 91–102, 107–12, 115–24; in liberal mission thought, 102, 107–12, 151–64; in Puritan missions to Indians, 15, 23–33; in Quaker missions to Indians, 33–37
Evarts, Jeremiah, 65–67

Fairbank, John K.: on Chinese Communism, 1; on neglect of missionary history, 3n
Fiji, 201

Finney, Charles G., 67
Fleming, Daniel Johnson, 150–58; "If Buddhists Came to Our Town," 154–55; *Whither Bound in Missions?* 150; mentioned, 177, 180
Foreign aid (American), 14, 60, 124, 177
Formosa, Dutch missions to, 24
Fosdick, Harry Emerson, 148, 173; "Shall the Fundamentalists Win?" 148, 149
Fox, George, 36
Francke, August Hermann, 39
French missions, 15–23, 27
Frick, Heinrich, 136–38, 146, 185
Frost, Henry, 115
Fundamentalism, 147, 150–51, 165–66, 175, 177, 194; and critique of mainline missions, 125, 138–45, 150, 171–75

Gabriel, Father, 17
German missions, 25, 40, 93; critique of Americanism, 125, 129–38
Gilbert, Sir Humphrey, 24
Goodall, Norman, 176, 182–83
Gordon, A. J., 188
Gordon, George Angier, 103–4, 106, 107, 112, 188
Graham, Billy, 191–92, 207
Greece, missions to, 46
Gregory XV, 15
Griffin, Edward Dorr, 43, 54–57, 59; *The Kingdom of Christ*, 55
Guess, George (or Sequoya), 68

Hamlin, Cyrus, 98
Hardie, Keir, 192
Hawaii, missions to, 62–63, 69–77, 86–89; as success and problem, 45, 97, 100; mentioned, 45, 46, 48, 51, 67, 68, 102
Hawes, Joel, 59
Hennepin, Father Louis, 19, 22–24, 31
Henry, Carl F. H., 189, 192
Hersey, John, *The Call*, 3, 71, 72n
Higham, John, 14
Hinduism: Catholic accommodation to, 22; missionary views of, 97, 106, 122, 157
Hispaniola, 20
Hocking, William Ernest, 148, 156n, 158–64, 167–71, 177, 180; *The Meaning of God in Human Experience*, 159. *See also* Layman's Inquiry on Missions

Hoekendijk, Johannes, 183–87; *The Church Inside Out*, 183; *Evangelism in France*, 183
Hogg, Richie, 133, 136
Holiness missions, 127, 174–75
Hopkins, Samuel (and Hopkinsianism), 41, 49–51, 54, 61, 78; *Treatise on the Millennium*, 54
Horsch, John, 143–44; *The Modernist View of Missions*, 143
Hubbard, David, 187–88
Humphrey, Heman, 51–52
Hutchison, R. C., 156–58, 159, 195; "Christianity and Proselytism," 157–58; "Islam and Christianity," 156–57

India: American missions to, 46, 116, 128, 158, 175, 179; Anderson policy toward, 62–63, 80, 84–86, 96–98; Catholic missions to, 21–22; indigenous church, 202; missionary attitudes toward, 106, 151–52, 155; missions from, 198; mentioned, 48, 109, 150, 168, 197
Indians (North American): American missions to, 46, 54, 58, 62–69, 82–83, 86; Catholic missions to, 16–23; English colonial missions to, 23–41; removal under President Jackson, 63–64
Indigenization: and Anderson, 77, 80–90, 95–102; in Catholic missions, 15–16, 21–23; Edinburgh Conference (1910), 179; in evangelical missions, 192–96; Fleming on, 150–51; Speer on, 121–22; successful, 201, 202; Williams and, 36–37; Zinzendorf on, 26
Indonesia, Dutch missions to, 24–25
Ingoli, Francesco, 21
Institute for Social and Religious Research, 158
Interdenominational Foreign Mission Association (IFMA), 178
International Missionary Council, 172
Iran, historiography of missions to, 3
Islam, 13, 38, 47, 54, 156–57

James, Sydney, 36
James, William, 92
Japan: American missions to, 46, 106, 120, 151, 158, 174, 175; Catholic missions

Japan (*continued*)
to, 16, 21–22, 25; indigenous church,
202; missionary attitudes toward, 115–
16, 155
Jenkins, John, 96
Jerusalem Conference (1928), 180
Jesuit Relations, 20
Judaism, 38, 47, 141, 206
Judson, Adoniram, 21, 49, 188

Kagawa, Toyohiko, 173
Kähler, Martin, 185
Kennedy, J. H., 21
Kimball, Grace, 108
King Philip's War, 28
Kirkland, Samuel, 29
Korea: indigenous church, 201; missions
to, 3, 128, 155, 175
Kraemer, Hendrik, 180, 183; *Philosophy of
the Christian World Mission,* 180–81

Las Casas, Bartolomé de, 9, 19–20
Latin America: American missions to, 190;
American sense of "errand" to, 6; Catholic missions to, 16; missions from, 194,
196
Latourette, K. S., 100, 108n, 180
Lausanne Conference (1974), 194–95
Laymen's Inquiry on Missions, 158–74;
critics and supporters of, 164–74;
mentioned, 107, 148, 149, 152, 172,
180. *See also* Hocking, William Ernest
Laymen's Missionary Movement, 132
Liberalism: cooperation in civilizing missions, 95, 102–16; critique of missions, 148–75, 178–92, 196–99;
degree of enthusiasm for missions, 102–
11, 176–77; opposition to, in missions, 112–15, 138–45, 166, 169–75,
178–202; mentioned, 49, 147
Liberia, missions to, 46
Liddell, Eric, 71, 72n
Lutheran missions, 46, 127, 128, 138

McGavran, Donald, 176, 188–89; "Will
Uppsala Betray the Two Billion?" 188
Machen, J. Gresham, 150, 166, 171–75,
177
Mackay, John, 173
Madras Conference (1938), 180
Massachusetts Missionary Society, 61

Mather, Cotton, 28, 38–40; *Magnalia
Christi Americana,* 39
Maugham, Somerset, 71; "Rain," 156
Mayhew Family, 29, 64
Medical work in missions, 12–13, 80, 100,
111, 120, 139–40, 144, 163, 204–5
Melville, Herman, 156, 205; *Omoo* and *Ty-
pee,* 74–76
Membré, Zenobé, 17
Menéndez de Avilés, Pedro, 17–18
Mennonites, 127, 143
Methodist missions: and the ABCFM, 45–
46, in the early republic, 46; in the im-
perialist era, 127; post–World War I,
165, 201
Michener, James: *Hawaii,* 71–72
Micronesia, missions to, 46
Middle East, missions to, 46
Miller, Perry, 3n, 6, 24
Miller, Samuel, 53–54, 56
Missionaries (American): education of, 1,
163, 167; 1860–1918, 91, 93, 99–
101, 126–28; historical treatment of,
2–4, 176, 203–4; influence on American attitudes, 1; non-mainline, 3, 126–
29, 174–76, 200–201; offspring of,
1–2, 203; degree of sensitivity to foreign cultures, 1, 29–32, 105, 107–11,
116; statistics on, 14, 91, 93, 99–101,
126–28, 176, 190, 193, 202; women
as, 3, 101–2, 127
Missionary Review of the World, The, 99n,
113
Missionary thought (American Protestant): activism in, 7, 93, 118, 125–38,
145, 148, 171–72; about America,
9, 31, 48, 140, 145, 180; Anglo-
American connection in, 9, 44, 55–57,
116, 125–38, 146; biblical themes in,
5, 46–47, 51–53, 104, 106, 199;
compassion as theme in, 48–49, 55,
113; chosen nation theme in, 3, 5, 52–
53, 56, 61, 88, 208–9; church growth
in, 187, 194, 197, 199; conquest as
theme in, 47, 51–52, 60, 79, 105–6,
111, 152, 154–55, 162, 198, 205–8;
"errand" theme in, 5–9, 42, 44, 207–
8; the glory of God as a theme in, 48;
Golden Rule in, 152, 154–55; Great
Commission in, 5, 48–49, 77, 112–
13, 122, 125, 133, 191, 196–97, 207;

the home church in, 8, 59, 204; millennialism in, 53–56, 61, 79; New England in, 46, 53, 56–59, 82; "Christian presence" in, 36, 181–82, 198; and Western technology in, 8, 13, 98, 103–4, 116, 204; "world mission" concept in, 179–82, 190, 202, 209. *See also* Evangelizing/civilizing tension; Indigenization; Non-Christian religions, attitude toward; Secular expansionism and imperialism

Modernism. *See* Liberalism

Mohawk nation, 25

Monroe Doctrine, 43

Montesinos, Antonio de, 20

Moody Bible Institute, 112

Moore, E. C., 144

Moral Re-Armament movement, 173

Moravian missions, 184; to North American Indians, 25–28, 33; in Tanzania, 201

Morse, Jedidiah, 65

Mother Goose Missionary Rhymes, 123

Mott, John R.: career after World War I, 147, 158; European reaction to, 131, 135; as leading statesman, 100, 102, 120–21, 128; and the Watchword, 119; mentioned, 93, 94, 177, 179, 188, 199

National Council of Churches, 178, 193

Neill, Stephen, 18, 21–22

Neo-orthodoxy, 165, 174, 180, 183

Nevius, John, 120

Newbigin, Lesslie, 197–99

Nobili, Robert de, 21–22

Non-Christian religions, attitude toward: of Brainerd, 32; of Buck, 169; of Catholic missions, 19, 22; of conservatives, 115, 173, 191, 196; in early republic, 47, 48, 54, 97; of Fleming, 152–55; in the imperialist era, 123; of Hocking, 159, 161–63; of R. C. Hutchison, 156–58; of liberals, 105–7, 110, 113, 140–44, 180, 206–7; of Quakers, 33

Norddeutsche Missionsgesellschaft, 133

Obookiah, Henry, 67

O'Brien, Conor Cruise, 203, 207–8

Padilla, René, 194

Pannell, William, 192

Peace Corps, 60, 177, 203–4

Peck, Solomon, 84

Penn, William, 36

Pentecostal missions, 3, 127, 174–75, 193

Philippines, Catholic missions to, 16

Pierson, A. T., 113–20; *Crisis of Missions,* 117; and the Watchword, 99, 119; mentioned, 184, 188

Pietism, 25, 40; attitude toward America, 39; critique of "Americanism," 125–38; mentioned, 184, 186

Poor, Daniel, 96

Portuguese missions, 16–23

Postmillennialism, 40–42, 53, 103, 111, 112

Premillennialism, 10, 53, 95, 111, 112–18, 120, 177

Presbyterian missions: with the ABCFM, 45; Board of Foreign Missions, 95–96, 123, 127; in the early republic, 46; in the imperialist era, 127, 132; and modernism, 139–40, 164, 166–72; to North American Indians, 25–26; post–World War I, 190, 201

Presbyterians, 110, 112

Princeton Seminary, 150, 166, 172–74; mentioned, 110

Princeton Theological Review, 139

Propaganda. *See* Sacred Congregation for the Propagation of the Faith

Protestant European missions, to North American Indians, 23–41

Puritan missions: the ABCFM as heir to, 45; to North American Indians, 5, 23–41

Quaker missions, 26, 33–37

Quay, James King, 157n

Rabe, Valentin, 91

Rauschenbusch, Walter, 141

Reformed church missions: and the ABCFM, 45; and denominational mission boards, 95–97; in the imperialist era, 127; post–World War I, 165, 199

Reischauer, A. K., 174

Re-Thinking Missions. See Laymen's Inquiry on Missions

Ricci, Matthew, 21

Richter, Julius, 132; *History of Protestant Missions in the Near East,* 132

Rockefeller, John D., Jr., 141, 148–50; "The Christian Church: What of Its Future?" 148–50; and Laymen's Inquiry, 158–59, 161

Roman Catholic missions: 15–23; accommodation in, 21–23; by Dominicans, 20; by Franciscans, 17, 25; by Jesuits, 15–23, 25

Rose, Arnold, 1

Sacred Congregation for the Propagation of the Faith, 15, 18, 21

Sanders, Elizabeth Elkins, 76–77

Sandwich Islands. See Hawaii, missions to

Sargeant, John, 29

Scandinavian missions, 93, 131–32

Schaff, Philip, 129–30, 132

Schreiber, August, 133

Schrotenboer, Paul B., 198–99

Scudder, Henry M., 96

Secular expansionism and imperialism: American missions as a chaplaincy to, 92–93, 146, 209; and American missions intertwined, 44–46, 52, 60, 123, 198, 204–5, 207; American missions juxtaposed to, 5, 136, 204; in Catholic missions, 18–23; missionaries' attitudes toward, 9, 92–93, 98, 111, 116, 204

Sepulveda, Gines de, 19

Serra, Junipero, 20

Seventh Day Adventist missions, 128, 174–75

Shaftesbury, First Earl of, 192

Shelly, Maynard, 178

Shuffelton, Frank, 32

Simpson, A. B., 115–18, 120; Larger Outlooks on Missionary Lands, 115–16

Smith, Eugene, 178

Social Gospel, 9, 95, 108, 111, 112, 122, 141, 188; critics, 125, 136–38

Social service and reform in missions, 12–13, 177, 201, 204–5; and conservatives, 115–18; controversy over, 82, 125, 139–45; in Hawaii, 72–74, 77; in the imperialist era, 99–104, 107–11, 115–18, 122–23; and liberals, 102–4, 109–11, 151–53, 157–59, 163–64, 168, 181–86, 197–98; and post–1940 evangelicals, 191–92, 194–97

Society for the Propagation of the Gospel, 29

Sojourners, 195

Soper, Edmund, 180

South America, missions to, 46

Southern Baptist missions, 193

Spanish missions, 9, 15–23

Speer, Robert E.: on evangelizing/civilizing tension, 91, 94, 107–8, 121–24; Finality of Jesus Christ, 91, 172; and indigenization, 97, 122–23; on missionary motivation, 113, 122; and modernist controversy, 140, 166–67; as moderate spokesman, 147–48, 164, 167, 172–74; "Re-Thinking Missions" Examined, 169–71; as statistician, 99–100; and sectarian bodies, 128; on the Watchword, 119, 121; mentioned, 102, 157, 177, 188, 191

Stark, Rodney, 200

Stockholm Conference (1925), 172

Stott, John R. W., 191, 195, 196, 198, 207

Strong, Augustus, 140–43

Strong, Josiah, 60–61

Stuart, J. Leighton, 140

Student Volunteer Movement for Foreign Missions, 7, 119, 130, 131, 133, 147, 164

Syria, missions to, 46, 82, 84

Tanzania, missions to, 201

Thomas, W. H. Griffith, 139–41; A Tour of the Missions, 141, 144

Thompson, A. E., 118

Thompson, Augustus, 84–85

Thurston, Asa, 51, 71–72, 74

Turkey, missions to, 46, 84, 98

Twain, Mark, 74, 156, 205

Unitarianism, 144

Universalist missions, 127

Vendanta Society, 106

Venn, Henry, 78, 122, 192

Versailles Peace Conference, 136–37, 146

Vietnam: missions to, 16; war, 2, 208

Vivekananda, 106

Wagner, C. Peter, 199

Warneck, Gustav, 125, 133–38; History of Protestant Missions, 135; mentioned, 184

Watchword, 91; apologetic for, 100, 117, 121; explained variously, 118–21; reactions to, 104, 126, 131, 133, 136, 147, 181; reappropriation of, 189–90; Wilder as early formulator, 99, 99n

Wayland, Francis, 62, 78, 84, 88, 90

Wesley, John, 186

West Indies, missions to, 46

Westminster Seminary, 166, 174

Wheaton Declaration, 178, 190–91, 192

Wheelock, Eleazer, 29

Whitney, Sam, 71

Wilberforce, William, 192

Wilder, Robert, 102, 119, 135

Wilder, Royal, 97, 133; *Mission Schools in India,* 99

Wilkinson, William, 106

Williams, George, 192

Williams, Roger, 10, 15, 33–38, 40, 198

Wilson, Woodrow, 146

Winslow, Miron, 97–98

Winthrop, John, 6

Woods, Leonard, 47, 48, 59

Woolman, John, 33, 36, 38

Worcester, Samuel, 47, 48, 65–66

World Council of Churches, 81, 178, 183, 187, 193, 202; Bangkok Conference (1973), 192; *The Church for Others and the Church for the World,* 186, 195; Uppsala Assembly (1968), 176, 182, 186, 188–89, 192

World Missionary Conference, Edinburgh (1910), 125, 127, 135–36, 148, 179, 190–91

World Missionary Conference, London (1888), 133, 136

World's Parliament of Religions, 105–6, 109

World Student Christian Federation, 181–82

World War I, 125, 129, 136–38

Wycliffe Bible Translators, 193

Xavier, Francis, 21

Young Men's and Women's Christian Association: Association Press, 102, 156n; and social service, 139, 141, 172; mentioned, 147, 150, 177, 192

Zeisberger, David, 29

Zinzendorf, Count Nicolaus Ludwig von, 26–27, 184, 186